Poison Woman

Poison Woman

Figuring Female Transgression
in Modern Japanese Culture

Christine L. Marran

University of Minnesota Press   Minneapolis • London

Portions of chapter 4 were previously published in slightly different form as "So Bad She's Good: The Masochist's Heroine in Japan, Abe Sada," in *Bad Girls of Japan,* edited by Laura Miller and Jan Bardsley (London: Palgrave Macmillan, 2005), 141–67.

Published by the University of Minnesota Press
111 Third Avenue South, Suite 290
Minneapolis, MN 55401-2520
http://www.upress.umn.edu

Library of Congress Cataloging-in-Publication Data

Marran, Christine L.
    Poison woman : figuring female transgression in modern Japanese culture / Christine L. Marran.
        p.   cm.
    Includes bibliographical references and index.
    ISBN-13: 978-0-8166-4726-2 (hc : alk. paper)
    ISBN-10: 0-8166-4726-7 (hc : alk. paper)
    ISBN-13: 978-0-8166-4727-9 (pbk : alk. paper)
    ISBN-10: 0-8166-4727-5 (pbk : alk. paper)
    1. Women—Japan—Social conditions.   2. Women in popular culture—Japan.
3. Villains in popular culture—Japan.   4. Japan—Civilization—1868–1912.
I. Title.
    HQ1762.M3265 2007
    305.43'3643095209034—dc22

                                                                            2006037639

Printed in the United States of America on acid-free paper

The University of Minnesota is an equal-opportunity educator and employer.

15 14 13 12 11 10 09 08 07   10 9 8 7 6 5 4 3 2 1

This book is dedicated to the memory of
Andrew Lawrence Markus

Contents

Author's Note   ix

Acknowledgments   xi

Introduction   xiii

1. Anatomy of a Poison Woman   1

2. Newspaper Reading as Poison and Cure   36

3. Recollection and Remorse   65

4. How to Be a Woman and Not Kill in the Attempt   103

5. How to Be a Masochist and Not Get
   Castrated in the Attempt   136

Epilogue: By Way of Antidote   171

Notes   179

Index   207

Author's Note

Original newspaper titles are translated only once within the text; thereafter the original title is used. Book and magazine title translations are used throughout to make the text clearer to the general reader.

The last names of female criminals, their families, and their victims are used when discussing them as historical personages. When they are discussed as protagonists within a text, their first names are used.

Japanese name order is maintained.

Japanese books were published in Tokyo unless otherwise noted.

"Tokyo" and "Osaka" are not given macrons.

Translations are by the author unless otherwise noted.

Acknowledgments

This book would have been of a much narrower scope were it not for the advice of mentors at the University of Washington who encouraged me to expand my dissertation beyond Meiji literature. John Whittier Treat always managed to provide research funds for me and my peers where money was scarce. Marilyn Ivy was a source of inspiration during the early write-up stages of the material, and Motoo Kobayashi provided an insistent critical eye to the Meiji material. Andrew Markus's teaching of classical Japanese helped me tremendously in getting through the early Meiji material. Paul Berry helped in writing grants that enabled me to make multiple trips to Japan for research. I remember fondly the vibrant atmosphere at the University of Washington, where the Japanese literature cohort engaged in delightfully heated discussions. I especially thank my fellow graduate student Davinder Bhowmik for her warm encouragement in all matters.

Rinbara Sumio of Kobe University patiently answered hundreds of questions on Meiji literature over e-mail and Chinese food, and he shared his intimate bibliographic familiarity with even the smallest of bookstores. I appreciate his unstinting generosity during the research and writing of this book.

Ann Waltner provided invaluable advice for the book and university life, and Jan Bardsley was of great help in the later stages of writing. Livia Monnet's own work has always been an inspiration, and she offered useful advice, especially for chapter 1. I thank Sandra Buckley, John Lent, and Douglas Slaymaker for opportunities to present my work in print, and Dani Botsman, Rebecca Jennison, Hiromi Mizuno, Hideki Okada,

Gregory Pflugfelder, Alan Tansman, Dennis Washburn, and Janice Brown for the opportunity to present material in public forums.

I thank my colleagues at Princeton University for their encouragement and guidance in turning a dissertation into this book, and the Princeton librarian Yasuko Makino for availing me of her book-finding skills and for her acquisition of the invaluable Naha microfilm collection of early Meiji literature.

I would like to thank my colleagues at the University of Minnesota for creating a spot for me in the Department of Asian Languages and Literatures, especially Joseph Allen, who helped make it possible.

Others who have helped me in articulating this project are Micah Auerbach, Michael Bourdaghs, Steven Clark, Lee Friederich, David Howell, William Johnston, Margherita Long, Anne McKnight, John Mertz, Shigemi Nakagawa, Jim Reichert, and Atsuko Ueda.

Various grant institutions provided greatly appreciated funding for the project. Without these grants, I would not have had the chance to locate and consider the popular cultural texts discussed in this book. A Japan Foundation Dissertation Research Grant took me to Japan to begin re-search, and a Japan Society for the Promotion of Science Postdoctoral Research Grant enabled me to work further on chapter 1. A Social Science Research Council Advanced Research Grant provided much-needed sup-port for further research and writing. A travel grant from the University Committee on Research in the Humanities at Princeton University helped me in the final stages of the project, and Makoto Yamaguchi kindly invited me as a visiting scholar at Kansai University for one summer, during which time I found invaluable material for chapter 3.

At the University of Minnesota Press, I thank Andrea Kleinhuber for her terrific enthusiasm for the project, and Doug Armato and Nancy Sauro for their patience as I tried to make final editorial changes to the book with a hungry newborn, Lorenz Henry, in the house.

My greatest debt of gratitude is owed to Mark Anderson, who munifi-cently and enduringly allowed me to pester him with questions, concerns, and doubts and never failed to have an insightful response, regardless of the hour.

Finally, I thank my parents, Hank and Lucy, and brother, Keith, who never asked why but only asked when.

Introduction

This book addresses stories of women in Japan who were joined in history by the unflattering appellation *dokufu,* or "poison woman." Most of these women committed murder or robbery and often both. Most carried out their adult lives during the tumultuous decline of Shogunate rule and the rise of a new oligarchic government in the nineteenth century. The term "poison woman" blossomed during this period of dramatic social, cultural, and political change and remained a familiar cultural icon throughout the twentieth century. Originally penned as sensational temptress in Japan's first serialized novels in the 1870s, she traveled to the kabuki stage, to woodblock-printed books, to transcribed popular novels, to confessional podium and transcript, to psychoanalytic discourse, to memoir, to avant-garde theater and screen, and to the feminist short story and cultural criticism. She has contributed to the white noise of urban legend, docudrama, and tabloids about women. The literature written about her contributed to the development of a vernacular style and to the cultural fashioning of the modern heterosexual matrix.

The term "poison woman" suggests that the women designated by this term were convicted of administering toxins to their enemies. This was only occasionally the case. The most notorious of the poison women, "Demon" *(yasha)* Takahashi Oden, was said to have poisoned her leprosy-ridden husband to be free of having to care for him. But the crime for which she was arrested was the fatal stabbing of an acquaintance who had reneged on a business deal. Poison woman "Night Storm" *(yoarashi)* Okinu was said to have fatally poisoned her patron to be free to live with her lover, a kabuki actor. Other poison women strangled their victims, and still others were

guilty only of robbery or counterfeiting. While not all administered toxins, most are in some way connected with drugs. The heroine of the first
serialized poison woman story in 1878—singing street minstrel Omatsu,
whose fresh face temporarily gained her reprieve from a meager living as
a prostitute after the removal of class boundaries that had kept her in the
poverty of an outcast class—is eventually ravaged by boils that no medicine can cure. Drugs are rendered useless against the illness of a woman of
low origins who had grown accustomed to a middle-class lifestyle. Demon
Oden allegedly prostituted for drug money. The medicine she procured
for her leprosy-ridden husband kept him teetering on the verge of death
until he was mysteriously administered a fatal dose. Night Storm Okinu
of the same generation fell in love with a neighboring doctor cum pharma-
cologist whose self-medication by alcohol left him vulnerable to her intoxicating wiles. She drugged and kidnapped the failing doctor's "good girl"
girlfriend to alleviate him of the burden of a toxic sedentary life. Her male
cohort, rather than fatally poisoning the kidnapped girlfriend, kept the
beauty as a personal love slave. A poison woman of a later generation, Abe
Sada, fed pain pills to her lover to alleviate the silk burn around his neck
caused by orgiastic love play. When he insisted on returning home to his
wife, Abe threw the remaining capsules in dirty water, depriving him of
their anesthetizing effects.

As recalled by Avital Ronell, Nietzsche argued that the history of high
culture is the history of narcotica. For him, music, art, and theater worked
to "intoxicate the audience and force it to the height of a moment of strong
and elevated feelings," enabling the viewers and listeners to forget their
lives. Stories of poison women have provided readerly intoxication but at
no time have they been mistaken for high culture. And they may have been
escapist, but they also were policing. In their own time, they could work
to anesthetize populations to racial, gender, and economic biases through
false claims of inclusion. They purported to illuminate intoxicating elements that might lead to social and political bedlam. In retrospect, they
suggest the modern drive to detoxify the body and expel dangerous am-
biguities by creating clear classifications.[1] Ronell has argued that the increased intolerance of drugs in the United States reflects an increased intolerance for the marginal or "unproductive." Drugs signify more than civil
disobedience. During the peak of the Reagan era, a war against racial, gender, and class others was waged and articulated through drugs. The hysteria quickly snowballed into a national obsession though the war was not
waged equally on its enemies.[2] Similarly, we might wonder at this attention

to poisons and drugs in the unprecedented period of nation-building in 1870s Japan. The earliest modern newspapers featured abundant advertisements selling pharmaceutical drugs to the degree that the enlightenment proponent Fukuzawa Yukichi condemned the habit of resorting to drugs to cure all ills.[3] The same newspapers that ran the country's first drug ads also featured the unhappy "poison woman" in whom *toxin* and *woman* were allied.

The long and changing tradition of writing about female criminals began with the rise of the newspaper serial. With such colorful nicknames as Demon Oden, Night Storm Okinu, Viper Omasa, and Lightning Oshin, to name only a few, the first poison women appeared as anti-heroes in Japan's earliest serialized newspaper stories. These serials were based on the lives and crimes of real women. The attention to women's crimes, which in many cases did not include murder at all, was all out of proportion to the number and types of crimes committed by women in the 1870s and early 1880s. An arrest of a young woman for murder or thievery led to an all-out media blitz. Fictionalized stories about these women were serialized in small newspapers, recounted at informal corner theaters, and enacted in well-established kabuki theaters. Competing novels by multiple authors would be simultaneously published, colorful handbills announcing the arrested woman's crime were printed, and poets would dedicate Chinese poems to her story. The proof for this preponderance of attention to the female criminal lies in the simple fact that an entirely new category—the "poison woman tale" *(dokufumono)*—developed in literary history to account for the myriad serials and books (both soft multivolume and hardback single-volume) devoted to the female criminal during this era of reform. Since in most cases the subject of the poison woman story can be identified as based on historical personages, poison woman figures should be considered distinct from literary and film femmes fatales that are not based on historical figures. For example, the depraved seductresses of novelists Izumi Kyōka and Tanizaki Jun'ichirō haunt, but not with the uncanny power of a historical figure.

Why did a handful of women arrested for robbery and occasionally homicide during the brief Seinan war of 1877 and the early years of nation-building hold such interest for readers?[4] What national obsessions were articulated through this interest in the female convicts? Penal statistics do not support this hysterical interest in female criminality. There was no substantial increase in crimes by women in early Meiji. It also makes little sense to attribute interest in female criminals to their rarity. While thirty times more men were executed than women from 1876 to 1881, women were still put to death with surprising frequency, ranging from eight to seventeen times a year during this period.[5] Furthermore, reports of men committing homicide by poisoning do exist. A cursory look at *Tokyo E-Iri Shinbun* (Tokyo Illustrated Newspaper) reveals one story about two men from a samurai class family who served time in prison for being involved in the Seinan war and attempting to poison four family members (the article begins, "There are a lot of poison homicides in Korea but [we had a similar case here in Japan] . . .)." Nevertheless, it was the female criminal who garnered enough popular attention to produce the iconic figure of the "poison woman" though she only occasionally resorted to poison in committing crime.

Much literature on transgressive women in Victorian society and the turn-of-the-century United States takes as its fundamental basis the notion that charged representations of sexual difference and gender articulated in stories of deviant women do ideological labor, especially in times of political change. While Mary Poovey and Nancy Armstrong have illustrated that representations of gender generally constituted in Victorian England an important site "on which ideological systems were simultaneously constructed and contested [and] at which struggles for authority occurred," other studies show that often it is the transgressive or criminal woman who is most subjected to obsessions and concerns about sexual difference and female power.[6] As Ann-Louise Shapiro has argued regarding Parisian society:

> In the social imagination of the fin-de-siècle, the female criminal was never very far from debates about divorce reform and civil rights for women, or from heightened national anxieties about the viability of the traditional family and conventional gender roles on the one hand, and the perceived crises of depopulation and national decadence on the other. In sum, the story of female criminality was a story about the pain of social change. It was a story that often read like melodrama, casting deviant women in leading roles.[7]

Shapiro describes the expression of such anxieties regarding social change or a female invasion (she discusses narratives about feminists and female criminals) as *stories*. Lisa Duggan, in her discussion of the female sexual "deviant" and crime in the United States at the turn of the century,[8] emphasizes (following Lisa Lowe and others) that these stories of social deviants are "cultural narratives" that refuse a separation of social life and representation.

Poison Woman looks at various narratives in culture, but especially at the press, the novel, theater, essay, medical narrative, and other written representations of the female criminals who were specifically referred to as "poison women." It is curious that the poison woman also emerged as popular icon during a time of tremendous social and political upheaval that could potentially bring great changes to women's lives. The feminist historian Sharon Sievers describes how woman's social position and power was a source of debate in early Meiji, as well as in Western Europe and the United States:

> As the new government leaders moved to amend any social condition that seemed to justify Western criticism of Japan as uncivilized, they were immediately faced with one of the favored patriarchal myths of the nineteenth-century West: that the status of women was an important measure of any society's progress toward civilization. Though the irony of such a claim was obvious to women in the West who were struggling to improve their status in "civilized" societies, the Japanese were very sensitive to the issue and its potential implications.[9]

Some social and legal changes potentially improved women's status. Prostitutes were released from enslavement in 1872 following the Maria Luz incident, the Tokyo Girls' School was established the same year, formal (though not de facto) class boundaries were abolished in 1875, and some in the Freedom and Popular Rights Movement argued to extend voting rights to women who owned property and paid taxes. Heated debates about female suffrage, the right for women to participate in government, the need for equal access to education, the right to safer working conditions, and so on developed only after the publication of poison woman serials and novels. Still, the increasing evidence of impending political change was ample fodder for the imagination of contemporary writers who, not inconsequentially, turned their sights to the female criminal.

Nation-building brought with it different methods for sorting bodies. Matsuyama Iwao has argued in *The Perspective of Rumor* (Uwasa no enkinhō) that the rise of the poison woman marks a new interest in sexual difference as an essential category for interpreting social relationships and identities. It is not a coincidence that poison woman stories were invented during the installation of an emperor whose supporters purported to be invested in creating a national body. National bodies require spaces of exclusion. The denizens of this exclusionary zone will change, but it remains an important attribute for such a power-base. Those marginalized within society are symbolically central to how a society describes itself. If Madame Bovary, the eponymous heroine of the 1857 novel dubbed "poison" by contemporary courts, was "the clearing space, the translating machine through which an epoch rendered itself intelligible,"[10] as Avital Ronell suitably claims, how much more so the widely circulated, highly fabricated stories of real women whose very names reveal their toxicity? Like Flaubert's famous heroine, the Japanese poison woman in her time could be a vehicle for articulating the politics and position of the under-class woman, sex practices and reproductive morality, female subjectivity and suffrage during this time of upheaval. The women, of course, never spoke for themselves. Their tongues were deemed poisoned; they had no power through which to assert the veracity of one claim over another. But as a silent medium, they served to articulate the various claims of the new national subjects. The manifold articulations of gender and sexuality in poison woman narratives express concerns to create a coherent vision of gender in the formation of national ideals. In that sense, female transgres-sion and obsessive interest in it throughout the twentieth century in Japan has everything to do with configuring the modern Japanese subject, par-ticularly the female subject, through representations of female criminality in literature, theater, newspaper, and film.

Michel Foucault wrote that "criminals come in handy."[11] Criminals, in their many forms, do not just come in handy. They are essential to the pro-motion of a status quo and the reproduction of the symbolic order. Usually we imagine a transgressive act as a laudatory or deeply troubling distur-bance of a prevailing and even amorphous cultural, political, and economic order. In actuality, it is the opposite. The insistent systems of exclusion and classification that privilege and pathologize bodies to reproduce themselves are their own "economies of transgression."[12] One author on the poison woman, Asakura Kyōji, relates the rise of the poison woman story with the Seinan war, finding in both entities a featured "outlaw." In the case of the Seinan war, the outlaws were the anti-government forces from Satsuma who were ready to envelop Japan with flames if necessary and were vilified in the press as a "pirate army" *(zokugun)*. Newspapers reported that army members used the livers of dead soldiers as medicine *(kusuri)*. In this way, the "army pirates" were treated as spiritually "perverse" *(ijō)* in the press. In the creation of a stable unified nation, Asakura argues, the survivors of this "pirate army" had to be prosecuted in court, and while they were, a new kind of "pirate" to the national "economy of transgression" who was also treated as "perverse" emerged in newspapers and fiction in the form of the "poison woman."[13]

The term "economy" used by Stallybrass and White in describing "economies of transgression" is important because it denotes exchange. The social symbolic sells the transgressive and abject and in return buttresses its base of exchange, its status quo, its logic. The earliest writers of poison woman stories who themselves were on the verge of disenfranchisement could provide a place for themselves in the new symbolic and ideological order by reinventing themselves in the form of social guardians. The trouble with transgression is indeed its indispensability. The social symbolic needs its criminals.[14] It needs its terrorists, its sex addicts, its drug czars. But one way the discriminatory basis of a social semiotic might be disturbed is by revealing, through the study of transgression, the justifications for those discriminations.[15] The (albeit anachronistic) chalked profiles drawn around the poison woman's victims washed away long ago. The "common logic" that is left in the shadow of her curvaceous figure is what this book seeks to elucidate. The allure of the poison woman as an object of study resides in her capacity to illuminate not only the emerging social, sexual, and political mores but also the fundamental drive to read and consume the other in order to define the self.

Doku of *dokufu* (poison woman) supplies an all too convenient homonym. One reading of the character means "poison," the other "to read." The economy of transgression relies on the drive to consume the very thing that is deemed toxic. The inordinate attention in newspapers, medical studies, biographies, and fiction to every aspect of the female criminal's life illustrates an enigmatic drive to supplement everyday life with tales of the transgressive. From the Bakhtinian perspective of Stallybrass and White, who have considered at length this problem, the transgressive is an exoticized other that provides sustenance to the system and to the subject. The subject consumes the peripheral or the transgressive in order to feed and nourish the psychological self/subject:

> The "top" attempts to reject and eliminate the "bottom" for reasons of pres-
> tige and status, only to discover, not only that it is in some way frequently
> dependent upon that low-Other (in the classic way that Hegel describes in
> the master-slave section of the *Phenomenology*), but also that the top *in-
> cludes* that low symbolically, as a primary eroticized constituent of its own
> fantasy life. The result is a mobile, conflictual fusion of power, fear, and
> desire in the construction of subjectivity: a psychological dependence upon
> precisely those Others which are being rigorously opposed and excluded
> at the social level. It is for this reason that what is *socially* peripheral is so
> frequently *symbolically* central (like long hair in the 1960s).[16]

This eroticization of the other explains in part the impetus to so greedily consume the transgressive. Also at play in stimulating cultural fantasy is the notion of the transgressive itself, which is a charged subject burdened with the task of exciting and motivating the central symbolic.

The use of the transgressive woman as social symbolic appears in an essay invoking the poison woman by the fiction writer and essayist Nagai Kafū. In the short passage "Airing" (Mushiboshi) from his essay "After Tea" (Kōcha no ato, 1911), Kafū evokes the thrill of unpacking one's belongings and the flood of memories that surge when fondly poring over accumulated treasures. Laying out books on the *tatami* floor for their annual airing and cleansing of silverfish, the narrator waxes fondly over his possessions. Leafing through his collection of books provokes more than a nostalgic moment of remembrance. It yields an opportunity to comment on his colonialist present. The narrator spreading out his colorful old books on the floor is transported by images on their covers of poison women who had been so prominent in fiction, news, and theater during the tumult of the Meiji restoration. Recalling the figure of the poison woman as she stood defiant and proud on the kabuki stage in Kawatake Mokuami's plays *(sewamono)*, the narrator describes her as a colorful character exhibiting the prosaic tenacity and ingenuity of the commoners of the Meiji enlightenment coupled with the seduction and mystery of a femme fatale.

Kafū's narrator makes much of the combination of reportage, verisimilitude, and sinister allure of Mokuami's stage aesthetics. To him the poison woman evokes a lost air of youthful optimism alongside a dark but resolute struggle of the new underclass during the restoration: "Vigorously they imbibed the pure with the impure and boldly forged ahead. Comparing then and now of forty-four years later reveals the stifling conditions of thought under [the current] oppressive militarism."[17] Kafū nostalgically imagines the female criminal as representative of Japan's own marginal position in the geopolitical sphere prior to its evolution into a major player in the militarist struggle for power and prestige on the global stage. The staging of the poison woman in his memory is the restaging of the aesthetic libidinal body, which is wholly representative of a commoner's struggle within the nation. He implicitly critiques the newly oppressive militaristic body to which the populace has submitted. For Kafū, the poison woman of Mokuami's plays represented the counterhegemonic utopian body of "the people," which has been usurped by an authoritarian empire.[18]

Kafū's critique of the imperialist direction of the Japanese nation by way of the sexy poison woman of the stage exemplifies two general points when it comes to the poison woman. Sexuality and desire are at the heart of the poison woman's symbolic power but very different meanings are produced depending on the author, the historical context, and the medium in which she is drawn. In other words, there is a continuity of imagery—the poison woman is always portrayed as sexual and desirous so that female criminality is inevitably linked to female desire—and the journalistic, juridical, medical, novelistic, and film images of her went far beyond what the law had to say about her crime and its punishment. Her sexualization in these myriad texts is treated as inherent to the woman herself. Never innocent, she is always already guilty—of being sexual. One central goal of this book is to illustrate how violent acts by women were transformed into ideological, social, and moral crimes that deployed notions of female sexual desire in explaining her criminal acts, thereby charging sexuality with the power to dictate the parameters of womanhood. The pervasive depiction of the deviant woman as too sexual, too salacious, too modern casts a larger shadow over "woman," whether she kills or not. That the deviant woman gets described so often via gender, sexuality, and sexual desire is not necessarily a problem solely of modernity. However, the hysterical attention to female sexual desire of the convict, whether in the form of condemnation or fetishization, shows female sexuality to be a predominant mode through which morality or dubiousness was gauged in Japan.

Generally, through this process of tracing differentiation—that act of determining how "she" differs from "me" or "him"—I hold four general suppositions regarding transgression and writing (in the broad sense) about transgressive women. First, in the texts under discussion, the struggle to speak in the name of the social symbolic lies in the figuration of the poison woman. The depicted transgressive experience can be read for general social and political concerns, which get inscribed onto the transgressive body. However, each work of literature or representation potentially poses a different story of subjection that must be teased out. Second, the fantasy of the poison woman is in most cases not representative of that which specifically happens to a woman in Japan. Rather, she is symptomatic of the often textual processes of domination related to more general concerns like sexuality, nation, masculinity, science, and so on. Third, transgression does not often accomplish its name or what it promises—as Maurice Blanchot has illustrated—because it is supportive of and even produced by a nontransgressive hegemonic system and because it is not complete. The community or the writing subject can refuse or identify with the transgressor without itself engaging in any transgressive act or behavior, without any consequences. Therefore, perhaps especially within the context of popular culture, transgression, subject to consumption, does not usually signify a place of counterhegemonic struggle, though sometimes it does. Finally, it is supposed that the creation of subjectivity in Japanese modernity has occurred consistently (though not solely) through the specter of gender difference. Just as Butler and Scott have shown how the subject is so very often "constructed through acts of differentiation that distinguish the subject from its constitutive outside [with] a domain of abjected alterity conventionally associated with the feminine," the deviant woman is illustrative of the case in which the abject is associated with the feminine, though perhaps monstrously so.[19]

In delineating how the transgressive, poisoning female is inscribed over time, this book traces four main moments in her representation. Poison woman stories appeared throughout the twentieth century after their introduction in the 1870s. *Poison Woman* looks at the most intense moments of production of poison woman stories. Chapter 1 begins with the first and greatest "boom" in poison woman stories in the 1870s and 1880s. It explores the way in which female criminality is aligned with sexuality and gender, and illustrates how the female outlaw was useful in criminalizing a particular form of gender behavior. The chapter shows how the sexual, desirous body of the poison woman is created through biocentric discourse as a negative reference point mobilized to produce a national "civilized" body. Class and economic inequalities are justified in marginalizing the often impoverished female criminal as abnormal. It also argues that while authors of early Meiji fiction produced this sensational gender outlaw, *gesaku* writing itself—the stylistic form in which poison woman novels were first published—was made outlaw in Japanese literary history in articulating a new vision of modern literature. The point that emerges from this discussion is a theoretical and historical one: namely, that the gender outlaw and the "genre" outlaw are products of a broader cultural and political investment in a positivistic articulation of bodies, both literary and nonliterary. A new cultural logic is illustrated in poison woman fiction in which writing about the body (of the female criminal within fiction writing of this time) involved incorporating "practical learning" and "factual knowledge" into fiction and the rejection of the absurd or irrational deemed indicative of early Tokugawa-era *gesaku* (such as *kokkeibon* or "humorous literature"). "Practical learning" became its own plot device. This literary refashioning involved authors becoming "contemporary" through public self-regulating acts of classifying their own work. Fiction writers fervently advanced their writing as reformed and invested in the truthful and the practical, and through this rhetorical style assumed the authority to judge the outlaw, moving themselves from "popular" to "practical" and contemporarily relevant authors. This literary reform of early Meiji fiction has been largely discounted by literary historians as retrograde and distinctly unmodern in the course of defining modern literary language. Early Meiji writing, often referred to broadly as *gesaku,* in other words, has been fetishistically dismissed as a premodern form that must be marginalized (outlawed) in order for Japanese literature to assume a modern form. In examining three works of fiction by Kanagaki Robun, Kubota Hikosaku, and Itō Senzō this book's initial chapter illustrates how Meiji writers grappled with the contemporary rhetoric of the reformation in the creation of a gender outlaw through, especially, the reference to contemporary protosexological discourse and modern technologies. Explicitly arguing the writings' relevance to contemporary times is illustrated as part of the authors' drive to make their writing contemporary.

The second chapter continues with an analysis of the "civilizing" rhetoric associated with poison woman literature through a discussion of the context of the poison woman's original place of publication—the popular press medium of the small newspaper *(koshinbun).* This discussion of the layout of the popular newspaper, its idealized female reader, and the representation of crime and laws and regulations in the newspapers illustrates the centrality of crime *as well as the law* in storytelling during the reforms. This discussion focused on the birthing ground of the poison woman is included as an example of how and why journalistic elements are so predominant in longer, novelistic versions of poison woman stories.

At the turn of the century, a new kind of poison woman narrative emerged. The ex-convict's self-narrative joined previous fictionalized accounts of women's crime. These self-narratives were most often framed as *zange,* which might be translated variously as "repentance" or "confession." These personal tales of rehabilitation and literary memoir not only formed a new narrative mode for expressing female criminality but also suggest a new mode of self-narrative in formation. The confession enabled a full recitation of the thrilling life of the ex-con even while it offered an opportunity for the articulation of a different self that was not the fetishized deviant. The strange contemporaneous fixation on the concept of *zange* by both male literati and female ex-convicts serves as the basis for illustrating how confession by a woman might be written differently. In them, the subject assumes contradictory positions of self-affirmation, self-disgust, and insistence on rehabilitation. These texts are compared with confessional literature by male authors to illustrate the relevance of gender difference in articulating the modern self. This chapter includes testimonies by criminals who were not specifically referred to as poison women because they are suggestive of the way in which self-narrative by female writers convicted of a crime changes in the early twentieth century, though the insistence in the media on the female criminal as sexual does not.

During the 1920s and 1930s, the new sciences of sexology and criminology continued to develop a relationship between female criminality and sexuality. Chapter 4 returns to the question discussed in chapter 1 of how scientific knowledge was deployed to articulate motivations to crime by women. Exploring medical analyses of the murderess dubbed "poison woman" Abe Sada and popular medical and psychoanalytic literature from the 1920s and 1930s, this chapter illustrates the way in which psychosexual narratives speak of crime as a potential in every woman. Rather than the poison woman representing an anomalous outside that defines the center, the female criminal is deployed to show that any woman can be a criminal. Similar to earlier texts, however, is the continued insistence on sexual desire as the source of criminal behavior.

Also discussed briefly in this chapter is the shift in the 1920s and 1930s whereby the poison woman became a "historical" figure—a heroine of the historical novel (jidai shōsetsu), such as Kunieda Kanji's The Hell of Oden (Oden jigoku, 1934), and a central figure in cultural histories by writers such as Shinoda Kōzō, Ishii Kendō, Yokose Yau, and Umehara Hokumei. These works tend to take a much more sympathetic view of the poison woman—treating her as a victim of the press and social circumstances. It could persuasively be argued that the figure of the "modern girl" (moga) took the place of the poison woman as a figure emblematic of the dangers of female freedom, transgression, and sexuality. Since Poison Woman focuses on texts featuring actual women who have been convicted of crimes and dubbed "poison woman," the modern girl image of the 1920s will not be addressed, though the critique of the moga in popular culture as the overly sexual woman offers an interesting comparison to the poison woman.

The final chapter argues that a radical transformation took place in the portrayal of the poison woman in the postwar period. Exploring postwar portrayals of Abe Sada in the popular pulp fiction (kasutori) of the occupation period in Japan (1945–52) and in film and avant-garde theater of the 1970s, this chapter explores the ideological labor to which the female criminal is put in articulating a counterhegemonic, masochistic male subjectivity. In illustrating the prominence, especially in the 1970s, of a new kind of sexual subject—the masochistic male—this chapter also introduces texts that satirize this textual worship of the female transgressor.

Finally, the book closes with a brief examination of the postwar feminist writer Tomioka Taeko's implicit critique of narratives of the transgressive woman in her fiction, especially with regard to the dichotomies of the "sexual and transgressive" versus the "non-sexual and domestic" in so much writing on the bad girl.

The ubiquity of the poison woman in popular culture meant that she appeared in a variety of mediums. In addition to the so-called small newspaper and its serial novels *(tsuzukimono),* this book addresses a wide range of popular media from the 1870s to the 1970s, including *gōkan* literature and protosexological popular science, personal testimony and confession in both their written and staged forms at the turn of the century, popular criminological science writing of the 1920s and 1930s, *kasutori* or pulp fiction of the postwar, and film and political theater of the 1970s. Through a comparative discussion of the various manifestations of the poison woman in Japanese popular culture, this book elucidates the investment of popular culture in the transgressive and the reliance of "high culture" on such popular cultural texts.

Poison Woman shows that constructions of deviancy change dramatically in relation to their historical and political contexts and representational mode. In all cases, however, these narratives reveal the degree to which social relations are constructed around axes of domination. In this sense, as Judith Butler argues, "the subject is constituted through the force of exclusion and abjection, one which produces a constitutive outside to the subject, an abjected outside, which is, after all, 'inside' the subject as its own founding repudiation."[20] Poison woman narratives articulate disciplining discourses of gender, sexuality, and even class in their various literary and medical permutations. However, these narratives based on actual events do not just reiterate or perform regulatory but also counterhegemonic and nonhegemonic functions because they signal disruptive and irreconcilable differences. They disrupt because they reveal a lack of a rule of judgment applicable on all sides.[21] Eventually that disruption is reconciled into an idiom, but not before manifesting itself as an intoxifying way of poisoning the certainty of cultural truths.

1. Anatomy of a Poison Woman

Gender and Genre Outlaws

When I began considering the ubiquitous icon of the poison woman, I first considered her primarily as a literary fantasy that lured because she broke rules. She aroused anxieties and promised delights for her badness much like the blue-stockinged modern girl of the 1920s who succeeded her. But what sort of anxieties did the poison woman arouse and what delights did she promise? What sorts of rules did she break? Clearly more was at stake than simply a literary fantasy. My research convinces me that the poison woman created in early Meiji literary history was a persuasive body for articulating the politics of reproductive morality, female domesticity, sex practices, and the dilemma of the underclass woman. It seems there was for the poison woman no experience, no representation of her desire, which was not in some way pervaded and authorized by the law. Even her tongue was deemed poisoned; she had no discursive power through which to assert the veracity of one claim over another but served rather as a screen onto which various claims regarding gender, desire, and authority were projected. In dominant accounts, she was above all identified by her voracious sexual desire, which was nearly always claimed, explicitly or implicitly, to be the primary source for her criminality. We may conclude, therefore, that she was treacherous not only because she had murdered or stolen but because she exceeded the bounds of femininity and social propriety. The poison woman fiction discussed in this chapter marks the start of a longer exploration in this book of narratives that turn to female desire for their sensational condemnation of women who have made dubious choices.

1

The poison woman of the early Meiji period became tied to the law by means of sensationalizing gestures related to her *body*. The literary scholar Maeda Ai remarked as early as 1975, almost as an afterthought in one of the earliest of many academic studies of poison woman Takahashi Oden, that Kanagaki Robun ignored social circumstances to focus on the physiology of Oden in his story *The Tale of Demon Takahashi Oden* (Takahashi Oden yasha monogatari, 1879): "Robun consciously dropped the context in which Oden's crime was inseparably entangled with enlightenment society, simply minimizing it as a problem of physiology *[seiri]*."[1] As Maeda points out, such a focus on the female criminal's body—her sexual behavior and comportment—effectively diverted attention from any social or psychological motives for committing crimes. These female criminal narratives in the form of the newspaper novel, theatrical show, and handbill in Japan were similar to those in late-nineteenth-century America as described by Lisa Duggan when she relates how cultural narratives of deviant female love, written in the context of criminal activity, "worked to depoliticize, trivialize, and marginalize the aspirations of women for political equality, economic autonomy and alternative domesticities."[2] In early Meiji popular literature, the criminal was used to shore up conservative notions of sexuality and domestic life for women. The failures of self-promoting, transgressive women were made the stuff of murder and romance. The biocentrism of the discourse of the poison woman concealed or justified social and economic inequalities by expressing social discord as physiological and mental deviance.

This physiological discourse of the transgressive woman was articulated in language that was often factual, material, and written in an explanatory mode. Likely it was not just her sex and crime but their articulation through the fresh language of the newspapers and discourses of modernization that made the female criminal a sensational object of attention.[3] In the brave new world of the Meiji era, "reform" *(kairyō)* was the word of the day, and media and literature were two of the leading sites of its articulation. Woodblock-printed illustrated novels were still widely read and woodblock handbills were printed to spread news, but the number of movable type newspapers, where poison woman stories were first published in serialized form, was so great that lending libraries of the time complained that their woodblock-printed books—the literature of popular consumption of the Tokugawa era—were being abandoned for newspapers. During this reformative period in history, often referred to as the era of "civilization and enlightenment" *(bunmei kaika)*, the popular authors who published woodblock-printed stories that traditionally operated in the world of parody and neo-Confucian cosmology developed a new style that was informed by their profession both as writers of popular fiction and as Japan's first popular newspaper men.[4] These authors were the inventors of the first modern poison woman stories, which updated the traditional fictional forms to attribute a sense of the new circumstances surrounding the readers. Poison woman literature is often considered a subcategory of the unwieldy broader category of *gesaku*, literature that encompasses literary writing of the eighteenth to the nineteenth century that is polysemic, can contain wordplay and puns and vernacular speech, and may take the form of humorous satire or long story. This literature of the premodern period is usually categorized into the following broad "subgenres": *yomihon* ("reading books"—usually long-winded historical or fantastical fiction), *ninjōbon* (romance fiction), *sharebon* (literature on the haute couture of the pleasure quarters), and *kokkeibon* (humorous fiction featuring satire and parody). To use the term "genre" with regard to this literature is suspect since this mode of classification was not associated with literature in pre-Meiji Japan.[5]

The most appropriate term to describe the format and writing of the poison woman stories when they were written as novels after serialization in the newspaper is *gōkan*. As the Tokugawa literature scholar Andrew Markus has outlined, *gōkan* was the preeminent vehicle of fiction in nineteenth-century Japan. Virtually all authors before 1875 made it their life work or side work. From 1807 to 1867, fifty to sixty new titles were created every year and several hundred were written from the Meiji period.[6] Markus claims rightly that it is only *gōkan* that maintained such vitality through the bakumatsu and restoration periods in Japan, and *gōkan* even enjoyed a brief renaissance in the 1870s and 1880s—the heyday of poison woman fiction. According to the Tokugawa writer Shikitei Sanba, the *gōkan* was transformed from the *kusazōshi* format in 1807.[7] They were smaller in size than *yomihon,* contained illustrations straddling the page, and used relatively easy syntax and orthography. From 1807, *gōkan* frontispieces were printed on higher quality paper. Subjects included vendetta, divine retribution, criminal perpetrators, rape, torture, and execution in intricate plots that feature wordplay and sometimes the orthography of the theater—many of these subjects are not foreign to the poison woman *gōkan.*[8] As with poison woman literature, the *gōkan* chapters were usually released at different times. The chapters were divided into the *jō* (beginning), *chū* (middle), and *ge* (conclusion) groupings, each grouping receiving an illustrated casing *(fukuro),* and each grouping receiving a separate release, improving the chances for increasing the market for any one novel. As further reassurance that an audience could be found for a story, in the Meiji period many were published as *gōkan* only after they had been serialized in the newspaper and proved their popularity in the press. The scholar Mitamura Engyo has claimed that the adult elite readership for the *gōkan* increased when the novels were first serialized in newspapers, and this may have also been a result of the increased addition of Chinese characters into the text although *gōkan* always provided *kana* glosses for the less educated reader.[9]

Meiji authors of *gōkan* literature combined the satirical, fanciful, highly intertextual and polysemic writing of Tokugawa-era fiction with enlightenment thought and rhetoric that claimed the "truthfulness" of the narrative as one primary selling point in contemporizing the form. In many stories, the language of new fields of knowledge was incorporated into the fictional prose to create a convincing sense of the new reality surrounding the readers. As the reform of institutions, politics, education, and literature became a primary national imperative—at least as far as upper-class oligarchs and reformists were concerned—popular literature became yet another cultural manifestation deployed to mark the success or failure of conversion, either by the writers themselves or by their successors who sought to distinguish their own work as intellectual, serious, and therefore modern by vociferously and self-consciously rejecting earlier *gōkan* writing traditions.

This chapter explores how this Meiji-era "reformed" writing contributed to containing the imagination of female possibility during this time through discourses of physiology and enlightenment science. The discourses of empiricism and practical learning impacted not only conceptualizations of what writing could be and do in early Meiji but also what female bodies could be and do. I argue that the primary texts under discussion in this chapter, Kanagaki Robun's *The Tale of Demon Takahashi Oden* (Takahashi Oden yasha monogatari, 1879), Kubota Hikosaku's *The New Tale of Seafaring Street Minstrel Omatsu* (Torioi Omatsu kaijō shinwa, 1878), and Itō Senzō's *A Strange Story of Enlightenment: The Revenge of the Photograph* (Kaimei kidan: Shashin no ada-uchi, 1883), incorporated contemporary ideological imperatives of practical learning and are a testament to the new role that objects, facts, and physiology played in fabricating a literary world that conflated female desire and sexuality with criminality. It was precisely through this portrayal of the female criminal as a guilty, unenlightened sexual subject that the writer could reframe his work as reformed. The aggressively condemnatory rhetoric that structured these self-proclaimed true tales of the poison woman created for the narrators a position of authority from which to judge their heroines (and women generally) as unenlightened, and from which their authors could be judged as reformed. This examination of three poison woman stories will illustrate how Meiji *gōkan* writers grappled with the contemporary rhetoric of reform in the creation of a gender outlaw only to become excised themselves from a national narrative of literary progress a few years later.

Takahashi Oden: A Strange Tokyo Tale

Actual female criminals dubbed "poison woman" who remained in the popular imagination throughout the twentieth century number around twenty but the most popular, long-standing object of interest has been Takahashi Oden, or "Demon" *(yasha)* Oden. Takahashi, who sparked such widespread interest in female criminality, was beheaded in 1879 for the murder of Gotō Kichizō, a merchant of the Nihonbashi neighborhood in Tokyo. The details of Oden's biography change with each story told about her though a few factual details can be gleaned by comparing newspaper reports and trial records from the time. Oden was born in 1848 as the daughter of Takahashi Kanzaemon and his wife Oharu. In 1867, she was married to Naminosuke, who was brought into the family by Oden's father. The newly formed family enjoyed a relatively harmonious life in the small village of Numata in Kōzuke (present-day Gunma prefecture) until Naminosuke took ill with leprosy and the couple was forced to leave the village to find help. Oden and Naminosuke journeyed to Yokohama, where they hoped to receive treatment and medicine for Naminosuke's disease. The couple's finances were exhausted and eventually Naminosuke died. The circumstances of Naminosuke's death are treated differently in various Oden biographies. Robun assumed that she had poisoned him to be rid of such a heavy financial burden while Okamoto Kisen, in his version of the story, *Her Name Too Infamous: Poison Woman Takahashi Oden; A Strange Tokyo Tale* (Sono na mo Takahashi: Dokufu no Shōden: Tōkyō kibun, 1879), assumed that she accidentally poisoned him when she administered a toxic brew that she thought was medicine. After Naminosuke's death, Oden got involved in the silk trade among other business ventures, such as raising rabbits and selling planters. She met and cohabitated with Ogawa Ichitarō, and to ease his financial trouble she attempted to procure a loan from Gotō Kichizō.

Oden connived to make her victim invest in silk fabric. She convinced him to stay at an inn overnight in Asakusa to await the delivery of the fabric. Suspiciously, the fabric did not arrive. The two retired to bed, and while Kichizō was asleep, Oden slit his throat with a blade, stole his purse, and fled the inn. Kichizō's corpse was discovered later that evening by a maid who thought it strange that he had not left the room all day and went to check on him, only to find Kichizō's cold dead body lying atop blood-soaked sheets. Oden had left a note at the scene of the crime explaining the murder as a revenge killing in the name of her elder sister, who, the note claimed, had been murdered by Kichizō. This note, printed in various newspapers at the time, was signed with the name "Omatsu"—a famous name that harkened back to a notorious female pirate of the previous era, Kishin Omatsu or "Pirate Omatsu." Shinoda Kōzō and Hirata Yumi point out that this confessional note is written in a theatrical language and that the idea of a revenge killing itself was straight out of the theater (referring both to kabuki theater and public storytelling or *kōdan*).[10] The irony was that Takahashi's biography in a highly fictionalized and sentimental form was performed on stage as Kawatake Mokuami's kabuki play *The Binding of Oden's Letters* (Toji-awase Oden no kanabumi, 1879) and featured the popular kabuki star Kikugorō V in the role of Oden. As Hirata elaborates in her discussion of the lengths to which Takahashi had to go to speak at all in early Meiji, Takahashi framed herself in the confessional note and in court testimony as a "heroic woman" *(retsujo)* who killed for the honor of her family.

Takahashi was located and arrested soon after the murder. The courts, as well as her ever prolific biographers, were not convinced of her claims of revenge. In August 1877, the year the trial started, the *Tokyo Akebono* reported that an "obstinate" *(gōjō)* Oden had not confessed to the crime.[11] By October of the following year, newspapers reported that she had put a fourth thumbprint on her testimony, having changed it three times since the trial commenced.[12] Her refusal to "repent" of her crime and the court's attempt to run a thorough trial without recourse to its traditional practice of forced confession contributed to a two and half year wait before a verdict was reached. She was found guilty of the murder of Gotō and beheaded on the cold day of 31 January 1879 by the practiced eighth-generation executioner Yamada Asaemon.[13] Takahashi was one of the last persons convicted of a crime punishable by death to undergo beheading by sword, but she was one of the first women to be tried at such length in a rapidly modernizing system of law that was being constructed even as it was being used to provide lawful judgments.

Immediately after the execution, the satirical author and founder of the *Kanayomi* newspaper, Kanagaki Robun, began serialization in his newspaper of a story about Takahashi based on the testimony and court verdict. The serial, vaguely titled "The Story of Oden" (Oden no hanashi), was discontinued after only two installments so that it could be printed in longer form as a thread-bound woodblock-printed *gōkan* issued in eight separate volumes of three chapters each over the course of approximately three months. In most respects, the thread-tied version, *The Tale of Demon Takahashi Oden,* looked like a typical *gōkan* with its brightly colored red, pink, and purple covers decorated with images of a colorfully clad, seductively posed woman. Robun attempted a more modern look for the novel by using movable type for the first volume but switched back to the usual wood-block printed cursive *kana* with the next volume. The journalist and *gōkan* writer Okamoto Kisen, who wrote for the *Ukiyo Shinbun* (Floating World Newspaper), competed with Robun to produce his version of Oden's biography as *Her Name Too Infamous: Poison Woman Takahashi Oden; A Strange Tokyo Tale.* Two poison woman stories had already been published before serials of Oden. The *Kanayomi* newspaper had serialized a lengthy story about the outcast street minstrel Omatsu, which was extended to become a *gōkan* entitled *The New Tale of Seafaring Street Minstrel Omatsu,* and Kisen had serialized a story about Harada Okinu in the *Sakigake* newspaper in 1878 and also published the story as a five-volume *gōkan* about Harada with the title *Night Storm Okinu's Flowery Dream of Revenge* (Yoarashi Okinu hana no ada-yume, 1878) based on a poem she recited before her beheading for the poisoning of her patron Kobayashi Kinpei. However, neither of these stories had the immediacy of those written about Takahashi Oden. Omatsu's birthdate was not known, and while the story contained much about contemporary history to give it a sense of immediacy, the lack of a trial for Omatsu, who apparently died of natural causes, likely dimmed the urgency of the tale. The poison woman story by Kisen about Harada was based on a real beheading and public exhibition of Harada's severed head, but the event had taken place six years earlier, before the new juridical system was in place. It was likely the production of stories so soon after the lengthy trial and beheading of Takahashi that imbued them with a sense of urgency and excitement, igniting the boom in poison woman fiction and securing the place of the poison woman icon in Japanese literary and cultural history. In the ensuing years a flood of poison woman stories were published as serialized newspaper stories, ballads, colorful books, Chinese (*kanshi*) poems, and handbills, or performed as plays and corner shows. The poison woman literature in *gōkan* form—the primary form of poison woman story discussed in Japanese literary history—can only be understood in this popular cultural material context. As with much fictional literature in Japanese history, popular culture has been a fruitful harvesting ground for writers of so-called serious or high-brow literature. This point will be discussed further in chapters 2 and 3. In this chapter I focus on demonstrating how enlightenment discourses of science and empiricism were manipulated by writers in producing the poison woman who remained, after her inception in early Meiji, a major cultural icon that purportedly revealed an unequivocal relationship between female desire and transgressive behavior.

Bodily Evidence: Providing Proof of Oden's Criminal Nature

With her execution in 1879, the pieces of Oden's life were assembled into stories, which appeared as newspaper articles, plays, and novels. These texts, fictional and nonfictional, rationalized the execution through condemnation of her sexual behavior and unfeminine comportment and were thereby complicit in regulating female sexuality in the rapidly changing world of the restoration. While most poison woman stories linked sexuality to the poison woman's criminality, Robun's *Demon's Tale,* more dramatically than any other poison woman story, insisted on links between desire, sexuality, and female criminality. This suggests that in making the criminal woman sexual and gender deviant, concomitantly the nonsexual, feminine woman could be produced as the normative model of woman. Georges Canguilhem provides in his *The Normal and the Pathological* a useful description of the way in which trangression births the normative: "It is not just the exception which proves the rule as rule, it is the infraction which provides it with the occasion to be rule by making rules. In this sense the infraction is not the origin of the rule but the origin of regulation. It is in the nature of the normative that its beginning lies in its infraction."[14] It is not just that the infraction creates the normative but also that the rule is then misinterpreted to be the social good and normal. Any deviation from a rule is interpreted as pathological:

> The psychosocial definition of the normal in terms of adaptedness implies a concept of society which surreptitiously and wrongly assimilates it to an environment, that is, to a system of determinisms when it is a system of constraints which, already and before all relations between it and the environment, contains collective norms for evaluating the quality of these relations. To define abnormality in terms of social maladaptation is more or less to accept the idea that the individual must subscribe to the fact of

such society, hence must accommodate himself to it as to a reality which is at the same time a good.[15]

When the inability to adapt leads to an identification of abnormality, this identification involves submission to a system of society—a submission that is consequently interpreted as reasonable. It seems that the identification of Oden as pathologically sexual and gender deviant worked not only to promote the nonsexual, feminine woman as good; it also worked to depict the enlightenment movement as good and just. And it worked toward the self-promotion of the storyteller who, in writing about the female criminal as perverse, shaped himself as a productive citizen of the enlightenment.

The particular enlightenment-era discourses implicitly or explicitly developed in *Demon's Tale* to prove Oden's deviant nature were physiognomy, protosexology, and evolution. *Demon's Tale* begins with a detailed picture of the protagonist's suspect origins, positing the notion that Oden inherited a congenital evil nature. The first chapter is devoted to recounting details of Oden's out-of-wedlock conception to a gambling man and her mother Oharu, a "bold lawless strumpet" with "the nature of a harlot." Female promiscuity literally breeds evil. Though Oden is later educated by her adoptive father to become more proficient than he at Japanese *waka* composition and Chinese classics, it is only a matter of time before Oden's origins literally begin to infect her brain like a cancer *(masumasu nō ni shimi)*. This introductory chapter to Oden's biography teaches that female promiscuity, as practiced by Oden's mother, has devastating consequences. Robun's account insists that Oden's slow descent into criminality begins with her birth to a scandalously untrue woman. The child is doomed by her mother's innately promiscuous nature to a life of criminality that will eventually lead to the alleged deaths of at least two men (though she is only convicted of one murder—the murder of her husband Naminosuke is never proved).

Heredity as a source of criminal behavior is also the centerpiece of an earlier poison woman story by Kubota Hikosaku (and edited by Kanagaki Robun), *The New Tale of Seafaring Street Minstrel Omatsu* (Torioi Omatsu kaijō shinwa, 1878), which a year earlier had also been originally published as a serialized novel in the *Kanayomi* newspaper and then published as a woodblock-printed *gōkan*. The poison woman in this story, as the title suggests, is a street performer *(torioi)* eventually released from her *hinin* ("nonhuman") status, who travels and sings for a pittance to those enamored of her beauty and voice. Omatsu's story, like Oden's, is complicated. It begins when the restoration war brings soldiers into the new city of Tokyo, providing an ample string of clients willing to pay for her talents. She begins an affair with one of them, only to swindle him in cahoots with her lover of the same caste, Ōsaka Kichi. When a law is passed to end discrimination toward *hinin* in 1872, Omatsu dreams of marrying up and into a life of luxury but is unable to escape an innate tendency toward swindling, thievery, and violence. After a near-drowning when she leaps from a boat to escape a lecherous man, and later rolls down the side of a hill, only narrowly escaping death by shooting her pursuer, Omatsu finally decides to make atonement for her evil deeds by lacerating her face in repentance. The self-inflicted cuts become infected and she dies a grotesque, hysterical death. Like *Demon's Tale, Seafaring Omatsu* also portrays female transgression as rooted in the body, which in this case substantiates her lower-class position as appropriate. Social reasons for her crimes are ignored. Any mention of the politically driven harassment of *hinin* after their release from their outcast status, the trouble they faced finding employment, and the discriminatory aspect of the new social status itself—they were referred to as "new commoners" or *shin-heimin* rather than "commoners" or *heimin* in early Meiji—is elided.[16] Instead Omatsu is painted as an untrustworthy whore and unworthy recipient of new freedoms accorded by the enlightenment, thereby validating the existence of an untouchable class as something rightly inherent to a kind of a body, ergo to a social body in a suspicious association of class discrimination and dementia.[17]

Omatsu's degeneration is framed as a natural outcome of her "polluted" origins. Kubota Hikosaku's account insists that this seductively beautiful woman of the underclass is constitutionally *not adaptable* to the new, democratic order. The serialized narrative of the life story told in linear, chronological mode itself embodies a phylogenetic progress. The poison woman does not progress to a higher, more civilized state but rather devolves. The social evolutionary model at work here marks the imperative of the human and animal world to generate or degenerate. The lower-class, sexual, nonreproductive woman—were she to survive—would push society in a devolutionary direction opposite reform efforts. The extinction of Omatsu by the end of the tale predictably enables the progress of the nation. Her death as a hysterical woman running in circles like a dog chasing its own tail is described as a natural outcome for this woman struggling on the fringes of society. This implicit discourse of "natural selection" in poison woman fiction makes economic or class inequality irrelevant for explaining criminal motivation. The nondomestic, sexually available woman is presented as a sick perversion of femininity and the antithesis of "progress," "evolution," "enlightenment," and "civilization"—conceptions of progress in early Meiji whose ubiquity reveals the actual tumultuousness of the new age for their insistent appearance.

In the following chapter, I discuss other ways in which women in these stories are painted as unworthy of the freedoms that new laws allegedly bestowed upon them in backhanded denials of women's ability to participate productively in the foundation of enlightenment ideas. Here I continue to focus on the way in which enlightenment discourses of science are manipulated to prove that the *body* of the poison woman, which is described as unfeminine, assertive, and even masculine, is ill and barbaric. The historian Hirota Masaki has convincingly argued in an essay on women in the enlightenment that the portrayal of the assertive woman as barbaric *(yaban)* reveals a fear of the woman who speaks for herself against the state and society in this transformative period in Japan's modern history.[18] Poison woman stories assert again and again that sexuality and aggressiveness in woman leads to the corruption of the self and the state, thereby demonizing female sexuality and scapegoating female autonomy as unfeminine.

In addition to heredity, transgressive gender behavior is cited as a sign of impending descent into criminality. *Demon's Tale* introduces the notion that the physical body and gender comportment must be inherently related, and this begins an extended proof that any deviation from feminine gender behavior by someone of the female sex is abnormal: "The male and female sexes are different. This difference in essence follows the design of the Creator and it is only to increase the human seed that we have these subtle changes in our odd bodily design. If under the spirit of good and evil a girl is stronger or superior to a boy, she has been born as in western philosophy as a so-called hermaphrodite."[19] In this vulgarized reference to physiology and gender, the narrator stipulates that for the female to be physically weaker than the male is a necessary condition for the maintenance of the "natural" order. Not only should a woman be weaker than a man but if she is stronger or superior, then as a matter of common sense she will not physically resemble a female but will have the physical attributes of a man. This emphasis on physical distinction as determining behavior relegates the female sex to the "naturally determined" weak position. This type of discourse may even serve to inhibit particular sexual or gender behaviors since it suggests that any woman who does not accept the submissive position of the weaker sex is "unnatural" and doomed to a (nonsedentary) life of crime.

In *Demon's Tale,* Oden acts differently than her reproductive organs would dictate. As a child, Oden upsets the natural order, under which those sexed female should behave in a feminine fashion, by behaving like a boy.

In detailing her childhood the narrator describes Oden as a "hellion" who engaged in rough and rowdy play. She bullied the boys and broke fences (fences are frequently broken or climbed in poison woman literature, representing the transgressive nature of the heroines) in order to sneak through a garden where she would "break blossoming tree branches," "pluck the grass," or "scramble up trees to steal the fruit." Her unruliness as a child and the obeisance she demanded from neighborhood boys as well as her own boyish nature are further elaborated:

> During New Year's she didn't show an ounce of interest in playing shuttle-cocks or bounding balls [like the other girls] but mixed with the boys, fly-ing kites in the wind and challenging them to top-spinning contests. She picked fights with the boys, grabbing those who tried to challenge her. She would put up her dukes and land a strong punch. She was as threatening as Yamabuki and Tomoe likely were in their youth. Even the brats of the hometown and neighboring villages and gang leaders bowed their heads to Oden. Nobody dared defy her orders.[20]

Oden's rude and masculine behavior, as described in *Demon's Tale,* was a crime against the natural law in which the woman is naturally, physically, the "weaker sex." Her masculinity, or the perceived split between her female body and behavior, marked her as a "troublemaker."

This understanding of the female as physically predetermined to be the weaker sex had been recently circulated in Japan via a best-selling proto-sexological conduct book (*Fujo seiri ichidai kagami,* 1874) translated by Hori Seitarō, and originally written by George H. Napheys as *The Physical Life of Woman: Advice to the Maiden, Wife, and Mother,* and is quoted later in *Demon's Tale* in reference to the proper sexual behavior for a young woman, illustrating its popularity among Japanese readers. The inclusion of a foreword by Mori Arinori is offered as proof of the useful and scientific nature of the book, which is similarly emphasized in the English-language version in an insert by the editor of the Philadelphia *Medical and Surgical Reporter,* who wrote that *The Physical Life of Woman* was "a work at once thoroughly representing modern science, and eminently adapted for fam-ily instruction. It is well suited to female readers, to whom it is especially addressed both in the matter it contains and in the delicacy with which points relating to their physiological life are mentioned."[21] Despite Mori's contemporary arguments for the equal treatment of the sexes within the family, he endorsed a book that argued the superiority of the male body in, for example, infantilizing descriptions of the bone structure and skull size of the female as small and "like a child's."

In *Demon's Tale,* expression of female sexual desire in any form is presented as deviant. In a close adaptation of the "Secret Bad Habits" section of the popular *Physical Life of Woman,* translated as *The Mirror of Female Physiology,* the narrator assumes the role of medical adviser and sounds a gentle warning to female readers:

> *The Mirror of Female Physiology* instructs that the girls' secretive bad habit, which arouses the sickness of sexual desire in young women, inflicts damage to the body and soul when given free reign. Years ago, an American Miss So-and-So related this in a missive to the mothers of America. It stated that this secret vice drives one to the grave, the madhouse, or worse, to the brothel. This has only to do with dissolute behavior and not the crime of thievery and murder.[22]

The coinciding section in the original states regarding the woman's "maiden stage": "We refer to the disastrous consequences on soul and body to which young girls expose themselves by exciting and indulging morbid passions. Years ago, Miss Catharine E. Beecher sounded a note of warning to the mothers of America on this secret vice, which leads their daughters to the grave, the madhouse, or, worse yet, the brothel."[23] Beecher, a prominent advocate for the separation of work roles in the teaching of home economics, which she referred to as "domestic science," is invoked to instill the fear of sexual indulgence, which, girls are warned, leads to prostitution and hysteria. An illustration in the final pages of *Demon's Tale* of adult women and a girl gathered around the various poison woman *gōkan* strewn across the tatami-matted floor to read about such sexual women is its own kind of self-indulgent pleasure, rendered even titillating when the narrator promises that they are not at risk of becoming a murderess solely for indulging in the "unnatural acts" of masturbation. Nevertheless, the self-indulgence in onanistic pleasure is explicitly connected to bad living and dissolute behavior—the first tantalizing step a young woman destined for madness might take unless she internalizes the lessons of the crime story before her.

The most dramatic example of an attempt to make the source for the poison woman's crime bodily and a result of being oversexed was Robun's inclusion of a report of the actual autopsy of Takahashi's corpse.[24] After the execution, Oden's beheaded body was taken to the Fifth Hospital of the Metropolitan Police in Asakusa. This was reported in various newspapers, including the *Tokyo Nichi Nichi Shinbun* (Tokyo Daily), simply as "Poison woman Takahashi Oden's corpse was autopsied *[kaibō]* at Asakusa's Fifth Hospital of the Metropolitan Police."[25] The *Tokyo Akebono* newspaper reported these findings in a more sensational fashion: "The corpse of the recently beheaded evil woman [akufu] Oden was autopsied and according to a source, this bold, intrepid outlaw [kyōto] had an excessive amount of fatty tissue. Oden had been in prison for four years but her strength did not dwindle, she was in excellent health."[26] In turn, *Demon's Tale* describes the final days of Oden's life:

> As such an audacious [daitan] woman, the corpse was dispatched to the Fifth Hospital of the Metropolitan Police in Asakusa. That year from the first to the fourth of February an exhaustive autopsy was performed and it was discovered that her brain was large and she had evidence of much fatty tissue, which indicated a profound sexual desire. Although Oden had relatives, no one came to pick up the corpse so the hospital handled the funeral arrangements. The evil person comes to ruin while the good person prospers. The world's enlightenment progresses forward as the people shout their cheers of jubilation—hurrah and a hearty hurrah![27]

Okamoto Kisen, who wrote at the same time his own competing biography of Takahashi, similarly reported that "the excessive amount of fatty tissue in her brain proved the source of her wanton [tajō] nature." Later descriptions of the autopsy reveal that it was led by Dr. Osanai Takeshi, who was joined by three of his colleagues—Koizumi Chikamasa, Eguchi Yuzuru, and Takada Tadayoshi—and nine other male observers to discover the physical reasons for her criminality.[28] One postwar text quotes the original autopsy report as saying, "Takahashi Oden's genital area was autopsied. Discovered was excessive hypertrophy and fleshiness in the labia minora [shōinshin]. Moreover, the development of the clitoral area [inteibu] was remarkable and expansion of the vaginal interior and opening was visible."[29] Her body was the raw material for the production of scientific knowledge for these Meiji physicians, who, like many of their Victorian counterparts, seem to have believed that the origins of social ills might be found through empirical research into the body. The autopsy of Oden's corpse appeared to clear up questions remaining from the convoluted two-and-a-half year trial that had ended in execution. Ascribing to rudimentary biological determinism, differences detected through comparison of bodies seemed to provide contemporaries with evidence that criminality was physically determined rather than socially or otherwise. No proof of exactly how an excessive amount of fatty tissue might change behavior was suggested, but the stories by Robun and Kisen claim that this physical state marks excessive desire (jōyoku), which is then treated as the source for Oden's deviant behavior.

The equation of female sexuality with crime appears much earlier in Chinese seventeenth-century stories of fatal women or "castle topplers." Anne McLaren writes about three such stories that "reflect a particular strain of misogynistic thinking: that women who pursue their own sexual desires have a catastrophic effect on family and society. The heroines follow the dictates of their own passions and thereby bring about the ruin of their families and of those near them."[30] The stereotypical Chinese "castle toppler" or "one who ruins city and state" (*qing guo qing cheng*), however, is essentially a girl of a good family, sometimes based on a historical figure, who gives way to her passions and ruins her life, receiving divine retribution for her moral failings along with anyone else involved with her. While there are various comparisons that could be made between the premodern femme fatale of Ming fiction, which finds its way into Tokugawa-era literature, and the Meiji-era poison woman, here I would like to emphasize that while the poison woman is depicted as sexual like the Ming femme fatale, illicit sexual behavior is not the product of her evil nature; rather sexuality and gender deviance are a symptom of an essentially perverse nature, which manifests itself in the body. This perverse nature is the root cause of nonsexual crimes like murder and thievery. Furthermore, as dramatically distinct from Ming literature, the poison woman is identified empirically through the use of science and technology—and news of her perversity brought her great attention in the rapidly expanding media system.

Demon's Tale emphasizes its claim of Oden's sexual aberration through visual images.[31] An illustrative depiction of the autopsy covers four pages. The first shows Oden's corpse lying naked on a waist-high table, which stands on a decoratively tiled floor, with four doctors in attendance. The second woodblock image shows a scroll displaying a chart of a female body labeled "Autopsy chart of the female body, the thirty-first day of the second month, Meiji 12." The chart is labeled to designate that it is of a general female body although the inclusion of a date suggests that it represents Oden's body in particular. This chart hangs vertically behind a table holding a cup filled with scalpels. Implied in this woodblock print is the notion that Oden's crime was an expression of hidden abnormalities of the body. A woman's body, with the interrogating eye of science, could confirm her guilt or innocence, sanity or irrationality. Kisen's earlier poison woman story of "Night Storm" Okinu, who was executed in 1872 for the murder of her patron, depicts the severed head of Okinu, which had been displayed in the fashion of traditional Tokugawa punitive practices. In *Demon's Tale*, it is the *internal* body that is reproduced for public display.

The representation of Takahashi Oden as an ill body in an extended

Figure 1. Autopsy of Takahashi Oden. From Kanagaki Robun, *Takahashi Oden yasha monogatari* (The tale of demon Takahashi Oden) (Tsujibun, 1879).

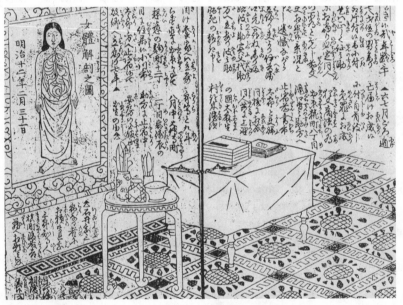

Figure 2. A chart of the autopsy of "a female body." From Robun, *Takahashi Oden yasha monogatari.*

media network points to the development of a new cultural logic related to female desire and behavior. Moral coercion is replaced by practical knowledge. Undesirable behavior in women is identified through the examination of "facts" and experimentation. Under this type of system, doctors and lab attendants could be imagined as ideologically uninvolved. Facts could be made to speak for themselves and the writer who invoked this evidence played the role of mere translator of the "natural" world, which was positivistically presented as neutral, factual, and unassailable. Under this semiotic system, facts were attributed a great deal of power while the notion that ideological conditions supported this reification of facts was ignored and the political or social aspects of acts of crime left unexamined.[32] The body was established as perhaps the most authoritative source for providing evidence of innocence or (usually) guilt. And the female deviant was created as a useful counterexample that could be manipulated in suggesting the proper development of a woman within the community and national body. In a similar case, Sander Gilman has shown how, for example, the Hottentot woman became the object of abnormalization in developing an image of a healthy (colonialist) nation. Her purported primitivism and sexual deviance were made signifier of the "appropriateness" of her inferior colonial status.[33]

In the postmortem study reported in Robun and Kisen's *gōkan,* Oden was found to have physical abnormalities that were determined to be the source of her deviant behavior. But what was the source of comparison? Where were the data for "normal" organs against which hers were compared? What sorts of classificatory systems of inclusion and exclusion (ones that continue to drive modernity) engaged the early Meiji reader? This attention to the body seemed to be premised on a popular understanding of the body as phrenological and embedded with signs, which indicated personal character once analyzed and decoded. Contemporaneous to poison woman stories, another publishing boom was taking place in a nascent field of sexological literature that also encouraged the analysis of the body, especially the sexual and reproductive capacities of the body. Called "books of nature" or *zōkakiron,* these studies of the reproductive organs cascaded onto the market in the 1870s and 1880s.[34] Ishii Kendō, founder of the Meiji Culture Research Society in pre–World War II Japan, writes in his multivolume *The Origin of Things Meiji* (Meiji jibutsu kigen) that *zōkakiron* marked the beginning of translated literature on sex *(sei)* and he refers to the *Tokyo Shinshi* journal, which stated that by 1879 (the year that *Demon's Tale* was published) *shunga* (erotic) books were in decline while *zōka* histories were all the rage.[35] Books of nature were introduced in Japan through the translation by Chiba Shigeru in 1875 of James Ashton's *Book of Nature* (1865). This scholarly text was republished a year later for the general populace as *The Layman's Book of Nature* (Tsūzoku zōkakiron*)* "with Japanese alphabetic script *[furigana]* for easy reading," as the *Kanayomi* newspaper reported.[36] Both versions of Ashton's *Book of Nature* enjoyed such success that another sexological tome by the prolific Dr. Edward Foote was translated under the same generic title *Book of Nature* (Zōkakiron, 1879).[37] The extraordinary popularity of these texts encouraged further translation and original writing of books of nature delineating desire, reproduction, sexual disease, and how to trace inherited traits. Some publishers cornered their share of the market by offering the cheapest volumes. Others provided intermittent illustrations of fallopian tubes, spermatozoa, and gynecological instruments to attract the prurient. Publication remained steady until around 1885 when the number of books of nature published began to drop. Oda Makoto cites nearly thirty titles, with at least one appearing annually, from 1875 to 1890.[38]

Robun's own *Kanayomi* newspaper, in which poison woman stories were first serialized, was a primary advertising site for books of nature. Between 1876 and 1880 at least thirty advertisements and articles about books of nature were published.[39] Some articles described the contents of books of nature as illustrative of the difference between the male and female sexual organs such as an article on 9 August 1876 lauding the preponderance of images in one discussion of the genital organs. Others simply reported the enormous popularity of the books of nature. An article of 13 July 1878 stated that the popularity of books of nature was "shocking" and told how one illustration from a book of nature displayed in a bookstore had been stolen. Yet other articles, such as one dated 5 December 1877, compared the sex manuals of the premodern period with these new sexological texts stating that the pillow books of old *(mukashi no makura sōshi)* and books of nature were different. One article discussed the importance of reading books of nature before marriage. An 18 August 1877 article suggested that a geisha engaged to be married should read books of nature, and a 31 August 1879 news story also in the *Kanayomi* suggested that those new to marriage should read books of nature. One letter from a reader even suggested that the books of nature were symbolic of the enlightenment (20 August 1877). One advertisement for the popularized version of Ashton's *Book of Nature* claimed that the book provided information on appropriate bedroom behavior, how to conceive, how to trace inherited traits to determine what sort of child a couple will give birth to, proper childbirth measures,

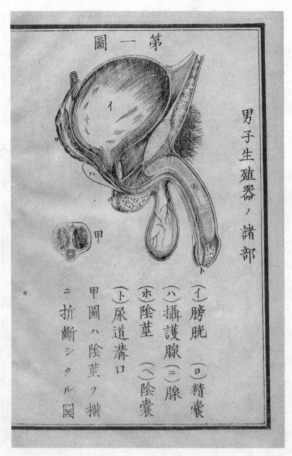

Figure 3. An illustration from a "book of nature." From Katayama Heisaburō, trans., *Zoku Zōka hiji* (The Secrets of Nature) (Tōyodō, 1877).

the prevention and treatment of sexually transmitted diseases, the dangers of masturbation, and other "practical" information. An extended description of a book of nature in the *Kanayomi* newspaper said that illness in children was the result of sexual passion *(jōyoku)*. In this same article the ills of masturbation were repeatedly suggested.[40] In appealing to the female reader, the advertisements emphasized the books' accessibility for all types of women "from the wife, to the experienced geisha, to the prostitute." In short, books of nature were early perpetrators of a new popular interest in bodily functions, desire, generation, and heredity referenced repeatedly within *Demon's Tale*.[41]

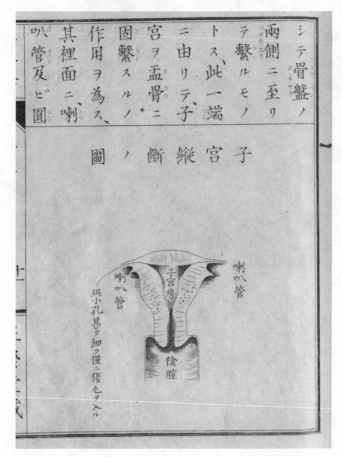

Figure 4. An illustration from a "book of nature." From Tashiro Kidoku, *Zōka: Seisei shinron* (Nature: A new treatise on life) (Sei'eidō, 1879).

Recent scholarly discussions of books of nature are concerned with placing them within a broader diachronic historiography of sexology in Japan and analyzing the impact of books of nature on attitudes toward sex and gender within a binary framework of nativist versus Western sexological knowledge.[42] As Ueno Chizuko has remarked plaintively in conversation with the Tokugawa literature and culture scholar Tanaka Yuko, the introduction of this type of sexual knowledge supplanted a (nostalgic) age of an uninhibited eros with a "Weberian" style of sex ruled by Protestant ethics of conservation and controlled use. In an informative introductory essay on *zōkakiron,* Ueno outlines four sexological literature categories that frame them as nativist, imported, or nativized translated sexology texts; Japanese sexology texts (often only loosely) based on Western models; books on *ars erotica* inherited from Edo literature; and conduct books for men and women in the tradition of Kaibara Ekiken's *Yōjōkun* (Lessons for a Cultivated Life, 1713), which described the general methods of health maintenance including advice on nutritional intake, exercise, and sexual activity.[43] At the same time, Ueno does note that the language of books of nature is a hybrid mix of Sino-Japanese lexicon and Western concepts. The historian Gregory Pflugfelder observed that the books of nature drew on Confucian and Shinto language and the male-female coitus represented in them related to the Sino-Japanese notion of the encounter of yin and yang "whose interaction served as the moving force behind the entire universe."[44] In this sense, the *zōka* of *zōkakiron* refers to the celestial and natural order much in the way that "nature" in the initial *Book of Nature* by Ashton refers to a transcendental cosmos that is also aligned with the laws of evolution. The simultaneous inclusion of references to a Western nature and the mythical progenitors of Japan, Izanami and Izanagi, constitutes only one example of the hybrid nature of this new scientific discourse that combined nativist knowledge with Western knowledge. My concern, however, is not to consider books of nature within a retrospective diachronic history of sexology within a nativist / Western dichotomy but rather to explore the way in which discussions of the body in books of nature dovetail with those in poison woman fiction and suggest that in both we see a physiocentric discourse that identifies every type of body as an integral part of the natural order through an appeal to positivist thought. It is precisely this logic that enabled a physiological explication of transgressive behavior and an elision of the political underpinnings of that transgression. Books of nature identified human bodies as desiring subjects in a larger generative social order. In them, the libidinal and reproductive functions of the individual body are part of an integrated natural and social system. This enabled a new logic of exclusion and difference and the development of a system of normalization premised on a popular new understanding of the body as phrenological and embedded with signs whose meanings could be interpreted through empirical analysis.

A comparison of a book of nature illustration with the second woodblock print of the autopsy chart in *Demon's Tale* shows the image to be clearly modeled after the lithographic and woodblock images of male and female generative organs common to books of nature, which were so popular at the time of Oden's execution. This image links reports of Oden's physical abnormalities, which provided illustrative proof of an unusual, excessive sexual energy, with the new science of books of nature, for which size did often matter, and not exclusively in female cases. One example from

Chiba's translation *The Layman's Book of Nature* states that men with large testes tire less when having sexual relations: "The testes are large or small depending on the person. Among them are those with large ones, but testes the size of a pigeon egg are most usual. It can be said that men with large testes can take advantage of the joys of the bedroom without exhausting their vigor in the bedroom but there is no real difference in terms of producing a child."[45]

The books of nature implicitly encouraged an appeal to the body, and size within the body, to understand behavior. In the case of Takahashi Oden, the findings of the autopsy were proffered as evidence of the physical aberrations that produced criminal behavior. This is not only true for early Meiji but continued to be important into the 1930s, as discussed in chapter 4, when somatic analyses of female deviants were discussed with little recourse to ideological or social concerns. That Takahashi Oden's reproductive organs were preserved in formaldehyde by the original doctor presiding over the 1879 autopsy and passed from research collection to research collection to be once again analyzed in 1935 (!) illustrates that early Meiji marks the halting, amateurish start of a long-lived popular science that sought to explain crime by women via the body.[46]

The interest in Oden's physiology and sexuality reignited in 1935 when an army surgeon from Keiō University's medical school remeasured Takahashi's reproductive and sex-related body parts, which had been kept in formaldehyde in the Toyama-chō's Army Medical School. Oden's formaldehyde-secured organs were reexamined with the same concern about size. Perhaps not surprisingly, her genitals and reproductive organs were again found to be pathologically large. This time every detail from the inner labia to the clitoris to the length of the uterus was recorded in pages of measurements. The labia majora and minora, on both the right and left sides, and the thickness and length of the clitoris were measured in detail along with the ovaries, the womb, the kidneys, the distance from the labia majora to the anus, and so on. Some of these findings were charted in a table that compared the labia of three groups: the "Japanese," the "Europeans," and "Oden." Substantial differences arose in comparing the "height" of the labia majora, for which the "Europeans" measured 1.5–2 centimeters while "Japanese" measured 6.8 millimeters and "Oden" measured a mere 2 millimeters (right side) and 5 millimeters (left side). The differences in length were not discussed. However, the difference in length of the labia minora left "Oden" looking quite "abnormal" with a length of 63 millimeters (right) and 60 millimeters (left) and "Europeans" at 25–35 millimeters. Statistics were not offered for the "Japanese" labia

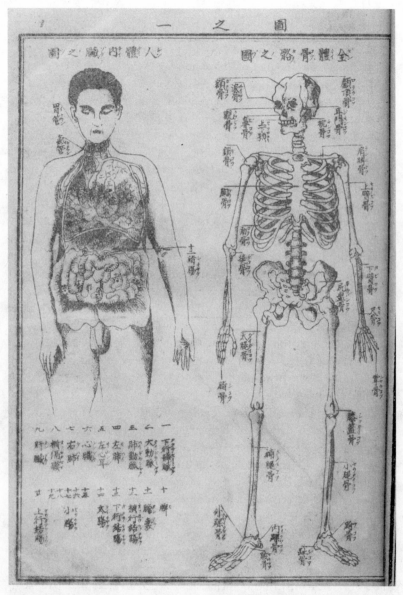

Figure 5. An illustration from a later "book of nature." Mutō Tadao, *Danjo jiei: Zōkaki-shinron* (On man and woman: A new treatise on the mechanics of nature) (Aoki Kosandō, 1894).

minora length. The "height" of the labia minora for "Oden" is also much greater at 27 millimeters (right) and 25 millimeters (left) and the "Japanese" at 18.2 millimeters with "Europeans" only measuring 8 to 15 millimeters.[47] This is presumably proof of Oden's abnormal sexual and therefore criminal nature.

The translation of transgression into physiological terms in Meiji offered an opportunity to settle the political position of women once and for all, ironically through the *exclusion* of women from political agency on pre-political grounds. The social and political contexts of the real woman Takahashi's crime were silenced in favor of isolating her as abject, inhuman, and grotesque. This new reliance on the body to figure the place of the individual in society appeared to displace previous social, class, and regional categories by bringing national bodies under the umbrella of a single all-encompassing generative order. In this way the proposed laws of nature allowed thinkers to imagine themselves working beyond and free from human prejudice. It is precisely the image of an integrated system within which the libidinal and reproductive functions of the individual body are imagined as mirroring a larger universal system that enabled a new logic of exclusion and definition of difference that were extended beyond the body of science into literature and media. The convicted woman was discounted as a worthy, political body through the identification of bodily "facts," repeated in the media by medical and newspapermen, which marked her as sexually monstrous.

The radical consequences of the demonization of female criminality through bodily evidence were her trivialization as a political body even while she was symbolically central to gender politics. The treatment of the "sexually deviant" female criminal in early Meiji is not so different from that of 1890s America, as evidenced by the historian Lisa Duggan's study of the murderess Alice Mitchell. According to Duggan, "the populations and subjects trivialized as 'merely' sexual or disruptively violent . . . have been at the center of politics, imbricated among the defining terms of democratic possibility, all along."[48] The exclusion of particular bodies by deeming them deviant points toward the way that so-called egalitarian rule is always circumscribed. Oden is imagined as atypical, even pathologically sick, but her atypicality is dependent on the coordination of bodies to represent the standard "citizen" and particularly the healthy female citizen. Similar to Michel Foucault's *scienza sexualis* for which sex "is subordinated in the main to the imperatives of a morality whose divisions it reiterated under the guise of the medical norm," in Japan, as early as 1878, a proto-sexological science was used to ascribe a morality by speaking of bodily phenomena in terms of social evil.[49] The discourse of vice is combined with genetic disease to minimize and trivialize the social aspects of transgressive acts by women through sensationalism. It should not be surprising that this projection of a social fantasy (or nightmare) back onto a domestic crime occurred at a critical time in history when women's social position and political rights, from the right to own property to their future inclusion in governmental politics, were under debate.

Enlightenment Science, Early Meiji Literature, and the Poison Woman

The way that literature and criticism by *gōkan* writers of the time engaged with contemporaneous enlightenment discourses illustrated the literary flexibility that had been the hallmark of the broader body of *gesaku* writing before Meiji. The references to factuality, heredity, education, and sexological knowledge in a narrative celebrating enlightenment ideas suggest an attempt by writers of the early modern form of *gōkan* to remain relevant during this era of modernization. The often-cited incident used to mark a shift in Robun and his cohort's writing in Meiji is a pledge made by Robun and Sansantei Arindo in response to three proclamations *(sanjō no kyōken)* issued by the government in 1872. Robun and Arindo promised the Ministry of Education that they would reform their writing by ridding it of "falsehoods."[50] The success of this "conversion" is perhaps best measured by the extent to which Robun was able to rid his writing of its distinctive and highly refined satirical style. As certain sections of his *Kanayomi* newspaper bear out (the "Myō-myō chinbun" section in particular), despite their claims to the contrary Robun and fellow writers resisted completely dropping their sardonic style, which traditionally could be employed in glossing criticisms of government in the Tokugawa period and the new Meiji oligarchs. The *Kanayomi* was in fact renowned for its ironical, critical style. And newspaper "contributors" continued to put their sharp-witted tongues to effect. Nevertheless, the plea directed at writers by government and pro-enlightenment intellectuals to replace fiction or pedantic learning *(kyogaku)* with utilitarian and true learning *(jitsugaku)* and the pledge in 1872 by Robun and Arindo to participate actively in the affirmation of enlightenment ideology illustrate that even the prolific authors of parody and wordplay were not immune to the ideological pressures of enlightenment thought. In an early essay, the literary scholar Maeda Ai described how poison woman literature constituted one particular example of the way in which new stories by *gesaku* writers contributed to the promotion of modern social reforms:

In the midst of the "devil-may-care" *[eejanaika]* revelry, the suddenly re-leased hope and energy of the people was slowly but surely incorporated into the new systems, though the ignited desire to change the world con-tinued to smolder for some time. The poison women Oden, Okinu, and Omatsu were the criminal embodiment of the processes of the suppression, and punishment of the people's energy that overflowed in "devil-may-care" fashion. The *gesaku* writers who explained their demise through "reward virtue and punish vice" *(kanzen chōaku)* [morality] unwittingly affirmed the societal regulations and current practice.[51]

Robun expanded his literary talents to writing the news by founding the *Kanayomi* newspaper. Newspaper reports by such veteran writers not only encouraged literary experimentation (and indeed we find a dizzying array of literary and vernacular styles in any single newspaper edition at this time) but also encouraged the production and consumption of woodblock-printed books about "newsworthy" subjects, including murderous women. Through both types of publications, these Meiji writers revitalized their prose to a surprising extent, such that they appeared to be as invested in reform as other groups in Meiji society.

The writer Takabatake Ransen commented on the early Meiji impera-tive to reform even popular literature by characterizing the period as hos-tile to the irrational and nonsensical. His frustration with the increasing irrelevance of prior more inventive or fantastical forms of literature appears in the characteristic comical language of the "scribbler":

> Since the Restoration, every spectator is a scholar. Deviate in the slightest and they [the readers] impatiently charge that it's a lie, complaining if it's not a true story of the day *[tōji no jitsuroku]*. . . . A writer, if he wants to be in good graces with you, the readership, must turn to writing recent true records *[jikki]*. Clearly the most difficult aspect of this approach is first of all that revenge is prohibited, and practicing incantation is not based on natural principles *[ri]*, and as the metamorphosis of living and dead spirits is associated with the mysticism of Shintoism and Buddhism, they obvi-ously have no use. Were parents and siblings to be separated, with today's strict family records so unlike those of the past together with the postal ser-vice and telegraph system, they would not be apart for long. Since murders and disputes are the burden of police now, vagaries are not suitable as the stuff for fiction, so that writers have become silent on the matter. Writers can cry all they want about it but the world is now explained according to principles.

Ransen added as a satirical afterthought, "There's no reason to condemn the enlightenment though."[52] Ransen frames his argument squarely within the context of *jitsugaku* discourse, observing that the absurd and irrational are no longer viable as topics for writers of popular fiction because of a new regard for the empirical and technological. This quote rightly strikes the literary scholar Yamamoto Yoshiaki as an early realization that conventional approaches to fiction were no longer culturally meaningful. Yamamoto's comments suggest that Ransen was a step ahead of Tsubouchi Shōyō, who has been such a celebrated figure in modern literary history for his critique of "Meiji *gesaku* literature" and promotion of a new novelistic style, as discussed in the following excerpt from Shōyō's "Essence of the Novel" essay (Shōsetsu shinzui, 1885):

> This is indeed a "golden age" of *shōsetsu*. There is certainly no shortage of *gesaku* writers but most of them write adaptations. Not one can be called a writer in his own right. Every recently published *shōsetsu* and *haishi* has been a reworking of Bakin or Tanehiko, if not an imitation of Ikku or Shunsui. *Gesaku* writers of late have taken to heart the words of Li Yu— they regard didacticism as the main purpose of *shōsetsu* and *haishi,* and construct a moral framework within whose bounds they strive to devise a plot, with the result that even if they have not consciously set out to mimic earlier writers, the restricted scope of their *haishi* nevertheless forces them along already well-worn paths.[53]

Meiji *gesaku,* a category that Atsuko Ueda has shown to have been in great part created by Shōyō specifically as a category of derision, was in Shōyō's eyes stylistically retrograde, uncompelling, and wholly unreformed.[54]

Putting aside the dubiousness of Shōyō's claims, it is clear that critiques that Shōyō made regarding "Meiji *gesaku*" were not unprecedented. Ransen addresses the weaknesses of contemporary literature more specifically by pointing toward its overuse of claims to empiricism. Another writer of poison woman fiction and newspaper editor, Itō Kyōto, was also critical of the direction "*gesaku* writers" were taking modern Japanese literature:

> *Gesaku* writers who previously had appropriated past forms to richly embellish their fiction *[haishi shōsetsu]* which was considered to be lies *[uso],* all went down at once, as if ambushed, calling everything they wrote (and there were plenty of non-truths) "true stories!, true stories!" thinking that without waving the flag of "truth" *[jissetsu],* they wouldn't sell. Only half digesting the enlightenment they did not comprehend the mysteries of

fiction. In spite of that, recently human knowledge has progressed. Since there is less interest in empty stories *[hana-naki-mono]* disguised as true statements *[jissetsu]*, real flowers will develop and fiction will inevitably prosper.[55]

Jitsuroku is portrayed by Kyōtō as an only superficially reformed type of fiction and an "unenlightened" one that he predicted would see its demise shortly.[56] This author, who was a disciple of Kanagaki Robun and later criticized Robun's writing quite vigorously, was a reporter for the *Ukiyo* (Floating World) newspaper and wrote a poison woman novel around this time, *A Strange Story of Enlightenment: The Revenge of the Photograph* (Kaimei kidan shashin no adauchi, 1884), using the pen name Itō Senzō. In *Revenge of the Photograph* the narrator does not make explicit claims to historical truth in the fashion of Robun and Kisen in their poison woman stories. Instead, the author describes his story as akin to photography—as a mimetic copy or visual-based reproduction of reality.

The Revenge of the Photograph: Technology and Crime in Enlightenment Fiction

The story *Revenge of the Photograph*, which was included in one of the earliest collections of poison women tales, the *Newly Edited Poison Woman Tales of the Ages* (Shinpen kokon dokufu-den, 1887), begins with a preface to the story by the author. Senzō engages in traditional wordplay familiar to Tokugawa *gesaku*, using, however, the newer vocabulary of photography, signaling the degree to which science and technology will play an integral role in this story of a poison woman. In using the language of photography, Senzō promises that his story will capture *(utsusu)* like a photograph *(shashin)* a picture of the world, and that the publisher will reproduce *(fukusha)* multiple copies. Senzō apologizes that the job of writing at first did not go well because "human feelings *[ninjō]* are a thing of the darkroom." He continues, "But when they pressed me, as in glass photography, to hurry, I composed a landscape, portrait, and denouement despite the absence of light."[57] Senzō appeals to truth in a different fashion from previous poison woman authors. The emphasis is not on the inclusion of reportage to illustrate moral truths but on versimilitude in telling a story of the world *(yo no hanashi)* with reference to visual image.

Revenge of the Photograph features the search by the son of a doctor of Chinese medicine to find the killer of his father. At the start of the story, son Hikonojo itches to learn Western medicine and begs an official, Samon, to let him travel, despite his father's prohibition, with an official envoy to

America in order to learn Western medicine, which, he argues, "will be for the good of the family, the country, and all of mankind." Samon responds, "The parental love which seeks to detain you is to be expected where there is affection. That you should want to cross over to a distant land in spite of this and undergo medical training reveals your spirit to be one to which even a warrior could not lay claim."[58] Hikonojo's father is convinced later that morning by Samon to let his son travel: "You have a splendid son, surpassing all others in this world, which makes me envious. Do not mention your misgivings; give him your permission to travel abroad. When he has completed his studies, think of how famous he will become, bringing glory to the family name."[59] Hikonojo leaves with the envoy and, upon arriving in San Francisco, feigns illness so that he might introduce himself to the director of the hospital. The director is impressed with Hikonojo's ardor to learn Western medicine and readily agrees to take Hikonojo under his wing:

> "That a man with such perseverance and determination should come to our country is in itself a blessing for America. I will entirely impart to you the medical secrets of hundreds of scholars, and if you spread these in Japan, the honor it will bring to this country will be beyond words. . . . Medicine and natural philosophy were originally closely connected, and if one who practices medicine does not know natural philosophy, even though he may improve his medical skills it is all for nothing. So follow me and I will teach you.". . . [Hikonojo] worked under Dr. Elayman studying natural philosophy and exact science. As an introduction to these sciences, Dr. Elayman first taught the skill of photographic technology to his pupil.[60]

The narrative leaves San Francisco to return to Japan where, a year after Hikonojo had left for San Francisco, his father has begun an affair with a geisha, which sends his jealous wife Okinu into a rage. Sexual jealousy and desire for her male servant lead Okinu, now referred to as a poison woman within the text, to kill her husband. She and her lover Denji poison her husband with a mixture of opium and alcohol. After the murderous poisoning, Okinu begins investing in the raw silk trade and increases her wealth tenfold. Despite her financial success, Okinu grows increasingly guilty and finally has a nervous breakdown. The poison woman Okinu, in divine retribution, is herself poisoned and dies a gruesome death on the seventh anniversary of her husband's death from accidentally imbibing boiled spring chrysanthemum rife with the poisonous eggs of the tiger beetle.

Okinu's son, Hikonojo, returns to Japan after thirteen years of study in America and is soon renowned for his expertise in Western medicine.

Powerful lords are impressed especially with his knowledge of photography. Hikonojo eventually learns the full story of his mother's jealousy at his father's indiscretions and the poisoning of his father by his mother and Denji from a chance meeting with the previous caretaker of his father's house, Gen'an. Though Gen'an had been bribed by Okinu and Denji to keep their secret quiet, Hikonojo forgives his silence regarding the murder, to which Gen'an replies tearfully, "Maybe it's because you have lived for a long time in that country of America, which I hear is a country of culture and enlightenment, but you mercifully do not rebuke me for my conduct . . . even though I am dog-like in my lowliness."[61] Hikonojo generously decides to give Gen'an work, and here the narrative continues to promote Western science while deprecating Chinese medicine:

> "Chinese medicine will soon be obsolete so from now on you will learn Western medicine. Since the most difficult task will be to master Western medicine in three to five years, to help you, I will teach you the science of photography. You will become a master photographer in a year or two and then you will easily be able to make your way in the world."
>
> Gen'an was overjoyed at hearing Hikonojo say this. "I am grateful to you for teaching me this rare science of photography. In the foreign land, you have studied not just medicine, but have advanced your study as far as the field of photography." Hikonojo replied. "Since medicine and exact science are difficult to separate, they must be learned together. That's why I have learned the science of photography. Look at these carefully. They are all photographs I have taken myself."[62]

Gen'an, perusing the photographs, finds within them a picture of Okinu's ex-lover and accomplice Denji, whom Hikonojo by chance had healed of neuralgia at the Hakone spa. Gen'an identifies the subject of the photograph as Hikonojo's adulteress mother's lover and accomplice in the crime to kill his father. Hikonojo exacts a confession from Denji when he unexpectedly stays in the same inn. Denji attempts to murder Hikonojo with a pistol but is unsuccessful and turns the pistol on himself.

As with *Demon's Tale*, scientific knowledge takes the investigator to the source of the murder. *Revenge of the Photograph* also incorporates affirmations of the enlightenment and science in its tale of a poison woman, although it is written in a style that anticipates future detective fiction, unlike *Demon's Tale*, which more resembles a *jitsurokumono*, or true tale. The incorporation in both stories, however, of a new rhetoric of *evidence* is apparent when we compare it with a broadsheet, which tellingly does not include a date, featuring the poison woman "Night Storm" Okinu, who poi-

Figure 6. An illustration of a photo shoot by Hikonojo, trained in the West as a doctor. From *Kaimei kidan: Shashin no adauchi* (A strange story of enlightenment: The revenge of the photograph) (1883), in *Shinpen kokon dokufu den* (Newly edited poison woman tales of the ages) (Genkadō, 1887).

soned her patron in 1872. This colorful *Tokyo Nichi Nichi Shinbun* handbill *(shinbun nishiki-e)* relating the beheading of "Night Storm" Okinu compares the female criminal to a coppery pheasant drowning in her own beauty:

> The copper pheasant in love with the hues of her beautiful plumage, will inevitably drown in her own reflection in the mirror of water. While living stylishly in a house with a decorative bamboo lattice in the Komagata neighborhood, a mistress's unclouded spirit went crazy for love. She who had an affair with the handsome young actor was the wanton Harada Okinu, a retired geisha. A flower readily plucked at the wayside belongs with the sapphire crane's storm. Her nefarious intentions were spurred by her carnal desire to be a couple with him. . . . Pursuing an evil scheme that leads straight to hell she bought the blue box with white lettering of ratsbane, and fatally poisoned her patron. But how could she escape the nets of heaven? Caught by authorities, the man was sentenced to imprisonment, the woman, to death and public exposure of her severed head.[63]

This story is heavy with ornamental rhetoric even though its presumed objective is to report the news of a woman's poisoning of her patron. In contrast to later poison woman narratives in which the criminal is judged and punished explicitly by state institutions, the ruling arm of justice here is abstractly referred to as the "nets of heaven." Okinu is depicted as both a wanton narcissistic woman guilty of self-indulgence and passion and a delicate flower at the mercy of a young actor. Typical reward-virtue-and-punish-vice morality is used to explain that her crime will be divinely punished. The brief narrative is emplotted and incorporates reportage, but judgment focuses on the moral transgression performed by an opaque body stereotypically described as seductive, feminine, and beautiful. The handbill is concerned with the details of the criminal act but no special attention is paid to the female criminal's body as a source of "truth," as evidenced in the colorful but conventional characterization of the dangerous woman as seductively beautiful, even sultry.

In contrast to the handbill and the play, *Demon's Tale* and *Revenge of the Photograph* are informed by a rhetoric that emphasizes evidence as way of proving the woman's guilt. Robun's narrator prefaces *Demon's Tale* with a promise to employ empirical evidence in telling a true tale that will teach the secret of being an enlightened citizen of the new Meiji order:

> Basing their stories on the fiction of the poison woman's wicked lies, there is not a newspaper serial that has gotten at the truth. The fact that every reporter adds a postscript to that effect proves that the real news needs to be recorded. Hereafter, this volume, roughly speaking, will try to get at the truth with only a modicum of embellishment in certain passages. I offer this as a moral tale for boys, ladies, and girls.[64]

In addition to the insistence of the narrator that this story is true, the fact that the story was based on an actual incident and shares details with newspaper stories of the time also made it appear more closely aligned with the actual event. And *Demon's Tale* is only one well-known example of the extraordinarily common use of the rhetoric of factuality and truth in poison woman stories through which the narrator assumes authority. The "moral justice" proffered in this story is of a different nature from the Tokugawa *gesaku*-style *kanzen chōaku* morality. The point that the Meiji moral imparative to reward virtue and punish vice differed from that of the Tokugawa era has been made by Hirata Yumi, who argues that a shift occurred in Meiji newspapers in the interpretation of the "reward the virtuous, punish vice" morality whereby the doctrine could be interpreted anew under the recently introduced ideology of utilitarianism.[65] My comparison of the handbill with *Demon's Tale* illustrates that in *Demon's Tale* the narrator's claim to provide moral education is produced through evidentiary truths provided by the narrator. The "biography" speaks with authority, the narrator claiming to provide intelligibility to seemingly unconnected facts in a striking combination of literary prose and reportage. *Revenge of the Photograph* combines depictions of new technologies and Western learning and claims to mimetic writing to place the story directly within the contemporary ethos of enlightenment thought.

Clearly the writers and editors attempted to revitalize their prose in keeping with the dramatic social transformation in which the previous literary language was losing its signifying power, but this is not to say that poison woman fiction was free of literary convention.[66] The Meiji literature scholar Ino Kenji claimed that this push to proclaim practical learning as a worthy goal within literature—and evident in *Revenge of the Photograph* in the use of Western medicine and technology to solve the mystery of a murderous mother—impeded imaginative thought in general:

> From the outset, the Meiji government enlightenment policy prohibited the naive imagination of the common people to flutter in the direction of a truly radiant, extravagant investigation into the new possibilities for humankind. Just as the popularity of the soon to be inaugurated so-called true-stories *[jitsurokumono]* illustrates, in the adherence to trivial factuality, the people were obliged to express the so-called "practical learning" *[jitsugaku]* and the will to self-discipline from which the absurd was eliminated.[67]

While Ino laments the reliance upon "practical learning" discourse in literature, Hirata has critiqued the conventionality of the female characters, though she concludes that later novels were not free of this conventionality. Regarding the *monogatari* (story) and *shōsetsu* (novel), she concludes that portrayals of "woman," including the poison woman in early Meiji, were reduced to oversimplified stereotypes:

> The "modern" novel, dispensing with the geisha as heroine, did not free the woman from being a mirror of male desire, nor return the narrative to the woman herself. The great chorus of criticism of the habits of female students around 1890, appearing not only in newspapers and magazines but in novels, meant that the vulnerability imposed on the female "poison woman" to the "fallen geisha" now made its target the "female student," producing

a new narrative. Stories narrating woman were always appropriated stories narrated by men; and woman, torn between the chaste woman and evil woman, remained both the object of eulogy and chastisement.[68]

This argument that female characters were empty of a modern subjectivity and served distinct purposes in narrative is similar to one made by Nancy Armstrong on nineteenth-century English fiction regarding the transgressive woman. In Armstrong's analysis the "monstrous woman" is found to be "one step in a series of displacements that eventually relegated a whole realm of social practices to the status of disruption and deviance requiring containment and discipline."[69] Significantly, Hirata is disappointed not only by the conventionality of female characters in poison woman literature but in later novels, making the important point that early Meiji *gōkan* literature need not be considered to have embodied all that is retrograde and necessary to overcome in the production of "modern" Japanese literature.

It is evident that the inclusion of *kanzen chōaku* morality in *gōkan* and poison woman stories enabled character types. Poison woman fiction was not "realistic" in our contemporary understanding of the term. A number of recent articles have attempted to address the frequent dismissal of what is broadly referred to as *gesaku* as "unrealistic" or even "premodern" in response to so many literary studies that agree, influenced perhaps by Shōyō's seminal work, that poison woman fiction as a genre somehow failed—whether as poor imitation, as overly conventional, or as lacking in relevant ideological content in its anachronistic adherence to the encourage virtue, chastise vice morality.[70] While I am sympathetic to the desire to rethink the origins of the modern novel, I prefer to think of the rhetorical insistence on "truth" in *jitsurokumono* writing as responding to the contemporary ideological space of enlightenment policy rather than an attempt at novelistic verisimilitude. Studies arguing that the broader category of *"gesaku"* exhibits elements of future novels still interpret the literary form in a teleological manner that turns Shōyō's negation of *gesaku* on its head in order to posit its modern features.[71] Interpretations that see *"gesaku"* either as a premodern precursor to the novel or solely in a diachronic literary history of "development" are unsatisfying because not only do they limit an amorphous body of literature to a teleological narrative of literary history but they also relegate the fiction to a category based on an ideal of the past or future. Furthermore, for poison woman literature, ideological connotations of gender get subsumed by discussions of *"gesaku's"* position within a teleological vision of literary history. The narrative framing, the publication of the poison woman fiction in newspapers, the inclusion of scientific evidence, the labeling of the poison woman stories as "true tales," and the progressive narrative reminiscent of a Spencerian perspective of social evolution, all reveal a literature form revitalizing itself. *Gōkan* literature of early Meiji exemplifies the tremendous ideological, social, and economic tumult of that period when neo-Confucianism, enlightenment thought, technological advancement, and science joined together in one big river rushing into the deep shadows of modernity. Meiji writers' active appropriation of contemporary discourses of enlightenment and *jitsugaku* constitute rich examples of the way in which conflicts between new and old value systems get expressed and mediated in cultural representation.[72] In attempting to avoid the label "barbaric" or "backwards," writers created highly intertextual narratives that exhibited signs, explicitly or implicitly, of enlightenment thought. The problem is that the writer who wished to invite a new "enlightened" readership to his literary table created the sexual, desirous woman as a signifier of barbarity.

2. Newspaper Reading
as Poison and Cure

By remembering it he has made the story his; and insofar as I have
remembered it, it is mine; and now, if you like it, it's yours. In the tale,
in the telling, we are all one blood. Take the tale in your teeth, then,
bite it till the blood runs, hoping it's not poison.
— Ursula LeGuin, "It Was a Dark and Stormy Night;
or, Why Are We Huddling about the Campfire?"

Reading, Transgression, and the Law

In a provocative discussion of the amorphous relationship between drugs,
writing, and literary consumption, Avital Ronell examines why Gustave
Flaubert's *Madame Bovary* was denounced in court as "poison." The novel,
more than almost any other, "brought out evidence of the pharmaco-
dependency with which literature has always been secretly associated—as
sedative, as cure, as escape conduit or euphorizing substance, as mimetic
poisoning."[1] Madame Bovary's immorality and adultery are a natural outcome of *reading novels*. Her serial reading encouraged an immodest lifestyle, and the reading of her deplorable lifestyle, the courts argued, would
similarly promote such immoral behavior and social decay.

A similar tale, more widely read in its own time if less widely circulated
internationally, is *And Her Name Too Infamous: Poison Woman Takahashi
Oden: A Strange Tokyo Tale* (Sono na mo Takahashi: Dokufu no Shōden:
Tokyo kibun, 1879) by Okamoto Kisen.[2] This colorful, woodblock-printed
book contains one illustration that is markedly exaggerated in size. It is the
figure of a female reader engrossed in perusing the details of the murder

case of the recently executed Takahashi Oden. And is she not Oden herself, reading her own tale of demise? This intent reader is engraved on a scale larger than that of any other figure in the work's twenty-one chapters. She sits calm, satisfied, enraptured. Another portrait of the similarly engrossed female reader found in Robun's *Demon's Tale* discussed in the previous chapter shows girls gathered on tatami-matted floors engaged in reading. Behind them a cabinet vividly decorated with titles of poison woman novels functions as advertisement for contemporary tales of crime while showing the girls ensconced in a world of crime stories. *Madame Bovary, A Strange Tokyo Tale,* and *Demon's Tale* associate crime with reading. In both Flaubert's time and Robun's, the deleterious or positive effects of reading stories of adventure and romance were described via reference to the female reader. Authors of poison woman stories claimed that their stories in nineteenth-century Japan constituted an important literary source for the instruction of readers regarding the new social space of "civilization and enlightenment." Prefaces, postscripts, images, and intertextual commentary did not judge readers of novels as dangerous but as vulnerable. Transcendental first-person narrators spoke directly to the reader, invoking images of the female reader in need of guidance in the unfamiliar landscape of national reform.

From the perspective of the narrator, poison woman stories were not poison at all, but remedy—as long as policing efforts through the *counterexample* of the poison woman successfully encouraged self-education in the "civilizing" reforms. The deleterious effects of reading would not infect them as they had Madame Bovary, the great reader of romance who died amid the gaze of medical men while her limbs convulsed and she vomited blood, her whole body covered with brown spots.[3] Reading stories of wayward women would not poison readers but rather steer them onto the right path.[4] At least this is what the narrators claimed on behalf of their female readers, who were not anticipated to be reading against the grain.

As the subject of reading (as opposed to the reading subject), the female criminal proved to be a convenient counterexample to the self-edifying civilized reader. She embodied the unenlightened citizen who perverted reforms to her own personal and "selfish," rather than civic, ends.

This dichotomy of the good female reader and barbaric woman was developed in the rhetoric of the small newspapers, especially the *Kanayomi* where the poison woman serial originated. The newspaper produced rivalrous figures of good and evil, enlightened and unenlightened, criminal and lawful in competing fantasies of woman. The reading woman is enlightened, the subject of her reading barbaric. These fantasies did not

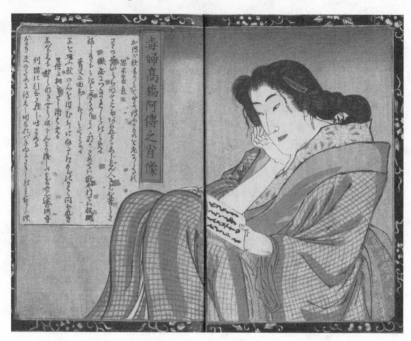

Figure 7. Takahashi Oden reading. From Okamoto Kisen, *Sono na mo Takahashi dokufu no Shōden: Tokyo kibun* (Her name too infamous: Poison woman Takahashi Oden; a strange Tokyo tale) (Tōsendō, 1879).

lead to the production of a meaningful female subject but rather closed down the articulation of an alternative idiom where women wouldn't need to be protected or warned, or conversely, paraded and punished. Both the transgressive woman and her reader were overdetermined figures of national potential under enlightenment thought disseminated through a rapidly industrializing press by enterprising editors. Images of the good and bad female citizen in popular newspapers were manipulated in the claims of the *Kanayomi* to be contributing to the "civilizing" agenda of the reforms and made part of a new cultural imagination of woman through the modern medium of the newspaper.

At the same time that the good reader and criminal woman were juxtaposed in the popular press, another binary emerged within the newspaper and newspaper serial—that of crime and law. The earliest poison woman stories serialized first in the *Kanayomi* exhibited a strange twist in their narrative. The crime committed by the barbaric poison woman was often an unanticipated result of new laws that had been put into place and of which she had availed herself. Transgression took the form of a

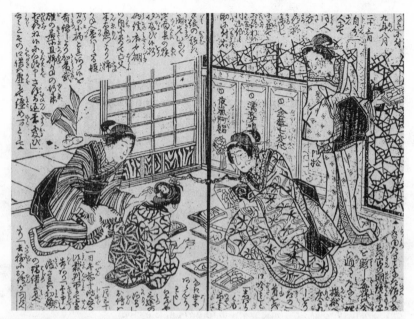

Figure 8. Female readers in front of a panel that displays the names of two poison women, Night Storm Okinu and Omatsu. From Robun, *Takahashi Oden yasha monogatari*.

woman's action against the state and state law, but also as action contra traditional practice, and the stories implicitly suggest that this transgression was *enabled* by new laws of the reformation. In this way, the poison woman story paradoxically critiqued the woman who would resist the law but also who would resist traditional practices by taking advantage of the new laws of the enlightenment, making law itself an important part of the storytelling—law that is represented both within the poison woman serial and in the newspaper running that serial.

This chapter examines the representations of the poison woman in serial form, her female newspaper reader, and crime and the law in the pulpy pages of the *Kanayomi* to illustrate that for all the explicit pro-enlightenment rhetoric that treats Meiji state authority as the proper source for control and judgment, the poison woman narrative relies implicitly on traditional practice (the confirmation of common sense) and superstition as a source of judgment. Not only does this narrative of the transgressive woman make state authority itself a primary subject of storytelling but it also suggests the misogynist question of whether women are as capable (as men) of interpreting and appropriately responding to the new environment of enlightenment modernity by treating the underclass woman as an unworthy recipient of new laws, especially regarding property ownership, social mobility, and travel.

"From Here On Out It's Newspapers! Newspapers!": Pro-Enlightenment Rhetoric in the *Kanayomi* Newspaper

In 1877 the *Kanayomi* newspaper published its first lengthy serial about a poison woman, "The Story of Omatsu," which marked the beginning of a popular genre of crime, the poison woman story *(dokufu-mono)*. These serials were often not completed within the newspaper, which is why studies of poison woman literature focus almost solely on the multivolume *gōkan* in which authors expanded on the newspaper biographies to increase their market. After stories were kick-started in the press, one had to buy the book to read about the gruesome demise of the poison woman, making the production of poison woman stories market driven in many respects. Nevertheless, the poison woman story enjoyed its initial meteoric rise to popularity within the newspaper not as straight fiction but as sensationally embellished news of women who had broken the law.

Japan's first modern, movable-type newspapers and the site of publication for serial poison woman stories were the so-called small newspapers *(koshinbun)* that were one of three types of newspapers: the "large" newspaper *(ōshinbun)*, the "small" newspaper, and the less frequently published, traditional woodblock-printed broadsheet printed in color *(shinbun nishiki-e)*. In this period of rapid industrialization of the press following the breakdown of the guild system of Tokugawa-era publishing, it was crucial to the new publishers to create a mass readership to provide for adequate return on the increasing amounts of capital required to produce a newspaper, and the small newspaper in particular sought such a broad audience. It can be argued that the Meiji press market contributed, in the way that Benedict Anderson has argued for other nations, to the development of a national imaginary. The small newspaper became a primary, if not *the* primary, medium that introduced into print a language that could more easily attribute a sense of reality to the new social and cultural circumstances in which the Japanese citizens and readers found themselves. This language, developed not only within the frame of a new print medium but within a changing social space created through the dismantling of the feudal class system and the creation of a restoration government, invited its people to imagine themselves as citizens of the new civic order.[5] However, the stylistic differences between the two types of newspapers—the "large" and the "small"—in terms of both style and content meant that the readers were not interpellated as an undifferentiated, horizontal readership. Rather, the newspapers perpetuated a hierarchy within the readership in their summoning of readers as connected and participant in the new modernizing national community. Readers were not imagined as equally participant.

Though the differences in content between the large and small newspapers should not be exaggerated, the disparity in language style between them was substantial. Small newspapers did not use Sinified characters and phrases to the extent of the large newspapers, and they provided syllabic glosses for less educated readers. They were less explicitly political in content and freely reported recent sensational events while employing rhetoric that was often complimentary of the Meiji oligarchy and its policies, though satire was by no means foreign to either the small newspaper or the large. While the large newspapers' attention to political events, debates among intellectuals, and disregard of gossip and sensationalist entertainment makes them an important source for understanding the dominant debates among the educated elite, the small newspapers, which eschewed their large counterparts' disregard of the abecedarian reader, provide insight into what was being consumed by the average reader, as well as the direction that mainstream newspapers would take later in the century.[6] The *Kanayomi* contained columns similar to those found in the many other small papers: a government proclamations column or the "ofure" column that headed the newspaper; a "shin-bun" or newly heard news column often glossed as "hanashi" (story) or "zappō" (miscellany) column; an editorial column that included letters to the editor *(tosho);* and special columns such as the *Kanayomi*'s gossip column "Myō-myō chinbun" about the world of flowers and willows. The idiosyncratic *Kanayomi* also included a column recording governmental fines and incarceration of newspaper reporters and editors, which no other small newspapers contained. This was the general format for most early small newspapers, and it grew increasingly sophisticated in content throughout the late 1870s and early 1880s, such that a prominent large newspaper editor, Narushima Ryūhoku, remarked in 1883 that the small newspaper and large newspaper differed primarily in size and linguistic presentation rather than in content itself.

The most widely read newspapers of the approximately 225 in circulation in 1877 (the year that poison woman serials were first published) were small newspapers. They had a wider circulation and were therefore more economically stable than their large counterparts.[7] The largest-selling newspaper was the *Yomiuri,* which was selling nearly 5.5 million copies annually by 1877.[8] The *Kanayomi,* where the poison woman serials originated, was among the top sellers according to a 29 January 1878 article in the *Jiji Hyōron,* which claimed that "the theoretically-minded large newspapers are the *[Tokyo] Nichi Nichi,* the *Chōya,* the *Hōchi,* and the *Akebono* and those providing *kana* glosses are the small newspapers the *Yomiuri,* the *Kanayomi,* the *E-iri,* and the *Sakigake.*"[9] The small newspaper industry boomed in the 1880s with the successes of the *E-iri Jiyū, Jiyūto,* the *Ukiyo* (later called the *Kaishin*), the *Mezamashi* (later the *Tokyo Asahi*), the *Sakigake,* the *Azuma,* the *Konnichi* (later the *Miyako Shinbun*), the *E-iri Chōya* (later the *Chūō*), and the *Yamato,* but the *Kanayomi* was one of the first small newspapers in the medium's history and quickly found a large audience. It is reported to have sold 1,561,120 copies in the year 1876 and 2,771,250 copies in 1877, making the *Kanayomi* in 1877 the third-highest-selling paper that year after the best-selling small newspaper, the *Yomiuri,* and the best-selling large newspaper, the *Tokyo Daily* (Tokyo Nichi Nichi).[10]

The popularity of the *Kanayomi* newspaper was helped by the entrepreneurial fervor of Kanagaki Robun, who was the only editor to open his own reading house where a customer could read and have a cup of tea for one *sen,*[11] and he was quick to locate sellers for his newspaper in various regions outside Tokyo, including Wakayama, Kobe, Ishimaki, Niigata, Fukuoka, Hokkaidō, and Shizuoka, among others. Second, the inclusion common to small newspapers of pronunciation guides in the form of vertical syllabary *(rubi)* and the employment of a more colloquial language common to *gesaku* vernacular fiction and staged storytelling *(rakugo)* of the time contributed to the accessibility of the *Kanayomi.* Much of the language of the *Kanayomi* was also indicative of speech and in that sense was an important precursor, along with other small newspapers, to the later modern vernacular form of writing *(genbun'itchi).* At the same time, the parodic quality of Robun's earlier writing also found its way into the paper, providing ample entertainment for the general reader.

As far as the readership went, the national rate of literacy at this time cannot be ascertained with certainty because no substantial statistics were recorded under a stable definition of "literacy." Reading levels varied according to age, location, educational opportunities, and the object of reading. Tsuchiya Reiko estimates, based on a study held in Tokyo in 1876, that 75.8 percent of the public in the city of Tokyo was literate. Of those readers, 64.8 percent were *heimin* (commoners) while 11.0 percent were *shizoku* (elites). 34.8 percent were women and 41.2 percent were men.[12] These statistics show basically that in terms of literacy, there was not a very substantial difference between the genders. Tsuchiya further estimates that in 1876 22.9 percent of the literate population read small newspapers, primarily commoners, though elite educated women too opted to read small over large newspapers.[13] This may help explain why the *Kanayomi* seemed invested in promoting itself as useful for the commoner and female reader. While literacy rate and level can only be surmised, these figures suggest that there was a vast market of potential readers, and editors sought to attract readers by providing entertaining and educational reading.

During this formative period in newspaper history and enlightenment thought, newspaper editors and reporters assumed the paternal role of teacher and supporter of Meiji reforms toward the general reader in formation. The editors aligned themselves with enlightenment ideology in encouraging the reading of their newspapers by claiming that newspapers could clarify the confusion of the new world surrounding the readers. The *Kanayomi*, for example, rigorously espoused progressivism and enlightenment by presenting itself as instrumental in building a shared linguistic and national space—one in which the heretofore disenfranchised lower classes were encouraged to participate. In commemorating the founding of the newspaper, the celebrated reporter of the *Tokyo Nichi Nichi Shinbun*, Kishida Ginkō, enthusiastically congratulated the *Kanayomi* on its entrance into the national press market:

> From Ginkō of the Nippō Company, a hearty congratulations on the start of the *Kanayomi* newspaper. I offer my heartfelt congratulations. Well, well! Is there anything to do but offer my congratulations! Listen everyone. Until now we suffered for 2000 years having to read the Chinese classics, jumping to the back and then front [of the sentence]. While neither the teacher nor the student knew exactly what they meant, they became scholars anyway. . . . During the years when we did not have *"kana,"* we only studied books using the angular letters brought over from China, and that habit has stuck with us until very recently. Now that we have the easy-to-read, easy-to-write *hiragana* and *katakana* scripts, we no longer need to mimic the difficult angular characters. After all, isn't our Japanese *kana* writing system the best option? Westerners study using the western scripts, Chinese study using Chinese characters, India, Arabia and all other countries study to be scholars using their own alphabets. With this in mind, Kanagaki of Kanagawa prefecture determined *kana* to be crucial to the *Kanayomi* newspaper in reporting news items of interest for the people, developing our minds, and contributing to the enlightenment of society with its publications every other day. Today publication begins. Hurrah! And a hearty hurrah![14]

In a rousing alliterative invocation, Ginkō lauds the *Kanayomi* as a place where the Japanese nation can strengthen itself by helping all the citizens to read their own letters. In the ensuing issue (2 November 1875), the writer of "virtuous and heroic woman" stories (*reppu-den* and *retsujo-den*), Matsumura Shunsuke, sustained this nation-building rhetoric, enjoining *Kanayomi* readers to compete with their international counterparts in Western Europe: "They say that in the capital of England there are four or five hundred newspaper companies. Everyone here does well to mimic London. Study, study!"[15] This reference to a shared national space promoted the idea of linguistic unification that had yet to be achieved since the large newspapers continued to print stories in sinified Japanese *(kanbun)*, which was less intelligible to the new readers of the newspaper. In promoting this agenda of creating an educated readership through the newspaper, the *Kanayomi,* along with the *Yomiuri,* provided useful glosses for reading. The Sino-Japanese characters were accompanied by *kana* readings and therefore contributed mightily, albeit in a rather ad hoc fashion, to the eventual maturation of a standard national language. Nevertheless, the classification of newspapers—small versus large—and its readers perpetuated class and gender distinctions.

The *Kanayomi* primarily targeted the general female reader and the male underclass reader in promoting the formation of a reading public to strengthen Japan as a nation:

> It is a must, for the progress of the country, that the general populace becomes clever *[rikō]*. The *Kanayomi Shinbun* is perfect for that. Verily, for the wife, the mistress, the masseuse, the geisha, the various prostitutes, the maid, the houseboy, the rickshaw driver, the old woman in the country, the retired man in Tokyo . . . for no one is there a faster way than with this easy-to-understand newspaper that tells about the official proclamations and rare things regarding domestic and international affairs, encourages virtue and chastises vice *[kanzen chōaku],* and teaches the path to scholarship and helps civilization and enlightenment.[16]

Here the *Kanayomi* speaks not to the solitary reader but to a community of men and women of various classes and generations ideologically constructed by a promise that all readers can participate as new citizens of the country through their exposure to national and international news. Through this rhetoric, the newspaper positioned itself as a modern consumer product of the new citizenry in the making.

In his pioneering study of the modern Japanese newspaper, Yamamoto Taketoshi proposes that the enlightenment rhetoric appealed to readers' desire to participate in the new era. In making his point, Yamamoto culls an excerpt from a small newspaper, prefacing it with the following remarks:

> That the civilization and enlightenment *[bunmei kaika]* activities of the small newspapers *[koshinbun]* were welcome by the downtown *[shitamachi]* merchants, geisha, common folk *[shomin]*, and soldiers is well illustrated in a menu that appeared in an Asakusa restaurant after the Seinan war which read, "We call it Newspaper Enlightenment cuisine, with boiled miscellaneous news, offical proclamation appetizers, contributions soup, steamed advertisements, and fried rejected manuscripts." Even if the newspaper was not subscribed to by the common folk, it became of interest and intrigue as a product of civilization and enlightenment *[bunmei kaika]*.[17]

This menu linking the newspaper with the enlightenment assumes that everyone will get the joke—that the reader too identifies the small newspapers as constantly touting their status as a participant in the national enlightenment project. It portrays the small newspapers as encouraging the imagination of a readership that included men and women of various stations, a variegated landscape of readers unified by the reforms. The solitary newspaper reader is thus invited to imagine others reading at the same time, thereby developing a consciousness of shared time, a phenomenon that Benedict Anderson has argued contributed to a sense of national community.[18]

However, Anderson's discussion of the importance of print technology in producing an imagination of a national community does not account for the way in which gender might inform and consequently divide the identity of readers along the lines of gender difference. Early small newspapers treated especially the female reader as vulnerable and unformed and communicated an urgent need to remedy the situation by cultivating the self through reading newspapers. In fact, the rhetoric of the *Kanayomi* suggested that the success of the government reforms depended upon the female reader's willingness to become comfortable reading newspapers. The newspaper as a mass medium was comparatively new, but this was true for both male and female readers. Woman is made, in this new mass publication, symbolic of the reader in formation, as evidenced, for example, in one letter to the editor in which the contributor claims to read three small newspapers a day. In conversational style she relates what she told her spouse: "Husband, nowadays the newspapers are terribly popular but I can't get through even half of an *ōshinbun* because I don't understand them a whit. And since they come out every day, there's never enough time to read them! But I can finish the *Yomiuri, E-iri,* and the new *Kanayomi.*

They almost don't give me enough to read, leaving me anxiously await-
ing next day's paper!" Her husband responds, "That's right, dear! It's just
like you say."[19] This and other examples in the *Kanayomi* depict the female
reader as symbolic of a premature stage of enlightened citizenship. The
woman is portrayed as the ideal reader who is not quite interpellated but
aspires to be part of a national body of readers. Makihara Norio has argued
that in the production of the nation everyone is made to feel liminal and it
is that distance that produces the desire to be part of the national order.[20]
In the small newspapers, however, women were targeted as those in a state
of *becoming* enlightened citizens of a newly progressive nation.

Within this pedagogical press hierarchy, the newspaper editor placed
himself in the role of authority. In convincing this new readership to purchase his newspaper, one *Kanayomi* author authoritatively warned his readers how wanting they are of guidance:

> Listen all you daughters, honorable prostitutes, geisha. Pardon my dis-
> respect but it is a shame that since most women make no room in their
> heart for learning, the disease of folly is worsening as you arrogantly ignore
> your lack of achievements and blame others or get angry at newspapers
> that report your mischief. Without looking in front or behind you, you
> become agitated and commit love suicide, hang yourself, throw yourself
> in the Umegawa river or lure wastrels. You wave around knives at the drop
> of a hat worrying strangers and your parents and causing trouble for the
> government just adding to your shame. . . . Stop carrying your foolishness
> so far. This newspaper scolds because we care and want to make you sisters
> clever, arresting and correcting your imprudent souls, setting you forth on
> the right path.[21]

The depictions of women as readers in the making was precipitated by this
first widespread market of print capitalism. This new age of the print medium capitalized on the rhetoric of reform, encouraging the perception of
the newspaper as an inevitable and necessary disseminator of enlightenment thought. The espousal of self-education, which carried over into poison woman literature, appears to promote self-reliant thinking but actually
promotes paternalistic supervision. There is still a higher authority posited
outside the self. Self-learning, in this case, meant accepting the reforms of
the newly instituted imperial regime.[22] Woman was made symbolic of a
particular type of enlightenment ideology in Meiji—the type of enlightenment espoused by Ogawa Tameji and to a degree by those who encouraged
the kind of education that endorsed reforms initiated by the new government. Under this model of reform, the (female) citizen is an empty vessel

excitedly anticipating the intellectual nourishment of the country's leaders and thinkers.

Despite its claims, not everyone was satisfied that the *Kanayomi* was spreading education. The competing *Tokyo E-iri* (Tokyo Illustrated) newspaper, referring to an ungrammatical letter by an apprentice monk who claimed he had become literate reading the *Kanayomi,* remarked in what may be a subtle reference to the poison woman serials, "Rather, the *[Kanayomi]* appears to be spreading poison to women and children" *(doku o nagasu yō).*[23] Nevertheless, references to girls leaving the traditional arts to take up the modern practice of newspaper reader abound in early Meiji newspapers. An example from an essay by Maeda Ai depicts an impressionable girl, Morita Tora, living in Osaka's Honmachi, who has dropped traditional arts to take up newspaper reading: "A person named Murakami Shinsai loved newspapers and often read to neighborhood girls. Tora began to attend. She became so interested in newspapers that she quit the *shamisen* and dance, and began receiving the three *furigana* newspapers. Her parents, worried that their daughter might become conceited, asked her to stop but Tora persisted . . . and soon even her father was drawn in."[24] In his comments on this article about Tora's taking up of newspaper reading, Maeda Ai surmises that young Tora's new hobby is a result of the new trendy regard for practical learning *(jitsugaku sonchō).* Maeda's main concern in quoting this news story is to trace the growth of a modern readership and the earliest inclusion of women into the general readership, but this story is also an example of the new valorization of utilitarianism and the newspaper medium that paraded its own utilitarian value as a tool for self-reform within larger social and political reforms. The female reader was a much-manipulated marker of changing social conditions, but ironically only inasmuch as she was imagined as vulnerable and scrutinized. In the *Kanayomi* and other small newspapers, *woman* in particular was the subject made culturally and symbolically representative of a new classless national community in formation. She is the liminal figure brought into print not only as vulnerable reader but also as thick-skinned criminal—the unenlightened antithesis to the self-edifying female reader.

Asakura Kyōji has argued that the poison woman figure represented the marginalization of woman generally in the new social and political world of early Meiji, concluding that what poison woman fiction primarily illustrates is the transformation of gender as the primary marker of difference in early Meiji.[25] On the one hand, the barbaric poison woman was a central figure in espousing progress of the nation (in spite of realities on the ground), but the good reader too is a symbolically overdetermined figure through whom the enlightenment is envisioned as triumphant. The condemnation of the criminal woman occurred through rhetoric that implicated other women as judges in creating a new imaginary of an integrated community that could unite in mutual condemnation. The female reader played an important symbolic role in promoting a certain kind of reform, and in this context she was the positive charge against which the negatively charged transgressive female could be judged inappropriate. In the newspapers' stories of law and transgression, enlightenment rhetoric articulated through the signifier "woman" regulated conflict. What was left out of the newspaper, however, was woman as meaningful subject. Woman could be good (reading, judging, civilized) or bad (wandering, sexually active, nonreproductive, and occasionally murderous). This pervasive gendered idiom, which denied a stable place from which women could be treated as fully formed subjects in writing, denied room for articulating the female subject except via the charged terms of dissident or acquiescent, poison or cure.

Transgression and the Law in the *Kanayomi*

Despite the pervasiveness of pro-enlightenment rhetoric in the *Kanayomi*, the ubiquity and variety of expressions used to discuss crime and the law make it a curiously pluralistic and uneven text when it came to representing sovereign power and the law. At least three columns in the *Kanayomi* featured law or its transgression: a daily *ofure* column running proclamations of new laws of the new Meiji state; the "shin-bun" column of miscellaneous news, which included a daily plethora of crime reports including a regularly featured list of recent indictments and serial articles detailing biographies of criminals and serialized novels of crime *(tsuzukimono);* and a monthly report of fines and punishment levied upon newspaper editors and reporters for libel. From what unified place could the reader interpret or map this cacophony of references to law and its transgression? Was the newspaper's goal to project that plurality or to contain it? The contradictions at work in the representations of law in the newspaper create a drama that brings the new sovereign law of the nation into confrontation with traditional beliefs and practices; and they raise questions about the interpretation and status of personal autonomy, especially of women, under the new laws.

Among the manifold columns related to regulation and transgression, the required *ofure* column of new regulations promulgated by the Meiji government appeared without fail at the top of the front page. The *ofure* should likely be considered a continuation of the Tokugawa-era practice of hanging *ofure-gaki,* or public proclamations, by government officials for public viewing. In this column, announcements of various organizing government ministries, local authorities, and national government authorities were run. The contents varied from day to day, and they included a wide range of proclamations from all levels and arms of government such as daily reports of trial outcomes, lists of changes in inmate numbers categorized according to prison and sex, domestic larceny statistics, formal procedures for reporting foreign visitors who could now legally stay in local inns, military conscription height requirements, how epidemics were to be handled by governing authorities, and even orders that natural mulberry trees were not to be cut down. These are only a few of the hundreds of regulations introduced in the "proclamations" column by various government bodies. These new regulations were generated and printed daily in legal prose painstakingly supplied with tiny, detailed vertical glosses in syllabic form, making the formal proclamations legible to a broader audience, though the legalistic jargon often made for difficult reading despite the syllabic aid. This *ofure* column in the *Kanayomi* and other small and large newspapers figured enlightenment policies as a swelling regulatory system of new laws.

In what was likely an effort to make these proclamations of law on the front page more appealing, the *Kanayomi* ran one article that expressed a reader's thrill at finding *girls* reading about government and the new administrative and punitive systems: "When I visited relatives in Tokyo the other day, two girls of nine years and two months and seven years and ten months of age were jointly reading the official proclamations section of your company's fifth issue of the *Kanayomi*. How beneficial to have *kana* so that even these youngsters can comprehend the government's official pronouncements. I guarantee your eventual success."[26]

But criticism of the various new laws and regulations of the Meiji government was by no means absent in the press, and the *Kanayomi*, along with other small and large newspapers, was fined for printing information that was deemed injurious to state authority. James Huffman has described reporters' frustration with to the newspaper laws—the "shinbunshi jōrei"—promulgated on 28 June 1875 that established the first regulatory system for newspapers. Newspapers were instructed to refrain from advocating revolution, reviling "existing laws," confusing "the sense of duty of the people," and justifying the "offenses plainly contrary to the criminal law." The government, said one indignant press historian, had decided to treat reporters "like swindlers and thieves in the night." Another called the law a "literary prison" *(moji no goku).* And the journalist Suehiro Tetchō said he felt suddenly like a "caged bird" or "a wild horse that had been tamed."[27]

From 1875, editors of both types of newspaper, large and small, were jailed rather than merely fined for material that criticized government policy or slandered officials. In response, the *Kanayomi* ran its own unique monthly column reporting, without commentary, the fines and punishment of editors and reporters that had been levied each month. From March 1876 to the end of 1879, the *Kanayomi* ran over forty-two columns reporting over four hundred indictments during those years. Though this column was never attributed to a specific author, the newspaper scholar Tsuchiya surmises that Robun himself was the column's author for the attention that he paid in other articles to government regulation of speech in print and also because the column vanished when he left the *Kanayomi* for another small newspaper, the *Iroha*.[28] Tsuchiya interprets this column as critical of authority precisely for its lack of additional commentary. The stark presentation of unembellished facts appeared an implicit expression of disapproval of such centralized control over the press. This column alone illustrates that small newspaper editors were not strictly supporters of the national agenda despite the preponderance of pro-enlightenment rhetoric.

The numerous changes to legal codes and the invention of so many new laws made crime and punishment a natural topic for the popular press. In addition to writing about regulation and prohibition, the *Kanayomi* from its inception reported widely on law-breaking in one-time and serialized articles. These serialized articles eventually morphed into longer serialized stories. The 5 October 1876 edition of the *Kanayomi* is the second installment of what can be considered a precursor to the serial "The Story of Street Minstrel Omatsu." In it was a serialized article that ran for only two days as "The Story of Female Bandit Otsune" (Onna tōzoku Otsune no den, 4–5 October 1876),[29] which was not expanded to become an illustrated novel. In the ensuing paragraphs I give a short synopsis of the crime stories in this edition to illuminate how news and story bled into one another in the prose of the newspaper in the way that fictional prose and reportage would both be present in poison woman *gōkan* only a few years later. It offers a clear instance of the important connection between the writing of a crime reporter and a *gōkan* novelist.

The introduction of the new official proclamations in the *ofure* column is followed by the "newly heard news" *(shinbun)* section, which opens with a dramatic lead in—a report of an attempted jailbreak: "Street rumor has it that on the second of the month at eleven p.m., 150 or 160 criminals held in the Third Police Prison in Tokyo's Sakamoto-chō, set fire and tried to escape but the smoke revealed their plan, the fire was detected and quickly extinguished. They say none of the prisoners were able to escape." Following a story of the opening of the rice market and lengthy depiction of a fire is a report of the statistics of crime in Tokyo over the course of two days: "On the first day of the month in Tokyo, 53 households were victims of theft, and 1 household experienced robbery. Three thieves were captured and five were kept in custody for (other) crimes. On the second day of the same month, there were thefts in 54 households and two perpetrators were captured. Four people were robbed, three households were swindled, and thieves escaped from two households. One was kept in custody." This article is followed by a story mocking a former public servant arrested for thievery: "A former government official who was arrested and later fired stole 5000 ryo from a former clan chief. A guy like him is a disgrace to the upper-class society."[30] Another crime article in this issue reports foreigners committing crime: "It appears that two foreigners had a grudge match in the seventeenth hall of the foreigner's district. A few days ago, [a man] shattered the window of 'Biyato' and disappeared into the darkness. They have barbarians in the west too."[31] A longer crime news story on the second page of this issue read:

> At 8 pm on the second, responding to a report of a suspicious person [at the Kanagawa station], detective Isa Sadazō and officer Kawamura Hideharu and Murata dispatched to a disorderly rooming house at the station. . . . The suspect was none other than notorious bandit and armed robber Katō Fusakichi (25). His gang had been caught and beheaded last year at a Yokohama prison, but he escaped, hid himself and continued committing crimes. . . . While he was in the room getting intimate with entertainer Fujimoto Omatsu, he heard footsteps, so he got up and exited out onto the roof through the veranda. The officers chased him, pulling him back into a room on the second story. Detective Isa struggled to keep him from getting away, grabbing him from behind with the two officers' assistance.

The story continues to relate in detail the struggle between Katō and Isa as they tumbled down the stairs and Isa held on even with one finger broken in the fight. This dramatic tale of the capture of a runaway convict was followed by the second installment of "The Story of Female Bandit Otsune" (Onna tōzoku Otsune no den) that related how Otsune gained the trust of a foreigner for whom she was housekeeper. In this similarly action-packed story, Otsune learned through her employment that another foreigner would be absent from his home on 10 June and took advantage of his absence. She stole "20 yen (2 Japanese gold coins), 37 Western silvers (one silver is equivalent to our 4 yen 20 sen), a document written in a Western language, six drafts from a foreign bank, and two gold rings." The boundary between the crime stories of the day and the crime story of bandit Otsune reveals little difference in style, though "Female Bandit Otsune" is marked with a short title including the term *den* meaning "story" but also "biography" and the story is marked as serialized from the previous day while the other stories in the "news" section do not have headlines. Nevertheless, the tone, attention to detail, and language of the crime reports and the continued crime story overlap to a great degree, though the serialized article set the stage for the emergence of the serial *(tsuzukimono)* the following year, the format of which allowed relative room for narrative expansion.

The association of the small newspaper serial articles and serial novels *(tsuzukimono)* with the truthful reporting of crime is illustrated in a letter from a reader regarding a play about one of the first poison women to make the stage, the street minstrel Omatsu, which took as its subject Kubota Hikosaku's serial "The Story of Street Minstrel Omatsu" (Torioi Omatsu no den)—the first lengthy poison woman serial to be run in the *Kanayomi*.[32] This favorable review of one performance at the Matsuza theater in Yokohama appearing in the *Kanayomi* reported the strategic use of the *Kanayomi* newspaper in this play to illustrate the story's contemporary newsworthy origins. The audience bleachers near the back of the stage space were encircled by red lanterns with "Kanayomi" written on them and further newspaper references appear in a boisterous finale during which the scenery changed and a newspaper hawker emerged to sell vociferously his boxed stack of *Kanayomi* newspapers, while animated dancers sang in the background.[33]

Readers appear to have identified the serialized "Story of Street Minstrel Omatsu" as a real event as revealed in another contribution from a disappointed spectator of a theatrical version of a "The Story of Street Minstrel Omatsu" who complained that the play failed to be anything like the newspaper story or the three-volume *gōkan*. The contributor happily recalled how the event reported in the newspaper by Kubota Hikosaku (and later embellished for the *gōkan* version) coincided with the account *(jitsuroku)* that he had heard while living near Unumegahara, where the events took place. He derided the stage version performed in April 1878 for changing the scenes of the crime from outlying areas to the cosmopolitan space of Tokyo and for adding needless scenes of adultery and other superfluous dramatic effects such that the performance "was nothing more than old-style theatre *(kyogen)* with an emphasis on the 'kyo' (fiction)." The contributer specifically takes the playwright Kawatake Shinshichi, student of Mokuami, to task for not learning from his teacher to limit the fictionalization of event, arguing that even the veteran Mokuami knows that theater must be educational and factual.[34] Failing to emulate the serial in reporting something of the actual event, the play was a disappointment.

The new consistency of typographical reproduction, its ability to transform gossip to multiple print venues, helped confirm the prose as objective reality rather than subjective narrative. As Michael McKeon explains in his discussion of Elizabeth Eisenstein's study of the print revolution,

> the very conception of an "objective" history owes a great deal to print technology. By permanently preserving and reproducing what could be no more than transient productions in oral and even scribal culture, print stabilized culture itself and the past in particular as a realm of experience henceforth susceptible to objective study: that is, as a collection of objects. Print made common first the very notion of competing accounts of the same event and then the norm of "objective" research and understanding through the systematic collection, comparison, categorization, collation, editing, and indexing of documentary objects.[35]

Meiji newspapers promoted the notion of an objective history through emphatic claims to provide new information *(shin-bun)* and the production of the same story in multiple newspapers, which encouraged readers to examine and compare evidence. Readers must judge the truth for themselves. The publication of crime stories on the same pages as new laws likely encouraged their reading as actual events.

Furthermore, the *Kanayomi* newspaper, it could be argued, lent an air of truth to the stories through the use of a vernacular style that the *Kanayomi* called "vulgar vernacular speech" *(zokudan heiwa),* which was very close to the style of everyday speech and easily understood by the reader who did not have training in Chinese-style writing common in the large newspapers *(kanbun kango).* This style of writing in the *Kanayomi,* along with the *Yomiuri,* "had as its goal a prose that could be read aloud and understood by uneducated people; attempting a style that was closer to the spoken word" and should be considered an important precursor to the later nationalized vernacular style *(genbun' itchi)* as pointed out by Tsuchiya.[36] The question of the contributions the "realism" of poison woman fiction made to the development of a realistic novelistic literature in the Meiji period is usually discussed with regard to the woodblock-printed book versions of the poison woman story, but this vernacular prose is certainly connected to the stories' initial appearance in the *Kanayomi,* where vernacular speech patterns were commonly used in reporting the news.

"News" as a kind of prose in the small newspaper, however, was not a clear category. The serialization of biographies of criminals in the same column as the *shin-bun,* or "newly heard news," illustrates the flexibility of the journalistic framework for representing actual events. News stories made no pretense of neutrality. Moralistic judgments were perfectly acceptable within news reporting. There was no internal law of reporting that had established limits and regulations for reporting the news, therefore there could be no perversion, no contamination, no corruption of the news. This mixing of newly heard news with miscellaneous news *(zappō)* and rumor disabled the possibility of a strictly identifiable way of reading. Put differently, there were interpretative alternatives for reading, and truth and fiction were not strict interpretive categories. An article could presumably be read as truth or as story, especially when it came to the serialized poison woman story, which contained much that retrospectively might be considered literary but was run in the miscellaneous news section. In the newspaper context, reading and writing conventions clearly distinguishing truth and fiction were still in the making.

In the absence of established reading conventions especially for the small newspaper, stories of the transgression of the law could be read as news *and* story. That being the case, not only transgression but also the law that is transgressed could be subject to reportage and storytelling. In an introduction to Jacques Derrida's discussion of law in Franz Kafka's "Before the Law," Derek Attridge suggests what is at stake in representing law: "The strict notion of the law is predicated upon its absolute separability from anything like fiction, narrative, history, or literature; yet, as Derrida shows in his reading of Kafka's fiction, this separation cannot be sustained."[37] The question for both literature and the law is the degree to which features of a text or of law are put into question as stable or unstable. Derrida is interested in Kafka's text because it attempts to "make [the law] present, to enter into a relation with it, indeed, to enter it and become intrinsic to it."[38] The story attempts to make a story of the law, though it "seems that the law as such should never give rise to any story. To be invested with its categorical authority, the law must be without history, genesis, or any possible derivation."[39] This statement points toward the situation in which the law itself tends to escape storytelling. This tendency for law to escape story helps explain how an act of transgression invites storytelling about the perversion of the law rather than of the law itself, which is usually registered as permanent and "intolerant of its own history."

Texts can create the law: "However, this is on condition that the text itself can appear before the law of another, more powerful text protected by more powerful guardians."[40] In early Meiji, laws of literature were in flux, as were juridical laws. But here, rather than focus on the question of genre and convention in literature—literature's ability to overcome its own law through framing and referentiality—I focus on the interpretations in news and poison woman literature of the specific moral law and juridical law (which Derrida resists in his reading of Kafka). Because of the predilection of journalists to both critique and affirm new laws at this time, the question of how crime writers engaged with law is useful in understanding the deep connection between literature and the law (in their manifold manifestations) at this time.

During the peak of the production of poison woman serials, laws were explicitly in the making and presented to the public in the newspapers as newly formed, as illustrated in the plethora of proclamations listed daily in the *ofure* column. The serials about female criminals reiterated these laws by making law too the subject of storytelling, by enacting the new laws within the story. Contemporary changes in the law were deployed in portraying the poison woman's moral degradation, but the law itself was depicted as a changing entity and *not* outside the realm of storytelling. The serialized poison woman stories and those printed as novels cite the law as an essential feature in the motivations of the female criminal for the freedom it (wrongly) offered her. The new "enlightened" laws, in other words, are shown to have *negative* consequences by giving free rein to women who are carriers of death. These laws are marked in their stories by their novelty—the law is not ahistorical and neither is it successfully regulatory. The more powerful system of "law" that drives the narrative of condemnation of the woman in the major poison woman stories is that of convention and traditional practice. The narrative of the poison woman practically guarantees a place for tradition and superstition such that traditional morality ultimately prevails as that most fundamentally true law. In this sense, the poison woman tale indeed performs a regulative function, but it is not clear that such tales are necessarily aligned with the laws of government reform.[41]

The Story of the Law in Poison Woman Literature

This concluding section introduces specific instances in which poison woman narratives implicitly portray state law as having wrongly ruled for an illegitimate recipient who, under the law of convention, is rightly damned. The first instance of Meiji law providing freedoms of which the "poison woman" is unworthy involves new laws of travel. One of the prominent features of poison woman stories is the criminal woman as traveler. The metaphor of travel is a rich one. The traveling woman who transgresses previously bounded regional boundaries is depicted as transgressing social boundaries. Her travel is fundamentally antithetical to proper feminine behavior and thereby encroaches upon male social prerogatives. *Demon's Tale* devotes considerable attention to regulatory changes of the time related to travel as discussed by the Meiji literature scholar Kamei Hideo. Poison woman Takahashi Oden's decision to take advantage of the political unrest toward the end of the Tokugawa era by escaping the village *(kakeochi)* and the family's efforts to bring her back surreptitiously are, according to Kamei, a reference to the Tokugawa law that erased a person's name from the local register *(chōmen-hazushi)* and labeled them a runaway should they disappear for more than three days. Vagrancy had already been of tremendous concern in the 1800s to the degree that in 1842 Mizuno Tadakuni created the "Order for the Return of Unregistereds and Beggars."[42] The goal was to return people to their place in society and those who had no guarantors were sent to the stockade (when there was room for them). Wanderers who had no home to return to were demoted to the *hinin* sector of society. Toward the end of the Tokugawa reign, fears of rootlessness were even greater and the power vacuum created by the competing factions in this transitional period meant that there were increasingly powerful gambling gangs in the countryside.[43] The historian Daniel Botsman explains further that for most of the 1860s Edo was plagued by disruptive "numbers of unregistereds and masterless warriors entering the city, and taking advantage of the Bakufu's preoccupation with the political crisis to roam the streets as they pleased."[44] In this reference to the law and travel in *Demon's Tale,* young Oden is a transgressor for breaking a pre-restoration law against unregulated travel, though to avoid the attention of government officials, the family attempts to take care of the matter under the official radar to avoid suspicion and censure within the village.

A dramatic change in travel laws took place in 1868 when travel was allowed by anyone without a passport. However, at the same time, all citizens were ordered to register their names with local officials, and travelers and wanderers were allowed to return to their homeland to register (the revised legal code enacted some exceptions). *Demon's Tale* weaves this new law of travel into the biography of Oden. After Oden was received back at her home, Naminosuke was adopted into the family to be her husband. As Kamei points out, Naminosuke and Oden confessed to running away the year that their register was created, giving the impression that Oden not only took advantage of the new law of 1868 that allowed travel without a passport but that she and Naminosuke likely returned after the revised legal code of conduct was created and registered.[45] Kamei further points out how Oden and Naminosuke used the legal system to successfully procure land from her brother by taking him to trial under a new law that allowed for negotiation of property battles through the equally new juridical system (which proves that they registered). It is uncertain whether Takahashi was aware of these new laws, but Robun made it seem so in his interpretation of the law and Oden's "manipulation" of it.[46]

This story, which describes Oden as despicable and selfish for her "enlightened" ability to comprehend the new law and use it to her gain, implicates the new system of trial and negotiation itself as her accomplice in procuring wealth. What made her and Naminosuke even more despicable was that Oden's brother farmed the land while they were gone because he believed it belonged to him. The decision of Oden and Naminosuke to leave the village soon after their success in court suggests the lack of popularity—the unforgivable transgression—of a woman who had used the new law to obtain property from her elder brother legally. Oden and Naminosuke encountered such ill will that they eventually sold their land and left the village. In this episode dramatizing land rights and juridical law, the law is seen to have ruled wrongly for an illegitimate recipient who is eventually rightly damned within the narrative through depictions of her perpetual failures in marriage and business and her eventual beheading.

Oden is shown as trying to shield herself from the ultimate punishment of beheading during the trial for murder by using her knowledge of the new laws. In Robun's interpretation, Oden was a poison woman precisely because she could so efficiently appeal to the law to try to save herself, which she did rather than acquiesce to the "wisdom" of the courts. Specifically, Oden hoped to be charged with "manslaughter," which under the revised legal code was punished with imprisonment rather than death by sword. According to Kamei, it was likely the "thoroughness" with which Takahashi applied the law to her own case that invited the appellation of "poison woman." In stark contrast, Mokuami's more sympathetic rendering of Oden in his play *The Binding of Oden's Letters* of the same year treated her as a woman incapable of understanding the law, while Robun's created a link between the evil woman and a woman's ability to negotiate new laws.

The specter of the traveling, nondomestic woman as a likely perpetrator of crime appears in another poison woman story serialized in the *Kanayomi* newspaper about street minstrel Omatsu and its longer novelistic version, *The Seafaring Tale of Street Minstrel Omatsu*. The title itself illustrates doubly how crucial travel is to depicting a criminal woman. As we will see in the next chapter in a discussion of poison woman Shimazu Omasa, the poison woman is often a traveler of the sea. In *Seafaring Omatsu*, the protagonist is not only a street minstrel but a traveler of the violent seas as depicted on the cover of the opening chapter of the tale. The evil woman was ever on the run, free to direct her destiny, perpetually in motion. It is perhaps not a coincidence that the only illustration that accompanied the serialized story of Omatsu in the *Kanayomi* depicts her jumping into the sea. The heroine was an intrepid adventurer tossed about in a literal sea of uncontrollable circumstances. The poison woman ran, climbed walls, and even swam (sometimes like a champ, as did poison woman Shimazu Omasa who saved a woman from drowning with her aquatic athleticism).[47] In all, there is an implication that the woman who acted on the new ability to travel with relative freedom brings immorality and death. The fourth installment of the Omatsu serial reads, "The Meiji restoration law of 'new commoners' unexpectedly wiped away the pollution of the outcasts and so Omatsu became [Hamada] Shōji's wife. She lived luxuriously but since she had from the outset the nature of a poison woman she ran away again with Osaka Kichi and returned for a spell to Tokyo where, at her mother's house, she suffered another wave of troubles."[48] When Omatsu's new lover Chūzō falls ill and they are forced to rest at the Masaki-ya Inn at Ganbarajuku in Sunshū, his illness gets worse and "Omatsu by his side impatiently wonders whether to abandon him though the all-important travel money was scarce. Bored with caretaking and forgetting all sympathy, *poison woman that she was,* she wondered 'What to do?'"[49] A two-day article about female thief Otsune in the *Kanayomi* stated that "even as a woman she traveled the Tokaidō Road opening her legs for money to pay for inns, her perverse heart swerved to take the sideways, digressing path of the crab, here and there drifting, drifting" *(soko yo koko kashiko nagare nagare)*.[50] Mark Silver has remarked regarding *Demon's Tale* that "Oden seems able to cover large distances with little effort, and to pop up anywhere without warning. This heightens her power as a symbol of the possibilities and dangers associated with the new geographic mobility of the early Meiji period."[51] A woman who is able to travel regionally is able to travel socially as well. Poison woman Omasa, for example, took on various identities, including the wife of a judge in Kobe. She rode on a ship posing as a wealthy man's mistress and stole the purses of travelers. Her faked social advancement enabled her to blend into her surroundings, poison woman that she was. The new law of travel that is symbolically deployed to mark the progressive shift from feudal to imperial order invites chaos and death not only when a woman avails herself of it but especially when a *lower* class woman avails herself of it, perpetuating the image of the new laws of the reformation as inviting danger from the female sex and lower classes.

Men in travel narratives of the Meiji period have a different experience. According to Kyoko Kurita, the literary theme of wandering was developed in Japan during the early 1800s and those stories of sea "drifters" *(hyōryūsha)* were taken up again by writers in the second decade of Meiji.[52] These fictionalized biographies *(jitsuden)* were the occasionally tragic tales of ambitious men of unrecognized talent seeking fame or fortune. Kurita has argued that Iwata Itei's works, through the combination of the traditions of samurai literature (privileging history) and merchant literature (privileging fiction) especially "succeeded in capturing a symbolic metaphor for the intellectuals of the time."[53] The hero was a protagonist who, in the nature of the earliest romanticists in Japan, sought release from an oppressive, or "overly determined" situation for a just utopia:

> Thus in the Gōhei story, the metaphor of drifting signifies the carrying-over process in which one's spirit rejects its geographically, socially, and philosophically over-determined location, turns its back on both the oppression and the security of home and terra firma, and surrenders itself to the search, at risk of life and limb, for a topos/non-topos, a place beyond space, where truth reigns supreme, and justice is always fulfilled.[54]

Merchants are the subjects of these biographies in the second and third decades of the Meiji period until students took their place as romantic social and financial drifters and enterprising merchants seeking international ports became full-fledged businessmen later in the Meiji period.[55] Unlike most of the drifters in political novels in the early 1800s and Meiji political novels who drift away from a national home, the poison woman has no place to which to return. Drifting does not have the aura of a romantic quest inspired by a spiritual goal but is rather a series of unwinnable tests for the survival of the fittest. Men could be enterprising heroic drifters but the woman who wandered enjoyed no such fate. While in theory the new travel laws would apply equally to all citizens, in representation man and woman are not treated equally; social propriety seems to dictate this incongruity. The male traveler is heroic, while the woman who takes advantage of the freedom to travel perverts that freedom through a problem of character. The violence perpetrated during her travels and her ultimate demise illustrate the justice of a tighter degree of control (of women).

"The Story of Street Minstrel Omatsu" serialized in the *Kanayomi* performatively addresses another significant new law of the Meiji era—the erasure of *hinin* status. In the first installment of the serial a conscripted soldier *(chōheitai)* (another reference to a new law, one allowing the drafting of soldiers), Hamada Shōji, is smitten with Omatsu from the minute he sets eyes upon her. Shōji determines that he will be with her "even if he were to descend to being like her—a *hinin*—and drown in the same mountain stream." This daydream of Shōji's, along with references to rumors that Omatsu was a "despicable creature of fate," introduce Omatsu as a person of the "non-human" class whose ability to assimilate is a test of the new law promulgated in August of 1871, which disallowed the discriminatory status of the *hinin* and allowed that class of people to work the same jobs as normal citizens *(heimin)* and to enter their names into the public register.

Omatsu speaks to the discriminatory law of the feudal period that kept socially branded personages in the status of "outcast" on an evening when she shares a pillow with lover Chūzō, in her abode. Chūzō has trouble sleeping because he is worried that he might be discovered sleeping with a *hinin.* Omatsu's lover Kichi suddenly appears and when he sees Omatsu in Chūzō's arms threatens to kill him. Omatsu tearfully pleads with Kichi to spare Chūzō's life:

> "I have no excuse if you try to kill me now but you who were [also] born in a miserable station with nowhere to go, who tied a romantic knot with me, you gamble every day and don't take up a trade and can't keep the home fires burning, so I must stand at people's gates singing those familiar songs *[shinnaibushi]* for [a mere] one or two sen, leading a miserable existence. I was born without bodily defect but am still despised as an untouchable *[eta]* and beggar with no chance to mix with normal people *[shirōto-shū].* You have been distracted with your illusions and so I turned to one who spoke kindly to me. Out of duty and love, if only once in my life, I slept with a normal man *[shirōto]* as was fated for this body. Chūzō is guilty of nothing, so swiftly kill me if you please."[56]

This eloquent soliloquy emerges from a narrative that otherwise condemns the traveling Omatsu as a faithless whore. Omatsu discusses directly the sting of social discrimination she has borne her entire life and explicitly rejects the idea that her body is different from anyone else's. But this sorry plight that would otherwise evoke sympathy is undone when it is revealed that Omatsu has manipulated this discriminatory practice to her own ends. Her sad tale runs cover for an elaborate plan to extort money from Chūzō, who fears for his life before the "jealous" Kichi and cannot recuperate his loss without risking exposure of his tryst with an outcast.

This early scene of Omatsu's swindling nature presages others showing Omatsu as a morally unworthy recipient of the new law that would lift her out of her lowly status. After robbing Chūzō, Omatsu and Kichi determine to flee the city. In the longer *gōkan* story, time is marked with the following reference to the official name change of Edo to Tokyo on 17 July 1871: "It was the second year of Meiji at the beginning of the second month of the lunar calendar. The scent of the plum at the eaves blew in the eastern wind. Everything was alive with spring. At that time too the name of Tokyo replaced the age-old Edo during this time of the honorable new reform government that brought manifold changes, saving the people from their suffering—a truly gracious reign."[57] The touted benevolence of the new government is expressed in a depiction of the erasure of outcast status with a new law, reported in the story to have been passed on 4 November 1871, which accorded people of this status the right to marry a person of elite, samurai, or commoner status. Omatsu welcomes the new law that releases her from the embarrassment of being from the "non-human" class and determines to take advantage of her status in the new order with cunning and finesse. But as soon as Omatsu learns she is free to marry anyone, free to travel, free to engage in other types of labor, she devises ways to take advantage of this newfound opportunity to the detriment of others:

> In the old days existed a social status that disparaged those as "untouchable" *[eta]* and "non-human" *[hinin]* but recently the imperial state declared that henceforth the term "untouchable" *[eta]* shall be abolished and they shall be called "new commoners" *[shin-heimin]*, and furthermore it would be allowed that they could marry elites, samurai, and commoners. Those of such status were enormously grateful to hear such news and felt very fortunate. Following this news, Omatsu became even more immodest of heart. "When the time is right I will slander [Hamada Shōji's] official wife Yasuko and restore myself to a life of prosperity," strategized the eyeless snake blind with greed.[58]

Maeda Ai has argued regarding the woodblock-printed story of street minstrel Omatsu that "as a story of 'equality of four classes' and 'all people under one ruler', it stole the hearts of the people. It appears that the readers of poison woman novels *[dokufu shōsetsu]* projected their hopes to change the world by secretly applauding the extravagant criminal acts of Oden and Omatsu."[59] But this story is disturbingly pessimistic and extremely judgmental, and it is not only Omatsu who is suspect. Class discrimination haunts this narrative. In this tale of digression, the woman who uses the law to move beyond her literally and figuratively limited position in society is ultimately condemned. Class discrimination is validated as natural and transcending any new laws that might eliminate class discrimination, thereby confirming old prejudices over new laws. In this case, judgment and discipline come from outside state law. In *Seafaring Omatsu* there is no guarantee for the successful implementation of the new law, which retains its status of novelty. The story invokes the new law but also undercuts it by citing its failure to deliver. The preface of the final section of the novel states, "The story here tells of the blessed dawn of Meiji which shone even upon street minstrel Omatsu who joined the ranks of new commoner status but was unable to cleanse her polluted soul. Blame the self for sins of the self. She collapsed under the agony of a mental disease."[60] The body of the underclass woman, as in the case of Oden, expresses the validity of conventional social and political boundaries.

The Meiji literature scholar Sumio Rinbara, who is one of the first scholars to reassess the popularity of poison woman fiction and other serialized fiction within the context of the enlightenment, claims that poison woman literature signals an ideological conflict of interest—a popular literary response to contemporary political revisionism and progressivism. To illustrate his point, Rinbara introduces an exchange in the *E-iri Chōya Shinbun* (Illustrated Morning Newspaper) between a reader dissatisfied with the "old-fashioned" themes of the serials, and the editor who politely refuses to alter the serials, arguing that the "barbarian" stories of war, thieves, and other melodramatic stories set in the warring bedlam of the final years of the Tokugawa period are what sell. This exchange introduces what is perhaps the first contemporaneous identification of the literary form of the serial *(tsuzukimono)*. As Rinbara points out,

> It is questionable whether the process whereby "serialized fiction" *[tsuzukimono]*, which developed into poison woman stories, and the anti-enlightenment aspects of those works can simply be treated as a revival of early modern *[kinsei]* literature. . . . The small newspaper *[koshinbun]* "serialized fiction" was not a revival of early modern *gesaku*-style literature, but an expressive world encapsulating a sense of discomfort toward revisionism.

That is, small newspapers' "serialized fiction" became the place for expressing doubts about rapid westernization and modernization, and as such be-
longs to the domain of modern literature. In the eyes of the "reporter" who
tried to make enlightened female [newspaper contributor] "Shibaiku onna"
and the "small newspaper" "a tool for removing the social barbarisms and
guiding it to enlightenment," the phase of old-style serial fiction was ob-
stinately stagnant in contrast with revisionary and revolutionary trends.
This phase should not be considered simply a revival of early modern *gesaku*
literature for readers with low reading capabilities by small newspapers acting on the assumption of western intelligence and commoners' ignorance.
Rather, it should be considered as the consciousness of a literary expression
contra the contemporary enlightenment movement. . . . The serial novel
discussed in contemporary testimonials introduced grave doubts about
modernization practices.[61]

In historicizing the popularity of the "barbarous" serialized fiction and
publicized debates surrounding the fiction, Rinbara argues convincingly
that the so-called retrograde serialized stories of "pirates and thieves" ri-
valed discourses of modernization as an ideological antipode.[62] This discussion suggests that the serial should be interpreted as a site of engagement with the new enlightenment movement and laws rather than a simple
espousal or rejection of them, and certainly this was the case when it came
to the representation of women under the law in the poison woman serial. The law in poison woman stories is progressive in that it allows new
freedoms, but suspicious for having afforded freedoms to women with devastating consequences for social order. The references to law in delineating
the poison woman's criminality suggest suspicion not only of women who
take advantage of the new laws but also of the law that would accord them
what is ultimately deemed illegitimate agency. In attributing equal status
to the underclass woman, the law ascribed an agency that was not affirmed
by traditional prejudice. The law is shown to give her status of which her
inferior essence is not worthy.

The poison woman's demise within the narrative, rather than affirming
the righteousness of the law, affirms the naturalness of traditional practices
and insinuates a need to place limitations on female agency. The narrative does not express an anxiety as much about the law per se as about
women under the law. Of implicit interest in the narrative was the status
of female agency and the emergent social body that enabled women and
those of the lowest class to participate in the formation of a new society.
The merging of classes and the merging of gender that could be construed

as sanctified under the newly promulgated laws could have easily produced a fear of women and lower classes who appeared under the new law to be invading territory that had been the sole prerogative of men of a certain status. The stories articulate this through a tension between the rhetoric of mobility and a textual space that justified the constraint of women. That there was never a "poisonous man" further suggests that it was woman's incursion into the social sphere that was at stake. This does not mean that there was a determinate subject-position for women or a clearly delineated discourse of woman in literature of the female criminal at this time. As the Renaissance scholar Catherine Belsey points out in an extended discussion of sexual difference, "To be a subject is to be able to claim rights, to protest, and to be capable, therefore, of devising a mode of resistance more sharply focused than prophesying, witchcraft or murder. It is to be in a position to identify and analyse the nature of women's oppression."[63] There were female activists in early Meiji making claims for women and analyzing their inferior treatment, but the delineation of women under the law in the *Kanayomi* and poison woman fiction occurred within sensational storytelling in which these sorts of political claims for women were absent.

The portrayals of the poison woman and the good female reader in the newspapers were part of an implicit management of the female sex in articulating authority (on the part of the editors as well as the state) in a period when new laws had destabilized traditional practices. Street minstrel Omatsu, Demon Oden, and even enterprising reader Tora were caught up in a struggle larger than their chroniclers realized—a struggle to establish limits on female agency enabled by new laws. In the "enlightened" society of projected (though certainly not actualized) equals, new regulations themselves become the subject of storytelling, and in these stories, lust and murder are the metaphorical destiny of the unregulated female.

3. Recollection and Remorse

In ancient times, this simple assertion was enough to shake the foundations of Greek truth: "I lie." "I speak," on the other hand, puts the whole of modern fiction to the test.

—Michel Foucault, *Foucault/Blanchot*

Literary confessors are contemptible, like beggars who exhibit their sores for money, but not so contemptible as the public that buys their books.

—W. H. Auden, *The Dyer's Hand*

"Rehabilitation." I wonder if you know what the word means. *The Unabridged Webster's International Dictionary* says "to invest again with dignity." You consider that part of your job, Harvey? To give a man back the dignity he once had? Your only interest is in how he behaves. You told me that once a long time ago and I'll never forget it. "You'll conform to our ideas of how you should behave." And you haven't retreated from that stand one inch in thirty-five years. You want your prisoners to dance out the gates like puppets on a string with rubber-stamped values impressed by you. With *your* sense of conformity, *your* sense of behavior, even *your* sense of morality. That's why you're a failure Harvey. You and the whole science of penology. Because you rob prisoners of the most important thing in their lives—their individuality. On the outside they're lost. Automatons just going through the motions of living. But underneath is a deep deep hatred for what you did to them. First chance they get to attack society they do it. The result? More than half come back to prison. Now it's all here in my book. And I suggest you read it and you read it thoroughly.

—Burt Lancaster as the "Birdman" speaking to the prison
head warden in the film *The Birdman of Alcatraz*

The Confessing Ex-Convict

From the late 1890s, a number of women who had been dubbed "poison women" by the press and spoken of solely in third-person fictionalized biographies emerged from prison to speak for themselves. At times, the ex-convict ascended the stage to narrate her past and imaginatively project her enlightened future in dialogue with other actors or in a monologue. Shorthand specialists who had only recently perfected their art of speedily recording oral speech transcribed these performances for publication as serialized newspaper stories and books, producing additions to the new literary form of the transcribed text, the *sokkibon.* Other times, these tales of repentance went to print in newspapers as the personal story told by the ex-con with the aid of an editor.

While the number of poison woman tales being published had decreased substantially, the turn-of-the-century reader, it appears, was still interested in the poison woman. A number of lengthy detective stories were published, such as *Viper Omasa* (Mamushi no Omasa, 1899) about ex-con Uchida Omasa, serialized in the *Miyako Shinbun;* and *Night Storm Okinu* (Yoarashi Okinu, 1904), which was a text serialized in the *Central Newspaper* (Chūō Shinbun) supplement *(furoku)* after being transcribed from the oral performance of raconteur Shinryūsai Teisui by a shorthand specialist.[1] Various compilations of poison woman stories had been published, such as the *New Edition of the Meiji Poison Woman Stories* (Shinpen Meiji dokufu den, 1886, republished in 1887), and the *New Edition of Dokufu Stories Past and Present* (Shinpen kokon dokufu den, 1887), which included stories about "Demon" Oden by Kanagaki Robun, "Nightstorm" Okinu by Okamoto Kisen, "Lightning" Oshin by Itō Kyōtō, and others. In addition to detective stories, true tales *(jitsurokumono)* continued to be a popular genre, and among them stories of poison women were featured.

At the turn of the century, however, it was the criminal's *self-narrative* that was the latest thing in women's crime stories. These self-narratives were most often framed as *zange,* which might be translated variously as "repentance" or "confession." Within literary history, the term *zange* is curious because it was so *present* at turn of the century and so *absent* later, in the way that, for example, "sentimental" was in eighteenth-century Western European literature. *Zange* originally was a religious term used to describe tales of conversion. At the turn of the century, the term *zange* appeared in a diverse array of texts by political novelists, literati, critics, and by convicted women who produced under the umbrella of *zange* staged confessions, personal tales of rehabilitation, and literary memoirs. Until *kokuhaku* (confession) became a more familiar term, *zange* appears in secular and nonsecular writing in low and high literature at this time.

Repentance narratives of the female ex-con formed what we might consider a new narrative mode for expressing female criminality. The confession enabled a full recitation of the thrilling life of the ex-criminal, providing sensational entertainment for the listener or reader while it offered an opportunity for the articulation of a different self that was not the fetishized deviant. The speaker acknowledged her guilt and her perversity and in that sense the confession was about *revealing* the self in typical confessional style, but it was also about rearticulating the self as rehabilitated. The staged confessions, likely because of their built-in visual spectacularity, appear to have been consumed as acts of performed disclosure of the life of the artist. An article in the *Yomiuri* newspaper from 1890 entitled "Poison Woman Omasa Appears on the Vaudeville Stage *[yose]*" treats the ex-con as both poison woman and popular storyteller: "Dokufu Omasa whose repentance story *[zange-monogatari]* is being played at the Gion-kan theatre, joined with comic storytellers *[hanashika]*, and came to tell her story at the Ikuyo vaudeville theatre at Shinkyogoku. A board with her stage name Dokufu-tei Omasa was placed in front of the stage house."[2] The name *Dokufu-tei* contains a homonym for "poison" *(doku)*, though it takes the Sinified character "alone" instead of "poison." Nevertheless polysemy is at work here. Some time later it was reported that Uchida "Viper" Omasa had attempted to play herself on stage in the Araki neighborhood of Yotsuya at the Suehiro-za theater where professional storyteller "Enjō" had been performing her story. She was ostensibly arrested again, this time for performing without a license.[3] She literally needed a license to tell her story.

Written (nonstaged) *zange* narratives, which are the focus of this chapter, are less explicitly self-exploitative. Unlike previous poison woman stories that take the delinquent past of their protagonists as their sole source material, the self-narratives by "poison women" use the past to predict a new and enlightened future for the speaker. The speaking subject's self-proclaimed social rehabilitation plays an essential role in the narrative. The speaker insistently paints herself as having turned over a new leaf and ready to spend the rest of her days as a socially useful person contributing to the community. Telling the truth, the intimate details of one's life, knowing one's self by revealing oneself are not enough for the female confessor. She must aggressively prove the self to be socially essential. The *zange* texts also reveal resentment, but this antipathy is inevitably joined with a rhetoric of rehabilitation—claims by the speaker to be a functioning, integrated (that is, feminine and demure) subject of society. The memoir of the political criminal Fukuda Hideko, who was never called a "poison woman," will also be discussed here, both because she wrote about a confessing poison woman and because her memoir engaged to great effect the rhetoric of repentance and emphasized social participation even while it was startlingly revealing—marking it as an important transitional work in writing of the "self" in modern Japan.

In canonical confessional literature, written soon after these *zange* narratives by ex-convicts were published, the confessor is nearly always male, and he, at all costs, must not be repentant. He must have no regrets. He must be shameless and consistently unapologetic. His confession is marked by boldness. This is clear in the impassioned responses to Tayama Katai's confessional novel *The Quilt* (Futon, 1907). The literary scholar Tomi Suzuki, who has written extensively on modern confessional narrative, points out that the first readers of Katai's *The Quilt* regarded it as a confession precisely because they observed the author's self-criticism and self-condemnation in his portrayal of the protagonist.[4] Katai heatedly refuted the claim that his *The Quilt* was a "repentance narrative" *(zangeroku)*. Katai's extended thesis on why his writing was not repentant was written in response to a number of reviews finding within *The Quilt* the author's own self-doubt and guilt. The critic and author Shimamura Hōgetsu unambiguously called *The Quilt* "a bold and outspoken confession of a man of flesh," praising the revelation of "ugliness,"[5] while another writer, Hoshi Getsuya, specifically named *The Quilt* a *zangeroku* precisely because the speaker exposes his ugly self in a bold audacious fashion. It is not surprising that Katai's work might be considered a *zangeroku*. A few months before the release of *The Quilt,* one book review of Kinoshita Naoe's *Zange* described this story and contemporary "zange" as a recent approach to writing the "self": "The anguish of contemporary youth is a problem of the "self" *[ware]*; questioning what life is, is a question of the 'self,' and the consequences of a life is a pursuit of the consequences for the self."[6] Katai countered accusations that he was in any way an author of *zangeroku* in an essay "Confessional Narrative and the Novel" (Zangeroku to shōsetsu, 1909).[7] In this brief essay, Katai argued that the description of psychology overcomes moral judgment in a novel (and by extension in his novels). There is, in other words, an absence of judgment and fictionalization that one finds in a *zangeroku*. The novel, in contrast to the *zange,* takes up the study of natural psychological phenomena like a scientist, and here he names Charles Darwin's "cool, objectivity" as a model for the novelist. Specifically about *The Quilt* he wrote, "*The Quilt* . . . is not a confession *[zange]* nor did I purposefully choose ugly details to write. I only wrote the truths that I discovered in my own life and revealed them to the reader. Whether the reader finds it distasteful, or unpleasant, or seeks some valuable insight from the author, or learns something is not of concern to the author."[8] Katai argues that his approach to a life is more truthful for its unabashed revelations, mundane or otherwise, of a man's psyche and adamantly refuses any connection between confessional narrative and his own novelistic writing. The fact that a debate arose around whether *The Quilt* was a *zange* illustrates the looseness and ambiguity of the term at this time, making it imperative to be attentive to contemporaneous narratives of *zange* by an array of writers in order to understand more fully how interiority developed in modern representation.

This chapter focuses on confessional narratives that immediately preceded this debate and analyzes featuring ex-convicts Shimazu Omasa (*A Record of Miss Shimazu Masa's Repentance* [Shimazu Masa-jo kaishin-roku, 1891]), Hanai Oume (*Hanai Oume's Story of Repentance* [Hanai Oume zange monogatari, 1903]), Fukuda Hideko (*Half My Life* [Warawa no hanseigai, 1904]), and, briefly, Uchida Omasa (*Confession* [Zange-banashi, 1903–4]). Paying attention to gender, I ask how the confessing "I" of these narratives differs from the criminal subjects in earlier poison woman literature and what aspects of the confessing subject's discursive positionality are shared with later confessional literature, if any. The confessional narratives, in addition to offering another example of how female criminality was represented in the Meiji era, prove to be an interesting instance of how confession by a woman might be written differently. In them, the subject is aligned with seemingly contradictory positions and in that sense offers a metaphor for the process of becoming a subject. The introduction to *Feminists Theorize the Political* illustrates how speaking of the self invites complicity with authorial discourses as a matter of necessity:

> Indeed, how is it that a position becomes a position, for clearly not every
> utterance qualifies as such. It is clearly a matter of a certain authorizing
> power, and that clearly does not emanate from the position itself. . . . this

"I," is *constituted* by these positions, and these "positions" are not merely theoretical products, but fully embedded organizing principles of material practices and institutional arrangements, those matrices of power and discourse that produce me as a viable "subject." Indeed, this "I" would not be a thinking, speaking "I" if it were not for the very positions that "I" oppose, for those positions, the ones that claim that the subject must be given in advance, that discourse is an instrument or reflection of that subject, are already part of what constitutes me.

No subject is its own point of departure.[9]

If no subject is its own point of departure, then each time we speak, we speak upon assuming a stage that involves, though it may be wrested from power, complicity with normalizing discourses. It is through these that the speaker speaks or *performs* the self. What normalizing discourses did the female ex-convict cite in her narrative of the self?

Like the protagonist of the Latin American *testimonio,* the subject in these confessions is aligned with a group or collectivity and this collectivity is feminine (within an "empowered masculine / disempowered feminine" dichotomy) and disenfranchised. As John Beverly says of the *testimonio,* "[It] is concerned not so much with the life of a 'problematic hero'—the term Georg Lukacs uses to describe the nature of the hero of the bourgeois novel—as with a problematic collective social situation in which the narrator lives. The situation of the narrator in *testimonio* is one that must be representative of a social class or group."[10] Shimazu's, Hanai's, and Fukuda's texts explicitly invoke "women" and "women in society" as a collective group to which their situation speaks. In contrast, the "I" of the confessional bourgeois novel celebrated in Japanese modern literary history is one who is antagonistic toward his world. He is cynical about his community and human nature and developed to be a self-righteous hero. This confessional hero over the course of modern literary history has become an aestheticized abject figure expressive of an abstracted interiority. The male confessional figure who is anti-social and aloof (and authentic and authoritative for those very reasons) has served as paradigmatic example of the early expression of interiority in narrative.

The pretense of an aestheticized self-proclaimed abjection was not a discursive option for the female confessor. This aesthetic stance of abject social outcast is not available to her for several reasons: (1) because she is already in that position and writing about it would be "news" to no one; (2) the primary way to assume authority was not to speak of abjection but to speak of social responsibility as an individual; and (3) her self-narrative is not supported by a claim for artistic license and requires the frame of repentance. The Meiji literature scholar James Fujii sees the assertion of authenticity and authority in writing as "two imperatives that defined the environment of turn of the century prose writing in Japan."[11] While Fujii focuses on canonical literature, confessions by ex-convicts also reveal this imperative to create an authentic, authoritative subject. However, the speaking subject cannot produce the sort of "authentic interiority" that has been identified in modern confessional literature because she cannot sustain a sense of authenticity and authority despite the autobiographical nature of the story, since the subject (the perpetrator of the narrative) had already been identified as criminal and often as sexualized and therefore not to be consumed as authentic speaker but sensational spectacle. The "I" of the repentance text could never be "sincere" not only because she had committed crimes but because she had been vilified in the press and named a poison-tongued woman. The subject suggested in these narratives is one that posits itself as abject while attempting to deconstruct itself as abject by articulating a self that is socially engaged and responsible.

Shimazu Omasa Stages Her Confession

The first "poison woman" to narrate her own criminal history was Shimazu Omasa. According to the handbill advertising her publicly performed confessions, Shimazu had been arrested by the Osaka police in October of 1881 for various crimes including theft and counterfeiting. Handed down a life sentence, Shimazu busied herself in prison. She formally converted and practiced Shingaku Buddhism and during her final years attended meetings held by a visiting Shingaku priest.[12] Released on 11 December 1887 for good behavior, she shaved her head and went to Tokyo to get permission to proselytize. While in Tokyo she attended a play about her life story at the Kotobuki theater and determined to go on stage to speak for herself. Named the founder of modern confessional narrative *(zangeroku)* by the cultural historian Watatani Kiyoshi in his book on poison women, Shimazu was the first to tell her own tale of crime rather than remain the object of others' tales.[13] But at least one ex-con before Shimazu publicly spoke of her crimes on stage. Murakami Ume, nearly seventy years old, had been released from an Osaka prison on 19 February 1881 after being incarcerated for thievery. As with other female criminals, a biographical story about her was serialized in a major newspaper, the *Asahi,* and thereafter the Naka-za theater performed the story on stage. The staged performance was so popular that in July of that year the seventeen-day run was extended by ten days.[14] After those initial stories about Murakami were published, she was once again investigated for thievery and imprisoned. After three and a half more years in prison Murakami was released in December of 1887. Because of her initial press notoriety, Murakami ascended the stage after a request from the Shinmachi-za theater to tell her life story. Murakami appeared before the public in nun's garb to perform *Murakami Baiji's Story of Repentance* (Murakami Baiji zange-gatari), which was by all accounts a resounding success, even giving rise to sequels.

Shimazu, who had been released from prison in 1887 at the age of thirty-one, ascended the stage at the age of thirty-five to tell her life story, often in nun's garb, to countless audiences around the country for at least thirteen years. An earlier *Yomiuri* newspaper report had encouraged readers to see the story of "poison woman" Omasa, which was to appear on stage beginning on the first day of January of the new year.[15] Prior to her staged repentance tale, a play about Shimazu ran in 1888 and in the same year Shimazu's autobiography was edited by Yoshida Kou and serialized in the prominent *Asahi* newspaper. This story appears as a later publication entitled *Repentance of Evil Deeds: Shimazu Omasa's Personal History* (Akuji Kaishun: Shimazu Omasa no rireki, 1895). The staged confession by Shimazu herself was transcribed and published as a book by Kawamura Tai'ichi entitled *A Record of Miss Shimazu Masa's Conversion* (Shimazu Masa-jo kaishinroku, 1891).[16]

As far as garnering an audience for this sort of confessional story goes, the gender of the narrating subject seems to have mattered. When a male ex-con, Takeshima Takegorō, tried the similar feat of ascending the stage to recount his past after his release from a Kobe prison for robbery and attempted escape from prison, he failed miserably *(migoto ni shippai shita)*.[17] By all accounts, Takeshima's appearance at the Kyoto's Gion-kan hall on 3 July 1890 found no substantial audience interest. Another newspaper article from this time tells of how a promoter advised a different male prisoner, Ganjirō, not to ascend the stage after being released from prison, though Ganjirō insisted that it would be in the interest of helping others.[18] A few years later there is at least one example of an article about a male repentant from this time who spoke from the gallows in "Repentance on the Hanging Platform," which is suggestive of the sentiment inspiring Shimazu's confession but is much more religious and disengaged from social circumstances. This article quotes a criminal's religious repentance before his hanging in which he begs forgiveness of his family and Buddha for the pain and suffering he has caused. In a 5-7 rhythm waka poem ("waka

sanshu" or "three-necked" waka poem) he makes his plea to be rowed to
the "other side of the river," leaving his criminal self behind and this vulgar
world on the far shore: "Bathed in the light of my parents' wisdom and
mercy / I leave [forget] this wandering path / This criminal forsaken in this
world / For Amida's salvatory mercy / I wait, To be carried on the promised boat / Rowed to Amida's Pureland."[19]

In contrast, confessions by criminal women who had been released to
join the general public were of popular interest. Shimazu's staged and published confessions were much anticipated by the newspapers. On 18 April
1888 the *Theater Correspondence* (Gekijo Tsūshin) section included in
the Osaka version of the *Asahi* newspaper related that a play would soon
be performed about "poison woman" Shimazu Omasa and "Lightning"
(Kaminari) Oshin at the Kado no shibai stage. On 20 May 1888 the newspaper followed up the story with a report that the play concerning Omasa
would appear instead on 1 June as *Shimazu Masa's Prison Diary* (Shimazu
Masa kangoku nikki). Then a week later the same publication reported
that the performance had been postponed. Two more articles followed
in July again promising the story of her life, one titled *Shimazu Masa's
Life* (Shimazu Masa no rireki), which was to be performed in seven acts at
Dotonbori's Benten-za theater.[20] The term *zange* appears in the title of the
final published version of the transcribed performance. On 20 February
1904 the *Yokohama Bōeki Shinbun* (Yokohama Trade Newspaper) reported that Masa would tell and confess the true story of her time in prison,
and her philosophy on "home training." Furthermore, three years later
the Osaka *Asahi* newspaper reported that Shimazu's *The Record of Miss
Shimazu Masa's Conversion* began running on 20 September 1891 and
was a resounding success. Shimazu's confession was, in short, a highly anticipated story.

The Record of Miss Shimazu Masa's Conversion and other transcribed
confessions are difficult to categorize because they were sometimes produced in a collaborative situation since the ex-con was not a professional
writer. The conclusion to *Record of Conversion* explains how the text mate-
rialized, moving from oral to written text:

> On November 6, 1889 . . . [t]he poison woman of old, Masa, vanished along
> with her sins, and she was completely reborn as Sister Chikai, Sister with
> Knowledge as Deep as the Sea. Before becoming one of countless wastrels,
> she gave penance, and all of her sins were absolved. Her oral outpourings
> were stenographed, then made into a theatre script of twenty scenes, and
> performed in theatres. Masa herself went on stage to perform.[21]

In *Record of Conversion,* the life story first narrated orally is displaced in the process of transcription and the autobiographical "I" is replaced by a third-person narration. Occasionally the "transcriber" interrupts to speak in the first person to assure the reader that a true story is being told, functioning as collaborator to provide authority to the narrative as if the speaker herself were not trustworthy.

Record of Conversion is a modern version of the sorts of revelatory tales *(zangemono)* told in medieval Japan in which religious awakenings from "humiliation, betrayal, and from witnessing grossly malicious behavior" give rise to a realization of the ephemerality of this world. Margaret Childs explains the form these medieval stories of religious conversion took: "While stories of religious awakenings are recounted in the voice of an omniscient third person and focus on one main character, revelatory tales consist of first-hand accounts offered by a group of several monks or nuns who tell their tales in turn. The public sharing of these stories of private realizations is, in fact, a religious ritual by which means the storytellers hope to confirm their beliefs and strengthen their religious resolve."[22] *Record of Conversion* contains many aspects of conventional *zange* including looking back on one's bitter experiences and confessing one's sins in order to "clear away the clouds of delusion," as the protagonist in Ihara Saikaku's parody of *zange* in *Life of an Amorous Woman* (Kōshoku ichidai onna, 1686) put it, and announcing the impetus to confess as a desire to inspire piety in others.[23]

However, *Record of Conversion* is not a traditional *zange* narrative for a number of reasons. According to Childs, *zange* is a story of individuals revealing to each other their sins and regrets. These tales reject the mundane world for a spiritual state, rather than a material state of being. The reforming of this world, the improvement of others' lives, is not a concern. Shimazu's tale, while it was shared with others, was not told as part of group storytelling. More important, Shimazu was interested in the improvement of others' lives in this world. Public reform and not just private reform was of concern.

The events of protagonist Omasa's life are told in hurried detail in *Record of Conversion.* Omasa is described in the story as sexually active at a young age, involved in sex work, masculine at times, enterprisingly entreprenurial, and highly mobile, regularly traveling and changing living quarters, just as the earliest poison women were. The confession begins with Omasa's birth to Yamamoto Toshichi in Osaka. Shimazu was the last name of her stepmother, Sada, who raised Omasa. At the age of fourteen, Omasa was sent to serve as a maid for a wealthy family by the name of

Kōnoike where she was pursued by the second eldest son in the family, Hidejirō. In 1869, Omasa was dismissed from her post, the victim of her employer's son's amorous advances. Omasa's stepmother was without pity and talked of marrying her off. Omasa was so unhappy that she attempted suicide by jumping off of the Honmachi bridge, but she was saved by a carpenter, Seishichi, who was a "wolf in disguise."[24] Feeling indebted to her rescuer, she gave herself over to him sexually. Seishichi employed Omasa by getting her started in a kimono fabric store across the street from the Sakaisuji-za theater.[25] However, one evening when Omasa came home thinking of severing ties with Seishichi, she found that her fabric store had been robbed. Because the robber, Shimazu Yoshi, had the same surname as Omasa, eventually a strange rumor spread that Omasa had surreptitiously robbed her own store.[26]

Omasa is the victim of men and rumors. Very little in the early part of the story paints her as an aggressor or manipulator. She is simply in the wrong place at the wrong time. Nowhere is this more clear than in the story of her meeting with thief Kida Yasuzō. At the Umeda station, Omasa came across the bearded Yasuzō as he was being escorted by geisha. Suddenly fourteen detectives rushed in to capture him. Seeing them coming, Yasuzō left his suitcase with Omasa and jumped off of the Ebisu bridge. The detectives followed and eventually captured him. Omasa cut open the suitcase and was shocked to find 2,800 yen. She gave 50 yen to Seishichi's foster mother and 300 yen to Seishichi as severance money so that he would agree to end their relationship. The rest of the money she spent on wine and entertainment. Omasa later learned the suitcase owner's name and realized that Yasuzō had passed her tainted money while escaping the police, thereby implicating her in theft of an enormous sum of money.

The story then introduces the criminal exploits of Omasa as she begins extensive travel using her newfound wealth from Yasuzō. She is depicted taking on various identities including the wife of a judge in Kobe. She travels on a ship posing as a wealthy man's mistress to steal the purses of travelers. She becomes a mistress of Kanazawa Gohei and spends one spring and autumn in a state of boredom. Omasa at one point returns to her hometown, where she has an affair with a quack doctor. The doctor's wife is so upset at her husband's indiscretions that she falls ill with depression. The doctor sees this as an opportunity to poison his wife and get together with Omasa. Thus, while Omasa was not a poison woman herself, she caused the poisoning of another through her sexual affair with a married man.

Omasa and the doctor part ways for a time. After his death, Omasa returns to Osaka. In the *Record of Conversion,* she recalls, likely as a matter of sensational interest, her meeting and time in jail with another poison woman, "Lightning" Oshin, who had been touted in the press as having extraordinary tattoos. Just as Takahashi Oden's reproductive organs had been saved in formaldehyde for at least fifty years, Oshin's actual tattoos were memorialized in a museum after her death in the form of a grotesque human pelt. In one scene of the confession, Omasa describes saving a woman, Sue, who was about to jump off a bridge to her death, and giving her stolen clothes to change into. Wearing these clothes led to Sue's arrest, according to the confessional tale. Nevertheless, Omasa did not turn herself in but continued to steal and rob until she was finally arrested and put in prison.

Omasa escaped prison by climbing over its outer wall. She stole clothes, money, geta shoes, and an umbrella and managed to reach the Osaka castle moat where Mr. Okumura came for night fishing. He feared that Omasa would jump to her death in the moat so he took her home, where she stayed for six months. Omasa continued to steal and rob and opened a restaurant called Hatsuneya in Kobe. She was reunited with Yasuzō, who had recovered after receiving treatment for his arm, which was wounded during the jailbreak, from a foreigner. Realizing that the police had begun to watch her closely, and feeling sorry for having inadvertently sent innocent Sue to prison, Omasa turned herself in to the police. She was sentenced to hard labor for life and sent to the Osaka prison. Because she behaved herself, worked hard, and showed signs of rehabilitation, her sentence was downgraded from an indefinite term to a definite term. Omasa sent money that she made at the prison to her stepmother, became a model for other prisoners, and received four prizes while in prison. While prison guards and prisoners all admired her, Oshin resented Omasa and was arrogant toward her. Although Omasa apparently tried everything in her power to get Oshin's sentence reduced, Oshin remained aggressively ill-disposed toward Omasa, attacking her with a wedge from a loom and injuring her on the forehead. Despite this assault, Omasa "never stopped her good deeds" and was released by special pardon on 10 December 1889 after five years and ten months of hard labor.

In October of 1887, Omasa met yet another famous criminal, this time political prisoner Fukuda Hideo, who, feeling lonely and frightened, had requested company in her cell. Fukuda writes about Omasa in *Half My Life,* but Shimazu leaves out Fukuda, likely to spare the educated woman sensational attention. Omasa claims to have educated herself through reading books voraciously in prison and dedicating herself to encouraging other fellow prisoners to do the same during her five-year prison term. She further claims to have often listened to a priest of Shingaku philosophy, Okamoto Ichirobe, to atone for past deeds. And she claims to have become the pupil of the chief priest Ōtsuka of the Sumiyoshi Godairiki Jizō-ji temple and changed her name to Chikai.

As illustrated in this plot recap, *The Record of Miss Shimazu Masa's Conversion* has much in common with earlier poison woman literature in the sense that it details the adventures of a mobile woman involved with crime and deceit. The narrative echoes the condemnation of female sexuality found in earlier narratives of poison women. However, the subject condemns the self rather than being condemned by an outside authority. There is consequently a split in the discursive positioning of the speaker: the performer and the subject of the narrative are linked but not one and the same. There is a self-conscious splitting of the emotional, speaking "I" who seeks reintegration into the social order from the spoken "I" who is a bygone self. Her virtue and integrity are measured according to the degree to which she can refuse any sexualized identity. This Buddhist rhetoric of the refusal of desire is simultaneously a modern inflection of a female subject position. The mature, virtuous woman must refuse any sexual identity: this refusal took physical form on stage when Shimazu would dramatically remove her wig during the performance to reveal a shaved head. The exposure of her naked head literalized the transformation from perversely criminal and sexual to rehabilitated, asexual, and religious.

Nevertheless, there is still a suggestion that Omasa is perverse, in terms of gender, when the transcriber praises her performance with the claim that she outdid even the male actor: "Theatre-goers claimed that her performance and speech flowed like water, her physical expression and rhythm were better than a man's."[27] In claiming Shimazu's performance to be better than a man's, the transcriber may be referring to those cross-dressing *onnagata* actors who performed the roles of poison women on the kabuki stage beginning with the iconic figure's inception in the 1870s. The transcriber may even be referring specifically to an Osaka kabuki actor who performed Shimazu's biography as *The Diary of Shimazu's Soul* (Shimazu Masa bodai nikki), though the play was soon banned as injurious to public morals. The curious twist is that Shimazu is claimed to be as good as a man at acting like a woman. In skill she is the equivalent of the male actor; but as a woman she is a master of disguise. She is never what she seems; she is gender-enigmatic.[28]

In the process of speaking retrospectively of her past, the criminal, sexual Omasa is revived. The act of confessing ironically disables the attempt to transcend the deviant self. When the performative aspect of the confession is so emphasized by the transcriber, the deviant woman can conversely be imagined as retaining a hidden poisonous core that a mere ten years earlier could be "discovered" by literally peering inside the criminal body, as in the case of Takahashi Oden discussed in chapter 1.[29] The fantasy of the dominant woman is not interrupted by the confessing of her past. Omasa as self-proclaimed rehabilitant cannot traverse the fantasy of the sexual criminal woman. She remains in the position of object of fascination. There was little to differentiate her body in performance from that of the poison woman in print.

The cultural historian Matsuyama Iwao believes that it was precisely the theatrical behavior of earlier poison woman Takahashi Oden that led to the appellation of "poison woman."[30] The note written in blood to her lover Ogawa Ichitarō after her arrest, her histrionic crying, falling ill, and the changing of her testimony four times during the trial all contributed to an image of Takahashi as a deceitful actor. The emotions of the female criminal are interpreted as an *act,* therefore the speaker is already precluded from being a source of authenticity and authority. J. L. Austin's well-known treatise on pledges states that declarations and other similar speech acts specifically made on stage are "infelicitous" because they are mere acting and therefore inauthentic. The staged utterance Austin dismisses as "parasitic upon its normal use" and as an "etiolation of language." To him, that which is literally citational is void of effect and power: "[a] performative utterance will, for example, be in a peculiar way hollow or void if said by an actor on the stage, or introduced in a poem, or spoken in soliloquy. . . . Language in such circumstances is in special ways—intelligibly—used not seriously, but in many ways parasitic upon its normal use—ways which fall under the doctrine of the etiolations of language. All this we are excluding from consideration."[31] Austin makes a distinction between language performed on stage or in poetry, relegating the performative on stage to the realm of the weak and nonserious where language is only mimetic.[32] The promises made in these repentance tales performed on stage ("I promise to do good," "I promise to contribute to the improvement of the Japanese nation," "I promise that I am rehabilitated") under these terms would be infelicitous. Matsuyama's argument follows the same logic. It was precisely the verbal manifestation of Takahashi's story—Oden "live"—that erased the authority of the narrative. Takahashi's testimony as it was elicited from the lips of the accused was treated as lies—as an act. The authoritative version of Takahashi's life was that produced by the courts. In considering the question of articulation and power, the claim that some mediums do not enable meaningful utterances can have fairly radical consequences for determining who has the authority to be heard (and believed).

Shimazu made various attempts to overcome the assumed perversity of her staged confession by framing herself as the very spirit of reform. The handbills *(banzuke)* advertising her public appearances provided a short biography portraying Shimazu as a reformer par excellence. She was advertised as being involved in the promotion of education and the eradication of poverty for children. The caption under a portrait of Shimazu featured on the handbill advertising the Yokohama theater performance describes the show and its goals:

> We revised the play and steadily expanded the theaters and performed in many prefectures throughout Japan to say nothing of Tokyo, Osaka, and Kyoto. At every performance we received great applause. . . . It shows a detailed personal history without missing a thing—from the beginning of worldly crimes committed to today's repentance. . . . The main objective of our performance this time is, as previously mentioned, charity donation. This performance is a charity drama. Admission fees from everybody will be donated to the Education and School for the Poor Foundation initiated by the directory of our troop, Nakagawatsu. Everyone, good men and women, please feel compassion for the many children of the poor and support our mission. We beg you to please come see our play.[33]

The handbills introduce Omasa as a penitent woman who wants her experience to provide education and poverty relief to children. Recalling Judith Butler's notion of gender as performative and not essentially determined, the repentance situation can be considered a literal enactment of how being a socially proper, normal woman is a cultural performance, an act that is repeated to become a culturally recognizable identity. The dogged determination to depict the self as reformed suggests that in order to produce a position from which to speak authoritatively, one must be a woman without sexual desire, and the very spirit of social reform.

Hanai Oume: A Daughter in Rehab

Hanai Oume, who had spent fifteen years in prison from 1888 to 1903 for the fatal stabbing of her male assistant, Minekichi, on 9 June 1887, also published a confessional narrative detailing the events leading up to the murder and her time in prison. She had only been out of prison six months when the *Osaka Mainichi* reported that in the three months since the publication of the *Story of Repentance* Oume had become quite a celebrity. An unending stream of customers visited her restaurant near the location of the murder.[34] After the publication of the *Story of Repentance,* Hanai, like Shimazu, ascended the stage to tell her story (in 1905). The *Yomiuri* newspaper reported that Hanai expressed a desire to play herself on stage and that she had joined Mori Sannosuke's *shimpa* (new theater) actors to perform *Assistant-Killer* (Hakoya-goroshi).[35] In 1936, Tanizaki Jun'ichirō wrote the preface to a story about Hanai by Kawaguchi Matsutarō entitled *A Woman of Meiji* (Meiji ichidai onna) in which he recalled her stage shows: "Oume herself told her life's story on stage, and traveled around the country doing it. Once she even appeared in a film."[36] Tanizaki is likely referring to either the 1926 silent film directed by Yoshino Jirō entitled *Hanai Oume* or the 1929 film *Hanai Oume* directed by Oka Kōji.[37] Hanai's release from prison spawned more poison woman stories in the newspapers, including but certainly not limited to a five-installment story about Hanai entitled "Story of an Old Geisha from Shinbashi: Hanai Oume" (Shinbashi-jū Rōgi-banashi) and a long serialized confessional story about a different Omasa—Uchida "Viper" Omasa—entitled *Viper Omasa: A Confessional Story* (Mamushi no Omasa: Zange-banashi).[38] This long confessional narrative includes the perspective of an anonymous "transcriber." The serial begins: "Yesterday, on the 11th, a female prisoner Uchida Masa, known as Viper Omasa, was released from prison. It was seven in the morning when she was freed. Our reporter thought that she did not look like an evil, poisonous woman called 'Viper Omasa' so the reporter asked her if she had repented. Her tearful eyes showed a repentant heart when she raised her dropped head and started talking about her earlier years. We offer this story told word by word, by her." The *Yomiuri* also ran a shorter story, "Mitsuhoshi Oume," about "Viper Omasa's sister in crime."[39]

Hanai had become a popular subject for the press immediately upon her arrest. The *Yomiuri* newspaper alone published eighty-eight articles about the incident and the trial, which commenced 18 November 1887. Stories, articles, and plays portrayed Hanai as a new poison woman of the caliber of Takahashi Oden. One of the most circulated stories about Hanai was *The Strange Story of Hanai Oume at Suigetsu* (Hanai Oume suigetsu kibun, December 1887). Her court trial was transcribed and published as a book very soon after the trial. The Meiji literature scholar Hirata Yumi discusses in detail the difference between the contexts in which true tales about Takahashi Oden and Hanai Oume were published. In addition to changes in the newspaper reporting style and printing techniques, Hirata argues that the movement of literary style from serialized stories of poetic justice *(tsuzukimono)* to a novelistic fictional world *(shōsetsu)* determined a different style of narrative for the later fictionalized stories about Hanai.[40] It should also be noted that while the earlier poison women biographies were performed only on the kabuki stage, Hanai's was performed on the more modern *shimpa* stage.

Hanai, who had been convicted of murder, had far more to confess than Shimazu. The trial transcription serialized in the *Yomiuri* newspaper on 19 and 20 November relates the details of Hanai's crime, the murder of her employee, Minekichi. Hanai had been given up for adoption at a young age and was sent away from home to be employed as a geisha at the age of fifteen. She was popular with the guests and eventually hired a "box-man" *(hakoya)* to carry her shamisen and various items during working hours. This man, Minekichi, was to suffer the fate of being Oume's murder victim. As the repentance narrative discussed below illustrates, in 1885 at the age of twenty-two, Hanai moved to Shinbashi to continue entertaining and took the name Hidekichi. She steadily saved money and opened a teahouse called "Suigetsu" a month before the murder on 14 May 1887 in the neighborhood of Hama-chō. Within days it had become a booming success. But Hanai greatly resented that the property title of the teahouse was in her father's name, since the teahouse's existence and popularity were the result of her efforts alone. Exacerbating the situation was Minekichi's increasing alliance with her father, who was hardly more than a sponger, according to the repentance narrative. As the speaker "Oume" in *Hanai Oume's Story of Repentance* tells it, Oume felt that she had been taken advantage of by a father who had never really loved her. According to the court testimony, the two argued incessantly about money. Toward the end of May, the father, Sennosuke, who had been insisting on his rightful ownership, put a "closed" sign on the door of Suigetsu and locked Oume out of the restaurant. While staying with acquaintances, Oume strategized on how to get her restaurant back. On the evening of 9 June, she called out Minekichi, who had supported Sennosuke's decisions all along, and rebuked him for his increasing tendency to side with her father. The conversation escalated and Oume, angered by Minekichi's bold behavior, stabbed him in the back. The sentence the court would hand down hinged on whether she had committed premeditated murder. She bought a knife before the murder but her lawyers argued that since she had purchased scissors at the same time, it did not constitute evidence for premeditated murder. The lawyers also argued, in a relatively new type of plea in Japan, temporary insanity. On 21 November 1887 the court determined that Hanai had committed premeditated murder. She was not sentenced to execution but rather to life in prison. She appealed to the highest court (Daishin'in) but her appeal was denied on 10 April of the following year and she was sent to Ichigaya prison on 18 April 1888.

Hanai, who had become a journalistic and literary sensation comparable to Takahashi Oden, was portrayed in the media, in contradistinction to Takahashi and "street minstrel Omatsu," as mentally rather than physically diseased (although Omatsu died running in circles like a mad dog according to Hikosaku's *The New Story of Seafaring Omatsu*). The plea of temporary insanity levied by Hanai's lawyers contributed to the notion circulating in the press that she was mentally ill. Newspaper stories subsequently traced this madness to her mother, arguing that Hanai was the sorry victim of a genetically transmitted madness that made her unstable and potentially violent.[41]

Hanai was haunted in the press for decades by accusations of insanity. The *Yomiuri* newspaper reported on 7 August 1893 that Hanai had made progress toward rehabilitation. She "endeavored to stamp out the poisonous insect" by working hard at making thongs for hemp sandals. The following year, however, she is reported to have suffered a relapse. The *Yomiuri* reported on 22 May 1894 that at the Ichigaya prison, Hanai reportedly became mentally deranged *(sakuran jōtai)* each year around the time of the murder. This tendency to frame Hanai as insane is repeated throughout the years during and after her imprisonment. On 8 February 1896, the popular *Miyako* (Capital) newspaper reported that "on the evening of the 8th of every month, Oume becomes feverish and suffers great anguish *[hitogokochi mo naku kurushimu]* but returns to normal the following morning of the 9th. This habit dubbed 'Minekichi fever' by the inmates has continued unchanged for ten years."[42] The following year, the *Jiji* newspaper again reported her apparent lunacy in an article entitled "Oume Who Becomes Enraged When Teased":

> We hear from former inmates who recently left the Ichigaya prison that Oume has never had a mental illness although there had been a rumor that she had tended to go mad *[hakkyō no kimi ari]*. In actuality, she is not mentally ill. It is a result of her powerful innate temper *[seirai ganpeki no tsuyoki]*. She loses her temper when made fun of by inmates, goes off the deep end, and punches the culprit. She has also ripped her own clothing to shreds and is punished frequently. Consequently she has been kept in a cell alone. Even at her daily stint in the handiwork quarters, she separates herself by about two meters from other inmates while sewing handkerchiefs. She seats herself at the foot of the prison warden and it seems that her body bends to the left and her neck stretches out. She appears to sit slumped in the shape of a "ku" letter. She does not appear to be a novice.[43]

This article frames Hanai's anger as incurable. This question of whether Hanai is stricken with a disease *(byō ni kakaru)* recalls the Takahashi Oden case in which the sensationalized female criminal is, must be, categorically, ill though the reference to Hanai as having an innately crazed temperament *(seirai)* shows her to be not physically but mentally ill.

An incident that occurred soon after her release from prison provided more fodder for the image of Hanai as insane. In 1912, when a geisha performed a semi-impromptu play about the homicidal attack at the same spot where Hanai had murdered Minekichi, the real Hanai jumped up onstage and vociferously raged against the actress, demanding to know who had given her the right to restage the event. The incident created a commotion among the onlookers.[44] Hanai's insistence on her right to determine who may tell her story, albeit in a socially inappropriate way, is treated merely sensationally.

Another article reported that Hanai went mad after the doctor she requested did not make a house call:

> At about 1:00 a.m. yesterday, Hanai Oume (42), who lives in Ushigome-ku Goken-cho, with her hair disheveled like a mad woman, knocked at the door of doctor Kojimahara Yasutami of Kagurazaka 1-chome, 6 banchi. As she asked whether the doctor was home, Dr. Kojimahara came to the door thinking it may be an emergency. As the doctor entered the entryway, Oume suddenly grabbed his collar and yelled that he was untrustworthy. The doctor and his family were astonished and confused until the police arrived and they learned that the woman was Hanai Oume and that she had a grudge against the doctor because her illegitimate daughter had been sick for some days, but the doctor had not come to check on the daughter as Hanai had requested. She was deeply bitter and exhibited mental imbalance. . . . Her brother was called to retrieve her.[45]

These articles portray Hanai as a deranged, crazy woman more than a decade after her crime and suggest the near impossibility of conversion in terms of the social perception of the female criminal; they suggest the impossibility of Hanai ever achieving "authority" as a speaking subject. The madness of which she is accused renders her incapable of supplying an authoritative narrative of the self. That opportunity is only for those seamlessly integrated into society.

What sort of speaking subject could emerge from these suspicions of her mental stability? How could a woman deemed interminably insane carve out a self with authority in public discourse? Probably because of these accusations, Hanai agreed to speak of the murder and her experience in prison. In collaboration with a journalist she produced a self-narrative driven by the rhetoric of repentance and rehabilitation. The extended repentance narrative argues against an image of insanity in developing an image of the ex-convict as rehabilitated and socially useful, similar to the repentance story of Shimazu and the contemporaneous memoir of political prisoner Fukuda Hideko discussed below. But unlike Shimazu's confession, which is founded in religious conversion as well as a rhetoric of rehabilitation within the secular world, Hanai's confession is fully secular. Oume describes herself not as having undergone conversion but rehabilitation. Thus the speaker begins her repentance tale in the following fashion: "A chance mistake has resulted in sixteen years of grief and hardship. I am still ashamed of it now. Yes, this is a confession of my time since entering prison. I have many painful things, sad things, pitiful things [to share]— in penance I will tell all, leaving nothing out."[46] Oume's apologetic revealing of her evil deeds is accompanied by an insistence that the rehabilitation she seeks is not only for herself but for the social system, specifically the prison system. These claims for personal involvement in social reform are to be evidence of her rehabilitation, and a narrative strategy for creating an authoritative voice in writing.

Hanai's confession is not framed simply as a sincerely performed revelation as part of a hidden will to power by claiming to disclose the truth about the past or present.[47] The goal of the confession is not simply "exposure," for that is actually counterproductive because it makes the criminal woman spectacular. To achieve "authenticity" as a female speaker, the subject insists on her social usefulness. Thus Oume announces her desire to work toward prison reform through the "confession" of her experience in prison: "Though this is a confession, and in all respects is my shame, I endure the humiliation for society. . . . My opinion is that even if it is only minimal, if I can aid in the reform of women's prisons, it will be the happiness of all of my days."[48] The confession by the ex-con strives to eliminate perversity that would be a hallmark of later novels featuring male confessors. The narrative (albeit futilely) works to counter the spectacle of confession by framing the female speaking subject as rehabilitated. The preface, written by the editor who was also an employee of the *Kokueki Shinbun* (National Newspaper), works to substantiate the claims of the confession by categorizing it as both confession and social document:

> She tells secrets of the prison and stories about herself, which are incomparable to the usual novel. More than an interesting read, this is a resource for researchers of women's issues *[josei mondai]*. Head wardens will read and savor it. For those excited by the topic of prison reform, sitting down with

this book is a must, and it goes without saying that on the relationship of society and the criminal, this will profit anyone who reads it. Oume was a woman in prison. . . . Though we should despise the crime, still, we should not throw out the story of being in prison. And, we should especially shed a tear for the act of lament and confession by a criminal figure.[49]

In a dramatic shift in poison woman narrative, the repentance text stages social reintegration rather than emphasizing the confessing subject's marginality or deviance. Instead of moral, social, and aesthetic judgments converging upon the female body to promote a counterexample as in earlier fiction in which the poison woman is excluded as an exception to the rule, these new judgments converge on the repenting woman in forming a model of self-willed normativity. The subject that emerges is one who seeks to normalize herself ironically through the "spectacle" of her testimony. In the process of producing a new self, the female criminal acted out a mise-en-scène of a promise to reform or "normalize" the self. The speaker claims to have shed the old self and left behind the past. She embraces cultural norms through a dramatized disclosure of the deviant "interior" seeking normalization. Hanai earns her right to speak by using the language of social reform, by illustrating through her use of nation-building rhetoric that she herself can improve current disciplinary systems through her narrative of reform.

At the same time, the performative situation of repentance allows for communication of anger and resentment toward the patriarchal system, which seeks obedience from its daughters, as well as the prison system, which made rehabilitation all but impossible according to the speaker. The confession is more clearly than Shimazu's "double-sided discourse" revealing a troubling anger and resentment within a narrative of rehabilitation. The speaking subject more clearly exhibits agency in this narrative of the self through the critique of social and gender discrimination. According to the repentance narrative (and court testimony), the antagonism within the family, especially between Hanai and her father, escalated on the day that she discovered the "closed" sign on the door of Suigetsu. In *Hanai Oume's Story of Repentance,* Oume recalls the bad relationship that she had with her father over many long years. The relationship worsened when Oume's patron offered to invest in a tea house as long as it was in her father's name so that he, the patron, did not receive any notoriety for his relationship with Oume. Oume's father began to take over business decisions and to treat Oume as his employee, while Minekichi continued increasingly to side with Oume's father's decisions. The confession frames Oume as victim of an overbearing patriarch through relating her unsuccessful attempt to commit suicide by throwing herself into a well after her father's accusatory remarks, even as it unapologetically depicts Minekichi as an ungrateful and unfaithful employee and friend.

Hanai avoided disobedient statements in the public trial, going so far as to state that she believed it was unfilial to disobey her father. In the confessional narrative, however, a long-held resentment toward her father, Sennosuke, emerges with shocking intensity. The confession discusses how her father, who had turned her over to an adoptive family when she was eight, returns to sponge off Oume's lucrative success as a geisha and restaurant proprietor. In the description of their reunion after her release from prison, Oume states: "The story of my past has been nothing other than my confession. I feel broken up. My father and I visited since my release from prison. He's gotten old. When he saw me, outside of a single tear, he had nothing to say. He has always been my birth father and though I had no intention of keeping him as my lifelong enemy, that single tear washed away the past forever."[50] In this closing comment, the memory of the struggle of a single woman against a dominating father emerges. This resentment (which coincidentally James Fujii identifies as a central theme in highbrow literature of the same period) toward her father accompanies the speaker's inscription of the self as a productive citizen and filial daughter. The confession of anger toward the father is culturally tolerable only if the female subject is repentant and rehabilitated.

The collaborator's presence in the narrative structure contributes to producing a repentant Oume who commiserates with the interviewer over false gossip perpetuated in newspaper serials written at the time of her trial. The interviewer normalizes Oume, just as Hanai herself does in repentance, through portraying her as socially active but appropriately submissive: "Hanai Oume was not evil by nature. . . . so many people know that she was not a poison woman. . . . Though she was a geisha, Oume was fastidious in her character and conduct, and did not do things in order to be out of the ordinary."[51] In this statement the editor rejects the label of poison woman on behalf of Hanai, claiming that she is a "normal" woman who did not seek notoriety; she was, he argues, fastidiously feminine, for only the feminine woman can be harmless and therefore assimilable into society.

Fukuda Hideko: The Double-Voiced Memoir of the Ex-Convict

The memoir of released political prisoner Fukuda Hideko clearly expresses the desire portrayed in Hanai's confessional narrative to be imagined as a working, productive, and self-disciplined citizen after having been imprisoned. It is essential to point out that Fukuda was never named a poison woman. Quite the contrary, she was a celebrated political rights activist from the upper classes who was highly educated. Nevertheless, Fukuda's memoir proves an interesting comparison to the repentance tales by less educated women for its similar use of repentance rhetoric and insistence on rehabilitation through social action. Furthermore, Fukuda's approach to narrating one's life as an "ex-con" suggests the importance of *Half My Life* (1904) as a formative text in the creation of modern confessional literature.

Fukuda was arrested for involvement in planned terrorist activities that were labeled by the press the "Osaka Incident." This was a plan led by radical political rights activist Ōi Kentarō to perpetrate an attack on Japanese forces in protest of Japan's support of the authoritarian regime in Korea in the 1880s. It was also intended to foment political change at home. Sharon Sievers describes Fukuda's state of mind:

> Disgusted with the quality of leadership in the old Liberal Party, and convinced that she had the "will to struggle for the country, even to the point of death," Fukuda involved herself in a plan to challenge the Meiji government by setting up a reform government in exile—in Korea. When the plan failed she was picked up by the police in November 1885. . . . Later sentenced to a ten-month prison term as a state criminal, Fukuda's heroics and her self-proclaimed struggle for freedom made her the idol of young women throughout the country, who became avid readers of newspaper stories characterizing her as "Japan's Joan of Arc."[52]

Fukuda achieved notoriety for her strong sense of patriotism and moral fortitude and not inconsequently for being the only woman involved in the Osaka Incident. After her arrest, Fukuda was first incarcerated in the Nakanoshima prison in Osaka and then moved to the nearby Horikawa prison, and it was there that she met Shimazu. The two became friends though they had little in common. Unlike Hanai and Shimazu, who were unschooled, labored as children, and engaged in sex work, Fukuda was an educated woman who fought for female suffrage, taught, and worked for social justice. *Half My Life* is written in the prose of a scholar, with references from world literature including Chinese philosophy and Benjamin Franklin's autobiography, which Fukuda read with great pleasure.[53] No interlocutor interrupts her narrative. No transcriber receives credit for the story's publication. Fukuda's autobiographical confession—she refers to it both as a *zange* and *kokuhaku*—details a conversion from a wild-eyed, self-involved, and narcissistic youth to an ethical, concerned citizen of the nation.

Fukuda's text is less apologetic than Hanai's, expressing anger and frustration at the mistreatment of the female sex in society more aggressively. As gender-marginalized but highly educated and sophisticated in her use of language, Fukuda was able to interject into her tale of regret a more explicit "double discourse" in which regret *and* struggle, erasure *and* admittance of desire could coexist. Gender, in other words, cannot be the sole privileged category for reading differences in confessional narrative. Her class position, her educated status, her facility with language enabled the production of a much more complex subjectivity in confessional narrative. Significantly, though, Fukuda's memoir makes frequent reference to the concept of *zange*. The memoir portrays the transformation of a naive renegade activist into a rehabilitated socially active woman through the portrait of a humble self who is, insistent about the lessons that humble self can offer the public.

The speaker equates herself with the pragmatist Franklin even while she describes herself as "foolish" *(orokanaru hito)*, "deeply sinful" *(tsumi fukaki hito)*, and a "sinner" *(tsumi no hito)* full of regrets and anguish *(kushin* or *kumon)*—words frequently visited by naturalist confessional writers. The self-narrative begins,

> If you asked who it is that is deeply sinful in this world, I would truly be the most [deserving of that title]. If you are seeking a fool in this world, there would be no one as foolish as I. Having lived over half of my life, alas, in reflection I find that nothing I accomplished was not a crime, nothing I planned turned out right. Only feelings of shame and a desire to repent, followed by pain and anguish, flood my mind.
>
> The only path to curing the anguish of confession *[zange no kumon]* is to *reform* oneself. But how is one to reform this self? This is another source of anguish. . . . To write this book is not to forget this anguish. No, taking up this brush is also itself a seed of anguish. Character by character, line by line, the more I write the more the anguish intensifies.
>
> The anguish only intensifies, but by no means do I want to forget this. No, these nostalgic memories of the past increase, along with the anguish, with each character, each line. How nostalgic I feel! This remembrance of pain.[54]

In this opening passage, the speaker prepares the reader by presenting a self-portrait of humility and deference. In the creative process of articulating a self, the speaker resorts to self-abjection, and this anguish, which appears to be emotional and even physical, gives her validity and authority as a writer.[55]

Just as both Shimada and Hanai's confessions contain a discussion of sorrow and regret but also introduce a self that is motivated toward social action, Fukuda, in the preface, outlines a new plan for social action, which is part of her self-reform, while she insistently presents herself as at heart a mother and wife:

> Despite being a woman, in my youth I went delirious with shouts for the freedom and political rights of the people. While I frequently stumbled on the way, later in life I was able to start a family but before achieving plans I made for the family, I became a widow. I deeply felt the dreariness of the world seep into my bones. Those who sympathize with me must also be unfortunate souls. . . .
>
> Indignant about the monopolization of political rights, I now defy the monopolization of capital, and am predisposed to save the unhappy poor. Paying no mind to ridicule I dare to narrate honestly my youth without hiding a thing. This is not necessarily because I am trying to atone for my sins through repentance *[zange]*. It is to declare anew a struggle with the world and myself.[56]

The text speaks highly of Shimazu's atonement for her crimes in prison, claiming that Shimazu's reputation among Osaka prisons for being a model prisoner rang true to Hideko, who describes Omasa in the memoir as among the prisoners and generous toward others. Shimazu is claimed to have been highly motivated to learn Western letters, going so far as to suggest that she take on Fukuda's prison work in exchange for instruction.

The earliest discussion of "rehabilitation" in Fukuda's text traces her transformation from a tomboy to a proper woman. The narrator earnestly recounts on numerous occasions how she was considered a gender imposter but eventually reformed to become a feminine woman:

> On my way to school everyday, mischievous local kids would tease me yelling: "Here comes the imposter! Here comes the imposter *[magai]*!" As I think back on it today, it wasn't such an inappropriate term because I was a kind of imposter, a sham. . . . My teachers told me I was lively, and it's true that I behaved a bit like a tomboy. . . . Until I was sixteen, I kept my hair cut short with my bangs parted down the middle, and dressed like a boy. Yet I would walk to school with the other girls; apparently this caused some of the boys to feel strange so they took to calling me the "imposter."[57]

The author marks the transition from tomboy to woman in a rather sensational passage entitled "A Complete Physiological Transformation" in which she recounts getting her first period during her time in prison: "My body was not normal. Until my twenty-second year, while I was in prison, I had no knowledge of the thing that women should have monthly. I hear that normal girls usually have it from around the age of fifteen. My mother often worried how from birth I was unsociable like a boy without a trace of feminine tenderness."[58] After relating the surprise of her cohorts upon hearing this was her first period and the speaker's own surprise at her development as a woman, the author concludes, "As you can see, my masculine self developed early while my self as a woman developed extremely late."[59]

The narrator occasionally expresses a sad nostalgia for her years as the tomboy scholar and political rebel but does not linger on them:

> Is the public perception of me really this badly mistaken? Do I disgrace myself having been branded as a haughty and uncouth woman who tried persistently to outdo men? To tell the truth, ever since the embarrassing occasions in my youth when I dressed in men's clothing, my philosophy has been to try my best to develop the gifts that heaven bestows on women. But it seems that because I inadvertently became implicated in a tasteless incident, I have invited this kind of misperception. . . . If by some good fortune I have any of the feminine qualities like love, gentleness and compassion, then I would use these to support and encourage men of ability. . . . I would never think of trying to compete with men or fight for merit alongside men. Woman is, in the end, woman; man is man. When both sexes can work together and help each other out, we can be sure what the essence of male and female is. If I have inadvertently invited a misunderstanding of my views, I am very sorry.[60]

The literary strategy in this passage seems one of creating a humble self through an appeal to femininity that seeks indulgence in the listener. Through this relationship between the abased feminine self and the indulgent reader, which enables a bond with the reader, an "authentic" self is produced. This bond is created through a depiction of a kind of gender apostasy when the author dramatically gives up her masculine self to become a "natural," "feminine" self who derides the masculine self.

At the same time, far more than the previous self-narratives by ex-cons, *Half My Life* dares to discuss the body, love, and anger. The narrator brings up many topics regarding the body and desire that are absent in Shimazu's and Hanai's texts. One passage in *Half My Life* hints at sexual relations between people of the same sex in prison. In describing her most satisfying days in prison, Hideko recalls the "beautiful woman" with whom she shared a cell and developed an intimate friendship. Fukuda never reveals the woman's name though she does reveal that the two cared for each other deeply: "Whenever I bathed, she always washed me. When evening arrived, we shared a bed. She warmed the quilt that froze in the wintry air with her body's heat. We slept in opposite directions and she even warmed my feet by holding them under her arms."[61] The nature of the relationship is described through familial terms such as mother and daughter, sibling and sister, but one bitter event retold in the memoir illustrates dramatically the depth of the relationship with her cellmate.

When a jailer comes to remove Hideko's cellmate, telling her to bring her things because she is being released from prison, Hideko and her cherished friend shed parting tears of bittersweet joy only to find that the cell partner is taken two cells down and imprisoned in a new cell. The jailer laughs coldly at the young, unmarried Hideko: "Ms. Kageyama, I bet you'll be lonely tonight." Other jailers bait her, saying that she must hate being separated from her "wife" *(saikun)*.[62] Angered at the false accusations, the narrator reviles her keepers: "Far from being a place where criminals are rehabilitated, the prison leads the criminal to even greater evil!"[63] The jailers' attribution of a desire that she denies brings ire. The "I" of the text adamantly refutes any homosexual desire despite remarking upon a preponderance of same-sex relationships in both men and women's prisons: "Among male inmates, male love flourishes and female inmates too seek like minds and live like married couples *[fūfu]* with the more masculine of the two acting as the husband and the gentler counterpart as the wife. They become blissfully obsessed with the illicit love affair, forgetting their eternal chains."[64] She goes on to recall how jealous lovers in prison have often attempted to injure or even murder rivals. Still, it infuriates her that the prison guards considered her to be one of these devoted prison lovers: "It is a memory that is even now hard to forget."[65] The description of the jailers is perfectly contiguous with the childhood experience of walking with the girls and being taunted by the boys. In both cases, Hideko describes a perception from the outside that she has acted out male desires. But it is described only as something that is external to her own desires. She denies implicitly in her claims of innocence that she is entitled to have this desire fulfilled for reasons of sex and gender discrepancy.

This narrative of confession and resentment can be usefully described as "double-layered." This notion of "double-layered" *(nijūsei)* discourse in *Half My Life* is discussed by Saeki Shōichi in his *Modern Japanese Autobiography*.[66] He identifies the primary dyads in this double-layered discourse to be the political and the literary and the eventful and emotional. Another way of considering the double-layeredness of the narrative is to identify the conflicting rhetorical claims of the text. The intense pre-occupation with the self's struggles in a misogynistic world is combined with a portrait of innocence and social contribution. Sentiments of resentment, which signal social critique, are countered with claims of regret and an insistence on (gender) normalcy. In this writing strategy, feminine qualities of humility, naiveté, and innocence run cover for a more critical expression of frustration and anger at unfair social, political, and economic conditions. Her anger against the political system that outlawed public speech by women and denied women access to public government institutions, and toward the capitalist system that created so much poverty, especially for women, is balanced with a promotion of "gender appropriate" behavior and a denial of anything but heterosexual desire.

The confessional stance in literature by male contemporaries exhibits a substantial difference. The self-indulgent male confessional voice in naturalist and political novelistic texts is not balanced with a socially responsible self and a denial of "perverse" sexual leanings. The speaker links himself to perversion, which is ultimately an aesthetic position—an aesthetic choice to assume the position of recluse or social exile (one he could socially afford to assume). The confessional aspect of the narrative is marked by regret in Fukuda likely because she is not claiming artistic license and the writing of *art,* as later confessional novelists would, and works to veil her "perversion" as a tomboy and an ex-con and a feminist. Nevertheless, her work can be considered an important and influential precursor to canonical confessional literature for its marked boldness and intimacy in comparison to earlier narratives by female ex-cons.

Preceding the work of authors whose confessional alter-egos did not capitulate to dominant social mores but boldly flaunted their transgressional acts was a female confessional ego in writing that articulated dominant discourses of inclusion, perseverance, and productivity. The subject (the penitent woman) did not merely ventriloquize previous judgmental accounts of her behavior in the press and poison woman literature but actively promoted another self that was "normal." However, simply because the ex-convict seemed to seek inclusion into the dominant social order through repentance rhetoric or appeared to accept a submissive position within the dominant social framework by adopting the speech of the master in shifting from unruly woman to penitent does not mean that we should interpret the language used therein to be transparent. The very different situation for the female confessor is misread if considered nothing more than a capitulation to dominant gender discourses. Seki Reiko comes close to this when she laments that both Fukuda's and Shimazu's autobiographical narratives reproduce the gender-oppressive system of the Meiji state. For Seki, both Fukuda's and Shimazu's autobiographical narratives mark the end of an optimistic, forward-looking era and signal a regression in the expression of female subjectivity by way of their capitulation to dominant political and gender discourses.[67] Seki sees Fukuda as having abandoned her earlier naive idealism and revolutionary pursuit of social reconstruction, and she claims that Fukuda's memoirs merely reinscribe the law that had condemned her to a limited life. The woman who had circulated as a sign became the producer of that same sign, hardly disrupting the opinions and laws that had condemned her as gender ambivalent. Matsuyama Iwao implicitly shares Seki's view that later narratives by ex-cons reflected a conservative trend. Commenting on Shimazu, he writes, "Shimazu Omasa chants her repentance through Shingaku, similarly appearing regretful about her previous way of life. . . . Poison women in the Meiji 20s lost their poison."[68] Matsuyama is regretful—regretful that the transgressive woman did not live up to her sensational reputation.

The poet and writer Yokose Yau—one of the first cultural historians to write about poison women from a sympathetic perspective—notes how the convicts dubbed "poison women" were wronged in the press by false claims and gender-based prejudice. But in his otherwise sympathetic portrayal of these women, Yau says of Hanai Oume's confessional narrative: "Hanai Oume's confession appeared in the *Kokueki* newspaper but it is an inferior work whose transcriber remains nameless. Inasmuch as we can learn what sort of circumstances Oden and other women experienced in prison it is a useful confession but it has only that one single merit *[sono hitotsu dake toru kachi wa arou]*."[69] Yau finds the repentant woman displeasing. The question of why the reformed confessor should be disregarded is not clearly articulated by Yau who merely seems "turned off" by a repentant woman. In a final example of the disdain for the confessing woman, the historian of poison woman texts Watatani Kiyoshi determined that "Viper" Omasa's confession published by the newspaper historian Shinoda Kōzō was untrustworthy and that a serial in the *Miyako* newspaper was the version to be trusted: "Viper Omasa's own verbatim account is included in the final volume of Shinoda Kōzō's *One Hundred Stories of Women from the Bakumatsu and Meiji Eras* (Bakumatsu Meiji onna hyakuwa). . . . Even though it is considered to be Omasa's own words it doesn't jibe at all with the *Miyako* newspaper and Hasegawa's accounts; if hers is correct then the *Miyako* newspaper and Hasegawa's accounts in the first half are radically incorrect. However, I can't help but feeling that Omasa's story is the one that is contrived *[sakui]*."[70] Watatani's opinion of Omasa's account as fantastic is curious considering his description of Hasegawa's account in the Miyako newspaper as a "fascinating literary narrative."[71]

Attention brought to bear on oneself for the purpose of social re-integration and explaining one's own perspective in the process produced nothing worthy of interest to these men. But the confessional rhetoric can instead be seen as a stylistic strategy for creating an opportunity to speak. It appears that to speak at all required an exhibition of capitulation, which masked stronger sentiments of anger and resentment toward the treatment ex-cons at the hands of fathers and patriarchal society.

Self-Indulgent Writer or Social Reformer?
Confession and Gender Difference

In addition to the texts by ex-cons, a cursory glance at other literature produced at Japan's turn of the century reveals that the use of the term *zange* had broadened significantly beyond its original meaning of narrative of religious conversion. In the early years of the 1900s, a wide variety of writers experimented with the conceptual possibilities of *zange*, giving reason to consider the form as significant in efforts to produce a self in narrative, a concern that absorbed writers at the turn of the century (as Kamei Hideo said of Japan's touted "first modern novel," the narrator exhibits "somewhat discomfiting moments of self-exhibition"). Contra current scholarship, I find *zange* narrative to be evidence that the development of a narrative "I" in turn-of-the-century Japan occurred in other types of confessional narrative beyond the protonaturalist or nonsecular confessional *(kokuhaku)* writing. Some of the most well-known titles that are not specifically religious in nature and only sometimes novelistic include Yamaji Aizan's "Confession" (Zange, 1903); "A Record of Confession" (Zangeroku, 1905) by Chikasumi Jōkan; the novel *My Memories* (Warawa no omoide, 1906) by Fukuda Hideko; the poem "Confession" (Zange, 1906) by Mizuno Yōshū; the celebrated novel *Broken Commandment* (Hakai, 1906) by Shimazaki Tōson; the other celebrated first novel of sexual confession, *The Quilt*, by Tayama Katai (Futon, 1907); the political novel *Confession* (Zange, 1907) by Kinoshita Naoe; Okamura Tsukasa's reading of Rousseau's *Confessions* in *Shisō koshi,* in 1908; Futabatei Shimei's essay "A Confession of Half My Life" (Yo ga hansei no zange) in 1908, written after a visit to Fukuda, along with "A Record of Confession" (Zangeroku, 1909) by Tayama Katai, and Miyazaki Koshoshi's *Confession of Half My Life: My Hometown* (Hansei no zange: Kokyō-hen, 1908); the parody of a sexual confession in Mori

Ōgai's *Vita Sexualis* (1908); Kuga Chigaharu's *Little Confession* (Shō zange, 1909); and Kuramochi Eikichi's *Confessions from Prison* (Gokuchū zange sōtan, 1909). Among these authors of confessional narrative we find critics, political novelists and activists, and poets.[72]

The flexibility of the concept *zange* can be seen in comparing conflicting contemporaneous discussions of it at the turn of the century. While Tayama Katai argued vociferously that his novella *The Quilt* was not a *zangeroku* narrative, which he identified as a specifically premodern narrative form, a critical book review of Kinoshita Naoe's novel *Zange* was just as thoroughly convinced that *zange* was indeed synonymous with new writing by young male novelists. One review of the novel was dismissive of this new trend among "youth" *(seinen)* to write from the perspective of a self-loathing subject. These conflicting interpretations of *zange* suggest a transitional cultural or literary expression (one which preceded the more well-known "confessional novel" or *kokuhaku shōsetsu*) that, in its multifarious manifestations, could be described variously as autobiography, oral history, memoir, confession, interview, life history, testimony, or even documentary fiction. Since *zange* was a form not subject to definition by a normative literary establishment, and involved a variety of grammatical styles, I will not attempt to specify a single generic definition for it.

What fascinates is the degree to which *zange* in manifold forms is embraced by writers from various classes, from various schools of literature, and by both sexes. In canonical literary history, what has been remembered of confessional narrative that appeared in so many forms at the turn of the century is the confessional fiction of non-Buddhist male intellectuals, especially of the naturalist school, but their confessional writing did not emerge in a vacuum. The literary history of confessional literature, which is described variously as "confessional narrative," *zange,* "self-narrative," "personal narration systems," and *watakushi shōsetsu,* has had little to say about self-narrative that resides outside of the realm of canonical "pure" literature *(junbungaku).*[73] But the history of confessional writing and self-narrative is misinterpreted if it is seen exclusively through the bounded discussions of canonical literary history since there is a broader, specific context in which confessional literature developed, as illustrated above, that raises interesting questions about the role of the popular and of gender in the development of self-narrative. It should be made clear that my intent is not to define or promote the naturalization of such an ambiguous and dubious category as "confessional literature" in literary history.[74] In fact, the danger in writing about this discourse is to perpetuate its already inflated importance in literary history. Nevertheless, while a particular historical moment in literary criticism has passed, the fundamental story told about the development of modern subjectivity through confessional narrative has not been overturned but merely pushed to the background. One goal of this chapter has been to question this insistent return to confession by male literati in analyzing modern subjectivity in literature and to ask why the confessional novel written by upper-middle-class male dilettantes has so exclusively been the primary touchstone for such inquiry.

In literary history what has often been remembered of the narrating self that appeared in so many forms at the turn of the century is the early confessional fiction of intellectuals like Shimazaki Tōson and Tayama Katai. It can be argued, without much exaggeration, that this early confessional literature has been described retroactively in postwar literary history as nothing less than the foundation of modern Japanese literature. In a discussion of literary criticism on self-narration, Tomi Suzuki has shown how the first-person literary form has generated across the twentieth century a powerful literary and cultural metanarrative for its special mystique surrounding the notion of *watakushi,* the "I" or "self." A number of writers from Nakamura Mitsuo to Kamei Hideo describe this narrative of the self as *guilty* of taking Japanese literature down a "mistaken path" but nevertheless of having brought about the future of the novel in Japan.[75] This form of Japanese literature, Kamei illustrates, involves a self-centered and confessional sensibility derived from a long history of narratives in which the first-person narrator is the central figure in the story. This sensibility extends to postwar notions of individuality and this individuality is linked with critical thinking. The "mistaken path" to which Kamei refers involves the notion of what an individual is: the individual produced through the first-person narrative (and which is extended to include the broader conceptualization of what it means to be an individual) is seen as critical and honest and above all authentic. More important, this vision of the self limits any sense of the individual as necessarily involved with social community and having a sense of responsibility. Kobayashi Hideo similarly argued that this self woven into literature in confessional narrative is a form specific to Japanese culture and was developed for a lack of a socialized self.[76] That is, the modern subjectivity specific to Japanese culture is one that is not socially responsible. Kamei has argued that earlier literature, *fūzokushi,* thought of as vulgar, sought to develop a sense of a lived commonality with the reader but has been largely forgotten.

In the postwar years when the *shishōsetsu* or "I-novel" was again the source of much speculation about the Japanese modern self, this supposed "lack of a socialized self" was proffered as reason for the lack of resistance to the Japanese military's fascistic war. As Takeuchi Ryōchi obliquely put it, Japan's fictional self-narrative involved much more than the question of literary form: "The problem of *shishōsetsu* goes beyond literature to be a problem of the character of our country's 'modernity.'"[77] The question of responsibility and the self, raised by Takeuchi, Kamei, and others is integral to discerning at least one primary difference between confessional narratives by (male) literati and those by (female) ex-cons. The solipsistic view of the self in writing in the former at the turn of the century perpetuated the notion that an "I" must be anti-social in order to be authentic. The conceptualization of the confessor as romantically solipsistic is not one that is extended to the confessing woman. The problem with this conceptualization of subjectivity is that it enabled those in a position of power to assume a subaltern position. It erased anyone else in the name of personal experience (and in the sixties in the name of personal freedom). The position of sufferer, of the wounded, could be embraced unproblematically in this type of narrative in which the subject is victim of even his own sensitivity. From this perspective it is no wonder that confessional narratives written by men have figured so prominently in literary history. Without a doubt the primary focus when it comes to first-person discourse has been the confessional novel, which usually features a male protagonist whose life strongly resembles the bourgeois male author's life. Through self-narrative the empowered can convincingly disavow power because it is told from the tautological situation in which the self is made more authentic for (merely) being presented through an unapologetic first-person narrative.

Critic of the Confessing Woman: Hero Tokito Kensaku Meets Omasa, the Confessing Woman

A work that has been considered a confessional novel by many, *A Dark Night's Passing* by Shiga Naoya, includes suggestive portrayals of the confessing poison woman, which act as a mirror to the protagonist Tokito Kensaku, who is himself a confessing writer. *A Dark Night's Passing* features a number of scenes involving "Viper" Uchida Omasa and repentant Hanai Oume. The protagonist's encounters with these confessing, repentant women enable Kensaku's aestheticization of anti-sociality via reference to confessing women Omasa and Oume, whom he critiques for being repentant.[78]

Kensaku first espies Omasa at the outskirts of Gion's Yasaka Shrine "in a small theatre *[koya]* that resembles a storyteller's theatre *[yose]*." Kensaku is disgusted at the sight of the confessing woman, whom he finds unattractive and pathetic:

> [Kensaku] happened to pass by the theatre late at night and had stopped to look at the large, illustrated signboard outside. On it was the picture of a woman, her head shaved clean like a nun's, engaged in a monologue. According to the caption it was Omasa telling the true story of her life as "an act of confession," it said. Thinking no more of it he was about to walk on when he saw a tall figure, dressed in a long cloak and wearing a kind of lay priest's hat, coming out of the theatre at the head of a group of young women. If Kensaku had not seen the signboard, he would have assumed it was a man. But it was Omasa the Viper. . . . [I]n order to make a living, she traveled from town to town at the head of a cheap theatre troupe, vending her so-called confessions of past sins. . . . What a degrading life it must be, Kensaku thought, to have to feign repentance on the stage day after day for the pleasure of strangers."[79]

In the eyes of Kensaku, Omasa is a pitiable, manly figure. Her ritualized repentance is hollow. She is parasitic, preying upon the curiosity of inhabitants of nameless towns on her show circuit. Her confession is of so little interest that Kensaku initially hardly notices her presence. There is nothing useful or interesting that might be said by this confessional speaker according to Kensaku, himself a writer in what has been considered a supreme example of confessional literature. Omasa is merely disingenuous.

Yet Kensaku is haunted by this dark figure of the confessing woman. He later visits a performance by another female penitent, Hanai Oume. Upon his second visit to the female ex-con's site of confession, he is still unimpressed: "He had seen recently on the popular stage a woman by the name of Hanai Oume. She had killed a man who had been her assistant and, like Omasa, had become a professional penitent. He had found her act both pathetic and distasteful, and had come away feeling more sympathetic than ever toward the defiantly impenitent."[80] Kensaku prefers the defiant woman, the woman who refuses to betray herself; the woman who refuses to speak. This is evident in his response to his wife's confession of marital infidelity. Kensaku angrily informs his wife that it is the silent, defiant woman who is attractive. The masquerade of a pure monogamous marriage must be maintained because it is too unsophisticated, too inelegant, to know a woman's ugly truths—her feelings, her shame. Eihana, the unrepentant singer and geisha who had murdered her own child but never reflected upon that act nor expressed any regret for her action, is for Kensaku a superlative model of what a woman should be—mute and wanton. The desirable woman is the one who wordlessly maintains a mask, who allows fantasies about her to remain intact. She is akin to film noir's femme fatale, as described by Slavoj Žižek, who is not threatening "insofar as she enters the frame of a particular fantasy" but fearful only when she explicitly reveals the assumption of her own fate:

> What is so menacing about the *femme fatale* is not the boundless enjoyment that overwhelms the man and makes him woman's plaything or slave. It is not Woman as object of fascination that causes us to lose our sense of judgment and moral attitude but, on the contrary, that which remains hidden beneath this fascinating mask and which appears once the masks fall off . . . woman is not a threat to man insofar as she embodies pathological enjoyment, insofar as she enters the frame of a particular fantasy. The real dimension of the threat is revealed when we "traverse" the fantasy, when the coordinates of the fantasy space are lost. . . . In other words, what is really menacing about the *femme fatale* is not that she is fatal for men but that she presents a case of a "pure," non-pathological subject fully assuming her own fate.[81]

The moment that the fatal woman embraces her own situation, she becomes a decreasingly erotic spectacle. She is increasingly perverse and unerotic. Her unattractiveness is the result of her manifestation as a specter who speaks her own shame. She traverses the fantasy of the deviant woman as created by writers of poison woman fiction, for example, to become an unrecognizable character. In describing the dynamics of the femme fatale of film noir, Žižek proposes that as long as the bad woman is a dominant figure, as long as she is "pulling the strings" and in control, she remains an object of fascination (for male characters within the film). When she begins to give in, to break down, or to allow herself to be manipulated by outside forces, the fascinating evil woman "disintegrates" and "her whole ontological consistency is dissolved."[82] Similarly, the repentant stance intervenes and alters existing discourses of the deviant woman, essentially disassembling the "poison woman" trope, leaving in its wake something more perverse. The female criminal dissolves as the fascinating woman and it is at this moment that she also becomes truly threatening, because she transgresses the body of the imagined other. How then might a "deadly woman" step outside such a role? How might she assert an "I" outside a previous discourse considering that a "self" is not uttered in a void and that one cannot have pure sovereignty over meaning, its truth, the values it espouses, and the systems it avoids or represents.

It is not impossible to imagine that Shiga's portrayal of the confessor through the eyes of Kensaku is a cleverly posed criticism of the indulgent confessional writer and the prurient reader. Kensaku is repulsed by the thought of the repenting woman and yet attends the show. The disgust at seeing laid so bare the performative mechanics of confession by an ex-criminal on the dingy stage of a traveling show and the impulse to watch it captures the seedy side of the confessional writing-reading relationship and amounts to a critique of confessional literature as driven by mere prurient interest. It explains perhaps Shiga's own shame at self-revelation, which the lengthy time that it took him to write *A Dark Night's Passing* seems to confirm.

By engaging with this question of authenticity, this potential parody of the confessional male writer illustrates a usual reliance on the projection of an aura of integrity and authenticity in the confessional narrative. The scenes of disgust in *A Dark Night's Passing* point toward a fear of a slip-page in which the confessing intellectual and the sideshow spectacle would overlap. Kensaku seems disturbed by the thought that he himself is not so different from a traveling performer. This anxiety suggests the thinness of the line between highbrow male confessor and lowbrow female confessor. The critical responses to Katai's *The Quilt* as well as Ōgai's parody of the *The Quilt* in *Vita Sexualis* illustrate the thinness of that line. *A Dark Night's Passing* could well be a caricature of the self-aggrandizing confessional writer though the writer-protagonist in *A Dark Night's Passing* continually asserts narrative authority to determine who is the authentic confessor and who should or should nor speak/confess.

Another Look at Narrative Authority

An examination of discursive positionality (rather than the often fetishized grammar and literary style in determining categories or schools in litera-ture)[83] reveals a remarkable resonance among various confessional voices. The concept of confession or *zange* in writing clearly traversed a broad range of narrative styles, but wide differences existed in the discursive strategies for creating subjects with authority, subjects mandated to speak truths. As Fujii points out, the expansion of state power was a force in the conceptualization of the subject (and vice versa). Certainly gender differ-ence as well contributed to the way in which subjects were produced and interpreted in Japan at this time. What so many texts have in common at this time is a powerful textual affirmation of the speaking subject—a voice that speaks to the reader, an "I" who demands to be recognized. Often the reader is meant to experience this voice as a real person rather than a fictional one. To reiterate an earlier point, Fujii has determined at least two conventions in narrative literature as crucial in early-twentieth-century writing in promoting narrator to the status of speaking subject: authenticity and authority. Fujii provocatively ties authenticity, which he argues is essential to producing subjectivity in mid-Meiji, to the ubiquitous concern with authority during this time of national consolidation. The state was actively shoring up power at that time and this political climate could not help but engage its populace with questions of subjecthood. An intimate narrative voice could provide this sense of authority for being closer to the experience and authentic for the same reason. Shimazaki Tōson, according to Fujii, "address[ed] the demands placed upon the Meiji writer of appealing to a mass unknown readership [rather than an audience of fellow writers] by creating an emotive first person narrator."[84]

Forms that centered on the "I" and that came down through the religious tradition of a practitioner confessing the story of her life, or the defense speech at a trial when the accused tells the judge who she is and what she has done were more familiar forms for the novice writer (and reader). The author could provide a sense of "authenticity" through descriptions of mental anguish, social marginalization, poverty, and the trials of living as a woman in a patriarchal world through a developed first-person narrative, which was by no means foreign to the narrating ex-convicts who had already confessed her story in trial. Was this form then perhaps suggestive for literati who found within it a style through which to produce a new private subject? It is as if the male confessor in literature is the exact antithesis of preceding narratives by ex-convicts. The (celebrated) male confessor is anti-social, individualistic, proudly solipsistic, and desirous. This self-proclaimed marginal status produces authenticity. The pain of confession and a sense of marginalization (written by *non*-marginalized literati figures) drive the protagonist to a romantic heroic status. The female confessional narrative's sense of authenticity, on the other hand, is developed through the act of producing a shameful but socially respectable self that is safe, productive, and explicitly not marginal and not sexual. Authority is to be gleaned in the act of explicit self-interpellation.

Virginia Woolf once remarked to Ethel Smyth, "I was thinking the other night that there's never been a woman's biography. Nothing to compare with Rousseau. Chastity and modesty I suppose have been the reason. Now why shouldn't you be not only the first woman to write an opera but equally the first to tell the truths about herself? Isn't the great artist the only person to tell the truth? I should like an analysis of your sex life. As Rousseau did his. More introspection. More intimacy."[85] This insightful comment points to the constraints of gender, which limit the imagination of certain narrative positions. The speaking female—the speaking ex-convict—who attempted to constitute a believable subject in speech and writing, fictional or otherwise, illustrates how modern subjectivity has been—must have been—written differently in confessional narrative.

4. How to Be a Woman and Not Kill in the Attempt

Amongst the most crucial forms of mediation are the categories, concepts, and languages which organise sexual life, which tell us what is
"good" or "bad," "evil" or "healthy," "normal" or "abnormal," "appropriate" or "inappropriate" behaviour. These too have a complex history—
but the chief guardians of these definitions during this century have
been the "sexologists," the scientists of sex, the arbiters of desire.
—Jeffrey Weeks, *Sexuality and Its Discontents*

Into the twentieth century, memoirs by female criminals grew bolder.
Those by Kanno Suga and Kaneko Fumiko are decidedly unapologetic
political critiques of the nation. Kanno was a journalist and anarchist
hanged in 1911 for plotting the assassination of the Meiji emperor in
what came to be known as the Great Treason incident. When Kanno
explained her goals in interrogation, she said, "I had to show that the
emperor too was a human being whom blood could flow from just like
the rest of us."[1] Kanno brushed aside any sense of shame and passivity.
The prison essays she wrote while on death row represents a triumph of
the active, rebellious soul.

Kaneko, who in 1926 was sentenced to death for lèse-majesté for con-
spiring to import bombs from the mainland to use on the imperial family,
also lauded imperial patricide as a worthy act in the battle to fight the
paternalism and racism of the imperial system. Like the women dubbed
"poison woman," these jailed women too were the subject of scandalous
assertions of promiscuity. After Kaneko's death, for example, the press got

hold of a photograph of her in an intimate pose with her anarchist lover, Pak Yeol, alone in the courtroom where they were tried, with Kaneko sitting on Pak's lap. The photo was taken by the judge of the case (Tatematsu Kaisei). The press accused the judge of being lenient: "It was said that he left them alone in the courtroom to indulge in their 'scandalous behaviour,'" and allowed conjugal cell visits.[2] Nevertheless, as Helene Raddeker illustrates, the focus of their self-narratives was to create a particular vision of the self as unapologetically political: "Suga or even the very egoistic Fumiko was very much the creature of her world; thus each had a collective mission while simultaneously being engaged in carving out for herself a Subject-position that created her in the role of the autonomous individual."[3]

Since 1936, the most circulated confession by a female criminal in modern Japanese history has been the deposition by Abe Sada.[4] Abe's testimony, her confession to the murder of her lover, Ishida Kichizō, has engrossed readers over the last seventy years in its many manifestations in fiction, pornographic magazines, scholarly works on Abe Sada, and elsewhere. The narrator of Tomioka Taeko's short story "Another Dream" (1979) recalls her surprise at the style of the deposition:

> I don't know if it's like that with all of those sorts of documents or had something to do with the era, but the document was in question and answer form with no punctuation whatsoever. The text (or it might be better to say the narrative record) had no commas or periods, so no matter how long it got, it just continued on. That might have contributed to the peculiar force or strength of Abe Sada's narration.[5]

No confession by a female criminal has garnered so much attention. This confession was unapologetic and strikingly blunt. Unlike the confessors before her, Abe did not reject her sexual self. Rather, she embraced her sexuality, even flaunting her romantic feelings for her victim. It is not surprising, then, that like so many women criminals dubbed "poison woman," the discussions of Abe after her arrest for the murder of Ishida including police and medical reports, focused intently on her sexual desire and sexual experience from puberty.

The Abe Sada Incident

On 18 May 1936, a maid working at the Masaki inn in the red light district of Ogu in Tokyo's Arakawa neighborhood discovered the corpse of a man in one of the rooms where Abe Sada (thirty-two years old) and her lover, Ishida Kichizō (forty-two years old), spent a week making love.[6] The couple had been together for three months. Their relationship began as a playful romance. They met at the Yoshidaya inn run by Ishida's wife, Toku, and owned by her family. Abe had taken up employment there as a maid and host. One day, Abe was told to entertain a guest in one of the inn's rooms. Her guest turned out to be the inn's proprietor, Ishida. Their brief sexual encounter was followed by regular secret trysts. After being discovered one day among the cushions in the storage room, the couple took to meeting at inns. Abe would ask her employer, Toku, for leave to see her family and meet Ishida instead. In her long testimony, Abe described how difficult it was to part after spending the afternoon together.

The week of the murder was one filled with passion. The two checked in to the Masaki inn on 11 May 1936. The couple was inebriated for most of the week, drinking sixteen large bottles of beer and forty-four bottles of sake. The maid, Itō Moto, who served Abe and Ishida the endless parade of bottles, reported in an appalled tone how sexually active the couple had been. She complained that they left the bedding out all day and spent their days and nights in bed making love or drinking. Abe remembered in testimony the passion of their lovemaking in reflecting on one tryst at the Tagawa inn:

> We kept the bed out from the evening of the 27th to the morning of the 29th, and hardly slept at night doing every nasty deed possible. When I said I was tired Ishida would make love to me and even while sleeping he would massage my body very sweetly. It was the first time in my life that I had met a man who treated a woman so well and who made me so happy. I fell in love. I could never be separated from him.[7]

The couple experimented sexually. In testimony Abe spoke without reserve about the sex play they engaged in prior to the murder:

> The evening of May 16th I got on top of Ishida and at first we had sex while I pressed his throat with my hands but that didn't do anything for me so I wrapped my kimono sash around Ishida's neck and I pulled it tight and then loosened it and so on while we were having sex, and while I was doing it I kept looking down there so I didn't realize that I'd squeezed too hard; Ishida let out a moan and suddenly his thing got small. I was shocked and released the sash but Ishida's face [and neck] had turned red and didn't return to normal so I tried cooling his face by bathing it with water.[8]

At a drugstore Abe purchased the painkiller Calmotin and proceeded to give Ishida thirty pills in three hours. She later denied in testimony that she had any intention of fatally drugging him. In the sixth round of testimony police asked about the drug: "The accused had Ishida take Calmotin at the 'Masaki' inn on the evening of May 17th. Didn't you think that Ishida might die from this?" Abe responded, "I didn't think he would die. If there had been any danger of him dying then the pharmacy wouldn't sell the drug. I had read in the newspaper that you have to take at least 100 Calmotin pills to die."[9]

The lovers' relationship lasted more than three months but the near fatal choking incident perhaps encouraged Ishida to rethink his situation because soon thereafter he suggested that returning home to his wife might be the best course of action for the time being. This did not mean that Ishida would break off with Abe, just that he would be more discreet. He then suggested setting up Abe as his mistress in an apartment. Abe, unwilling to share her man's affections, erupted in anger. During the couple's sexual play later that evening of 18 May, Abe again wrapped Ishida's neck with the pink sash of her kimono, this time fatally asphyxiating him. She then used a kitchen knife to sever his penis from his body and carved in his left thigh *Sada Kichi futari*—"Sada and Kichi, the two of us." On the bedding she wrote the same sentiment in his blood, *Sada Kichi futari-kiri*. This choice of phrasing was gruesomely appropriate, for its literal meaning is "Sada Kichi the two who are cut [off from the rest of the world]." This concept had a history in the Tokugawa period when used by courtesans who promised their loyalty to patrons by offering a token of their affection, which in extreme cases was purported to be their own finger. Courtesans would even tattoo a sign of devotion on their upper arm. Abe reversed this practice of self-mutilation and inscribed Ishida's body with her love letter instead.

Abe claimed in her testimony that after phoning the maid to say that Ishida was not to be disturbed, she used her few hours of freedom before the discovery of the corpse to purchase a new kimono and pair of glasses as a disguise. In spite of having provided authorities with a grotesquely penned confession to the crime, Abe eluded police by wandering the streets of Tokyo for three days. Tokyo tabloids and newspaper journalists mapped the alleged killer's whereabouts for days before police finally apprehended her on 21 May, three days after the incident. During the search, citizens breathlessly reporting that they had spotted the slippery quarry made hundreds of calls to police. By the time all reports were in, Abe had been concurrently sighted in the Tokyo neighborhoods of Funabashi, Akasaka, Ginza, and Shinjuku. The *Tokyo Asahi* evening and morning newspapers of 20 and 21 May ran the article "Shadows of Abe Sada: The Deluge" (Abe Sada no kage: Hanran) reporting the comedy of errors that occurred in the rush to identify Abe. A case of mistaken identity in a beauty parlor incensed customers in the wealthy neighborhood of Ginza. Suspicious that a thin, unfamiliar patron spoke only to ask "How much?" at the end of a new hair styling, the Carson salon called detectives, who arrived immediately. The customer bore no resemblance to Abe; appalled patrons left with their hairdos only half-finished. In the Kanda area, a misapprehended subject of interrogation fainted in tears while another look-alike was chased from Tokyo station to Hibiya Park.[10] Each purported capture produced crowds that blocked traffic and slowed trains. The newspaper released a map tracing Abe's escape route plotted from calls made by people certain that they had sighted her. The embarrassing, unorganized flow of panic that developed out of the chase to find Abe is captured in a later illustration by Okamoto Shinjirō, embellishing Sekine Hiroshi's poem about the Abe Sada incident. Disembodied feet encased in white tabi socks float hauntingly underneath a clock.[11] Abe's profile, clothes, and hairstyle were deduced even before news cameras had photographed the seductress's embarrassed smile as police arrested her in a room at the Shinagawa inn.

The enigmatic Abe became the era's new and favored subject of the press soon after her arrest. In reference to early female criminals, the newspapers called her "Shōwa's poison woman," adding her to the ranks of the imaginative tradition of the disorderly woman in Japan. Reflecting on the case in 1947, eleven years after Abe's arrest in 1936, the renowned author Sakaguchi Ango declared that he had yet to see a crime gain as much attention in the newspapers. He criticized the melodramatic approach taken by the press, which he felt betrayed the feelings not only of the readers but the reporters as well: "The journalists writing in such a sensationalist tone were actually Sada's greatest sympathizers and empathizers, yet betraying their own hearts, they ardently sensationalized the crime as journalists are sadly wont to do. Indeed, even if there hadn't been Sada's incident, the country was at the gate of an intolerable crushing fascism. Sada too, thanks to the fascist era, was likely made scapegoat in an overly reactionary, sensational ruckus."[12]

The sensation around the incident clearly was not confined to the event of murder alone. Rather, the uproar was caused by the extraordinary "messiness" of the crime—the mingling of bodily fluids, the spilling of the victim's blood, the inscription of the assailant's name on the victim's skin with a knife, the dismemberment of his body. The blood flowing from the various wounds of the corpse was messy. The dismemberment of his body was messy, as was Abe's description of the victim's sexual proclivities. She argued, counterhegemonically, that he was responsive to *her* desires up to his death. In testimony, Abe recalled nostalgically how her dead lover's passion did not wane even when she admitted to him that it was that time of the month. Desire to her and allegedly to her lover meant connecting with another body through flows of blood and other bodily fluids. Abe claimed that she had planned to die alongside Ishida but was ultimately unable to take her own life. She spoke through her lover, using his blood as ink to emblazon the bloody bedroom with her name. The crime scene flushed red with fluids of desire stood in stark incongruity to the hallowed bloodshed of the February 26 incident *(Ni-ni-roku jiken)*—a coup attempted only three months earlier by fervent imperial soldiers dedicated to upholding the sovereignty of the emperor. Abe's release of a man's blood cited danger. In her hands, he was shown to be a permeable body, a site of masculine incohesion. The danger lay in the fact that his blood flowed, like a woman's.

Abe was usually compared specifically to poison woman Takahashi Oden in the press. The headlines of the *Tokyo Nichi Nichi Shinbun* on 20 May 1936 read, "Shōwa's Takahashi Oden / Bitch Scrounging about the Darkness" (Shōwa no Takahashi Oden / Yami o asaru mesu).[13] In the sixth round of police interrogation, Abe described how shocked she was to be compared to Takahashi Oden: "At around five in the afternoon I went to an inn called Shinagawa-kan, and after taking a bath, had a beer, and then had a masseuse called for me. It was such a relaxing massage that I fell asleep. I had a dream about Ishida and wondered if I hadn't talked in my sleep but the masseuse claimed that I hadn't said anything in my sleep, which was a relief. After dismissing the masseuse I ate and read the evening paper. I hadn't really considered my situation much until I saw that they had compared me to Takahashi Oden and that police were staked out at every station. I realized there was no way for me to go to Osaka now and though I felt badly about it I decided to die at this inn."[14] A 1947 pulp fiction novel about Abe picked up on this aspect of the testimony and recalled Abe's surprise at being compared with Meiji poison woman Takahashi Oden: "After the masseuse left, I ate my supper, and picked up the evening paper. I was the source of great commotion. I didn't think it would be such big news but there it was in bold headlines written as if a great incident had occurred. A photograph of me when I was young. A photograph of the inn 'Masaki.' And articles reporting things like 'Shōwa's Takahashi Oden has appeared / Detectives stand ready at every station.'"[15]

Sexual Desire and Murder

As with so many women dubbed "poison woman," early journalistic writing and medical reports made sexual desire the centerpiece for explaining what made Abe commit murder and the postmortem castration of her avowed lover. Questions asked by police and depositions by people who knew her without fail turned to Abe's sexual past. One of her patrons was asked to submit a deposition and the conversation focused on her sexual wants:

> The rent was fifteen yen a month and I paid that, and I paid for food. I didn't live with Sada but early in the relationship I went to her place every day or every other day and stayed the night. She was intense. Very powerful, so that even I was intimidated *[heikō shimashita]*.
>
> She wasn't satisfied unless we did it three or four times a night. She wanted me to have my hand working her private parts all night long. She didn't mind licking my tool *[dōgu]*. It's hard to put into words what it was like; I hardly slept the whole night. At first it was fun but after a couple of weeks I grew weak. . . .
>
> I told her that I couldn't keep up with all of her demands.
>
> She told me, "Well then get rid of your wife and make me your legal wife, and gratify me that way," but I didn't consent. When I replied, "I can't do something stupid like that!," she threatened to take a lover. That was January 29th of last year. . . .
>
> Luckily, I broke up with her soon enough to avoid having my important parts cut off *[yarareta]*. While I was together with Sada she never messed with knives or poison or talked about letting someone live or die. She's a tramp *[dai-inpu]* and a siren *[yōfu]*. Judging from appearances she's the kind of woman men love to fear.[16]

The police report also looked to Abe's youth and sexual experience to explain the crime in terms that frame her as a lascivious creature on the prowl: "She listened to dirty stories of the workers [at her home] and she was influenced by this and matured quickly. In the summer of 1919 she lost her virginity at the age of fifteen, grew despondent, and looked for friendships among the town's delinquents. . . . she prowled around *[asaru]* searching out the opposite sex, her licentious lifestyle became so excessive that her father Jūkichi thought it in her best interests to make her a geisha *[geigi]*."[17] The report did not describe Abe's reaction of despair at being sent away into prostitution. Her experience as a geisha and the different sex jobs she took out of financial desperation are described in detail four decades later in Tanaka Noboru's film *The True Story of Abe Sada* (Jitsuroku Abe Sada, 1975), especially in the following voice-over by "Sada" in the film explaining that after she lost her virginity at age fifteen to a university student she became "a geisha, a restaurant maid *[jochū]*, an entertainer *[geigi]*, a bar girl *[shakufu]*, a mistress *[mekake]*, a prostitute *[shōfu]*, café waitress *[café no jokyū]*, and an escort *[kōtō inbai]*. There wasn't a day I didn't spend with a man." Sada speaks of wandering from place to place—from Yokohama, Toyama, and Shinshū to Osaka, Nagoya, Tanba no Sasayama, and Kobe, as the film portrays a flashback of her running down railway tracks from pimps in pursuit.

Abe's motivation to murder seems explained by these depictions of her violation by a student, being forced into sex work, and abuse by underworld men. Her hopeless environment drove her to attach herself to the kind and loyal Ishida, and her wish to prolong that happiness led to murder. The reference to losing her virginity had actually been described by Abe at one point as rape by a Keiō university student, but in the police description, the victimization of Abe at the age of fifteen by a college student, the agony of losing her virginity outside of marriage, her forced entrance into prostitution by her father (Abe said in testimony that she cried for three days and begged her father not to send her out to be a sex worker but he was insistent), the various incidents in which she is tricked into greater and greater debt by acquaintance-cum–pimp Inaba Masatake, her contracting syphilis, her attempts to escape locked geisha houses in which she was imprisoned, and her vain attempts to have a sustained relationship are all treated as her own failures of character developed in response to early sexual maturation. Abe did not deny that she gained great pleasure from sex but specifically stated that sexual pleasure came to her only from the the time she was twenty-eight, after she no longer worked as an entertainer and primarily earned her keep as a mistress to various men. According to her testimony, the years prior to this were discouraging ones in which she was abused by various men. The final police summary glosses over these incidents to paint a picture of a loose woman. In this report it is Abe who is the sole source of her troubles.

The various medical studies about Abe repeatedly claim her physiological state and sexual desire as motivating factors in the murder. Abe's widely publicized murder and castration of Ishida incited a rash of medical analyses from forensic study to psychoanalytic diagnoses. In them, just as with Takahashi Oden, sexual desire was the primary focus in identifying the impetus to deviance. Nevertheless, whereas Takahashi's delinquency was analyzed using a biologically based etiology, Abe's delinquency was interpreted through a new multifold sexual science that drew on discourses of evolutionary science, physiology, and psychology. Sexual desire as the fundamental basis for explaining criminality by women can be seen at this time in the work of criminologists from Germany, England, Japan, and elsewhere who seemed convinced that sexual desire, as a biological and/ or psychical drive, provided the key to understanding transgression by women. The sexologist Sawada Junjirō had argued only a few years earlier for a connection between sexuality and crime when he declared that "there is no crime, large or small, that cannot be traced to the lust hidden beneath its surface."[18] The marathon sex that Ishida and Abe engaged in before his murder crassly confirmed for specialists precisely that idea. In the development of this discourse of libidinal normativity, Abe was a pivotal figure and consequently offers an interesting and instructive case for understanding how the female criminal is refashioned as a new type of sexual suspect through science.

The difference in representation between Meiji and later female criminals demonstrates that notions about what constitutes a proper body, an obedient body, a law-abiding body, and a healthy body (especially in the context of sexual difference) are dependent on the cultural era and its specific social systems and discourses, which determine what is disruptive or disturbing. Nothing is intrinsically subversive. As the ubiquity of the poison woman figure illustrates, it is often the physically "abnormal" or otherwise "unhealthy" woman who affronts the social body and is consequently deemed pollutant or poison. The deviant woman is the exception by which the rule is proved. Somatic narratives in the Meiji period proving the congenital "guilt" of poison woman Takahashi Oden by dissecting her reproductive organs or the presumption of hysteria of poison women Omatsu and Hanai and the assumed nymphomania of Abe illustrate how compelling the often "sick" or "abnormal" body can be in articulating cultural ideas about the social body. Omatsu from the "outcast" class, for example, described as ultimately driven to her death by insanity, is expediently deemed constitutionally unable to assimilate. This biased story of the inability of a particular group to cope with liberation, which gets articulated through corporeal metaphor, is a convenient narrative for a social body anxious about incorporating the underclass citizen into the purportedly democratizing national body.

These narratives about poison women function as "cultural diagnoses" because in them certain patterns of behavior, which derail usual social and political hierarchies, are codified as a sign of the illness of a culture or nation.[19] The representations of illness and health developed around the new so-called poison woman of 1936 take a much different form from that of previous years. The medical diagnoses of Abe treat her as symbolic of female potential—of the latent capacity in every woman to create trouble. In Meiji, the poison woman was an anomaly. She was a social and sexual pariah. She was poisonous because she could infect the social and domestic sphere and bring havoc to an otherwise healthy, modernizing community and nation. Criminological narratives of the 1930s, however, treat the female criminal as a manifestation of the potential for dangerous behavior in every woman.

This persistent method of interpreting motivations to crime through medicine enabled the depoliticization of crime by women. Furthermore, with the development of sexology and psychoanalysis, the criminal's psychological world, rather than physical body, became the new key to understanding female deviancy. At the same time, the development of sexology and psychoanalysis meant that there was even greater impetus to make sexuality a primary touchstone for explaining crime by women.

Woman and Crime: An Evolutionary Model of Criminality

Abe emerged onto the media scene at a time when sexological and criminological studies had already been a source of popular reading by the general public, making her an iconographic figure through which theories of the relationship of female desire and deviance could be further proved. During this textual crime wave of the 1920s and early 1930s, journals and encyclopedic series like *Criminology* (Hanzai Kagaku), *Criminal Journal* (Hanzai Kōron), *True Stories of Crime* (Hanzai Jitsuwa), *The True Story Times* (Jitsuwa Jidai) and *Criminology Research* (Hanzai Kagaku Kenkyū), and the sixteen-volume encyclopedic *Collected Works of Modern Criminology* (Kindai Kagaku Zenshū) were published. As scholarly agenda, criminology enjoyed the status of new vital science. Medical associations and even private "clubs" dedicated to the study of crime formed to pontificate on the relationships between crime, desire, and the body, among other topics.

Various scholars have theorized the reasons for such an interest in criminology. Akita Masami has linked this interest in crime to the 1930s culture of "erotic grotesque nonsense," which included a culture of imperial modernity that wrote about technology, science, and sex, along with the occult, foreign, and bizarre. Sexual "license" of the 1920s was also cited as contributing to an extraordinary circulation of bizarre, often true-to-life sex and crime stories. This notion is perpetuated by the enduring reference to the period as one of moral decadence and social transgression that developed in the wake of the economic depression in 1929.[20]

Medical discourse on deviancy was another aspect of this interest in science, sex, and deviancy that manifested itself as bizarre and grotesque imagery and writing. Ōmi Hiroshi argued in the journal *Criminal Science* (Hanzai Kagaku) that a national increase in unemployment and the spread of poverty ignited this popular interest in criminological study. He claimed that as more and more crime studies emerged, crimes themselves increased.[21] Saitō Yozue also cited the economy as a source for criminological interest, saying that these new representations of sexuality and social manners were a result of increasingly hardened economic circumstances: "By this time, the circumstances of social life were too severe for merely considering human and sexual life as delectable bedroom play. 'Bizarre book' *[chinpon]* dealers' lowbrow erotic literature *[nanpa hon]* and publications appealing to individuals akin to Umehara Hokumei were no longer sufficient for knowing the true nature *[jissō]* of sexuality *[sei]*."[22] Hokumei is considered the founder of erotic grotesque literary culture in the 1920s with the publication of his novel *Society of Murderers: The Era of the Prosperity of Demonism* (Satsujin shakai: Akuma shugi zensei jidai, 1924), a novel lauding anarchistic activities as producing an aesthetic sublime.[23] Hokumei showed interest in poison women in the journal he edited, *Literary Marketplace* (Bungei Shijō), in which he ran newspaper articles from the Meiji period. In his June 1926 issue, he devoted thirty-three pages to rerunning articles about Takahashi Oden from various Meiji newspapers including the *Tokyo Akebono* (Tokyo Dawn), the *Tokyo E-iri* (Tokyo Illustrated), the *Yokohama Mainichi* (Yokohama Daily), and others. Hokumei is restrained in his commentary. His concern in revisiting reportage about Takahashi Oden is purportedly to reveal the falsity of so many of the claims about her in fiction, but the sensationalist aspects of her story were likely not lost on Hokumei or readers.

The following year, 1927, the poet and newspaper historian Yokose Yau published a book written with a similar goal of righting untruths spread about "poison women." *Stories of Early Modern Poison Women* (Kinsei dokufu den, 1928) was one of the publications produced for the group's series on "perversions" (Hentai jū-ni shi, The History of the Twelve Perversions). *Stories of Early Modern Poison Women* represents another cultural unearthing of early Meiji cultural artifacts. Culling articles from newspapers and books he discovered in his family storehouse in the aftermath of the Great Kanto earthquake of 1923, Yau edited and provided brief commentaries in his compilation of poison woman stories. In *Stories of Early Modern Poison Women* Yau plays the enlightened intellectual offended by the portrayals of female criminals in the Meiji press, which he critiques as insensitive, inflammatory portrayals of women who were in reality, he reminds the reader with a disgruntled gusto, downtrodden and desperate. Yau chooses sides in this book in unveiled language that takes early Meiji writers to task for what he considers to be unrelentingly simplistic portrayals of female criminals as headstrong women deserving of punishment. He criticizes on artistic grounds their meandering plots and unimaginative use of reward-virtue-and-punish-vice rhetoric whereby the socially improprietous unruly woman is literally and then figuratively punished by an omniscient narrator describing her punishment as a most felicitous event for the country.

Quoting Meiji sources on "poison women" including "Street minstrel Omatsu," "Night Storm Okinu," "Fusei Ito," "Takahashi Oden," "(Poisonous) Tiger Beetle Ohatsu," "Phantom Otake," "Hanai Oume," and "Ōnuma Kuma," Yau plays the role of detective, searching through the data for anomalies, elaborating on bizarre events while offering a more "truthful" version of them. About the story of Phantom Otake, Yau wrote, "She was not a delinquent girl hanging around near Asakusa. No matter how poor a daughter is in the country, no one would give their body over to three men for money. This is merely the result of a foolish author who tried to make Otake into a poison woman."[24] As earlier discussions of Robun's and Kubota's texts illustrate, Yau's vituperative commentary is not wholly unjustified. In the constructions of the female criminal in poison woman fiction, which set the tone for depictions of female deviancy in modern Japanese literature, the deviant woman was treated as a threat to the community for her gender-transgressive and sexual behavior. She bore the burden of playing out the role of threatening enemy to the enlightenment for her nonconforming sexuality and what was described as her masculine aggressiveness. As illustrated above this depiction of the female criminal as gender transgressive—masculine, sexually driven, and unrepentant (silent)—was one of the most salient characteristics of poison woman fiction. Yau addresses this treatment of the criminal woman and levels his harshest criticism at Robun's *Demon's Tale* for its unrelenting depiction of the female criminal as a social problem in judging her behavior in terms of the traditional morality of "reward virtue and punish vice."

Despite promises to reveal the sensationalism of claims made about women who committed crime in early Meiji, there remain in Yau's text provocative depictions of the women's sexual lives and unchecked descriptions of criminal woman as sexual and wanton. Yau's is one example of the many books on women's crime in this era of *ero guro nansensu* that took a deep interest in female criminality but continued to represent crime in grotesque discussions of female sexuality.

Yau was not immune to the popular art form of this day. In a discussion of Ōnuma Kuma, a woman who had committed multiple counts of homicide, Yau stresses that her crimes of murder began with a "natural" pursuit of pleasure, including sexual pleasure. Yau describes how Ōnuma had murdered two men and buried their bodies in a field only to move the putrid corpses a year later, and then he defers to the prolific scholar of sexology and criminology and editor of the journal *Psychology of Perversion* (Hentai Shinri), Nakamura Kokyō, for an assessment of the case: "Cannot Ōnuma Kuma be called a natural born poison woman? On top of the violent acts [of murder] was displayed a thoroughly fearsome cold-bloodedness [in later moving the corpses]."[25] Not showing the same disdain toward sensationalist descriptions of "poison women" as in previous chapters in which he discusses Meiji authors, Yau lauds his contemporary for his insightful prognosis, writing that "Nakamura was a fantastic scholar whose written work has no reason to be flawed."

As reflected by Yau's reliance on Nakamura Kokyō's scientific expertise in making less than scientific claims about female criminals, sexual science in the 1920s was incorporated into the sensationalist culture of the grotesque and nonsensical. Criminological science itself claimed that stories of the bizarre reveal much about biological life, as the following excerpt from the journal *Criminology* shows:

> The western reading world has already started a revolution in going from the pursuit of mechanical science to the mental sciences *[seishin kagaku]*. Criminal science research now has completely swept over the German and American reading world. Witness this magazine's aspiration to appropriate material beyond the usual magazine material that is academic and provides your fill of the bizarre through the monopolization of the academic. . . . The mission of this magazine is to expose the secrets of the human instinct that produces all social ills and social good, and to investigate thoroughly all aspects of human sciences. This magazine over the ensuing years will exhaust its energy in producing an encyclopedia that will gather resources on criminality, the scientific and the bizarre.[26]

This interest in sexual science had been building since the early twentieth century to reach its peak in the 1920s. Psychopathology had been introduced to Japan through the novelist and medical doctor Mori Ōgai's "Miscellaneous Conversations on Desire" (Seiyoku zatsuwa, 1902-3), which drew from nineteenth-century Western discourses of sexology and science and introduced from a medical perspective the term *seiyoku* or "sexual desire." The term "perversion" *(hentai)* was introduced broadly through the translation of Krafft-Ebing's *Psychopathia Sexualis* in 1913 by the Great Japan Cultural Association (Dai Nihon Bunmei Kyōkai) as *The*

Psychology of Perverted Sexual Desire (Hentai seiyoku shinri), a year after the introduction of Freud and Jung in Japan. Krafft-Ebing's book had been introduced much earlier in Japan 1894 by the Nihon Hoigakkai (Japan Forensics Association) as the *Book on Erotomaniacs* (Shikijō-kyō hen) but sales of this eighth volume were prohibited such that Krafft-Ebing remained in relative obscurity until the publication of a second translation. Nonfiction studies of sexuality in the form of sexual dictionaries or medical and forensics handbooks on crime found an even larger popular audience in the 1930s.

Deeply informed by sexology, psychology, and occasionally psychoanalysis, this new criminological discourse had a profound ideological impact on ideas of female sexuality because it operated both as scholastic agenda and mass cultural phenomenon. Of particular relevance in understanding both the popularity and the state of criminological discourse of woman during the time of the arrest and conviction of Abe at the height of this criminology boom is the sixteen-volume *Modern Criminology* series (Kindai hanzai kagaku) published beginning in 1929.[27] Within this series at least four volumes associate female sexuality with crime: Nozoe Atsuyoshi's *Women and Crime* (Josei to hanzai, 1930), Takada Giichirō's *Crime and Life / Sexual Perversion and Crime* (Hentai seiyoku to hanzai / Hanzai to jinsei, 1929), Nakamura Kokyō's *Perverse Psychology and Crime* (Hentai shinri to hanzai, 1930), and Kaneko Junji's *The Criminal Psychology* (Hanzaisha no shinri, 1930).

In the *Modern Criminology* series volume *Women and Crime,* woman is depicted as driven by her instincts and physiological drives. This association of female physiology and crime was made earlier by two of the most prolific scholars working in the fields of sexology and criminology, Habuto Eiji and Sawada Junjirō. In their 1916 *Crime Research* (Hanzai no kenkyū) the authors had argued that the tendency to commit crimes because of one's physiological makeup was greater for women than for men for the reason that their "reproductive functions are much more complicated than men's. There is a greater chance that they will a damaging effect on mental faculties with the result that crimes brought on by the reproductive functions in women are considerable."[28] These functions include puberty, menstruation, pregnancy, menopause, and so on. For Kaneko Junji, the very blood in a woman's veins drives her to animal passions man has never experienced. Blood is a literal sign of danger. The physiological "leakage" of the female body is named as a primary source of criminal behavior in women.[29] Kaneko argues on at least three occasions in his *The Psychology Criminal* that crime rates for women increase dramatically during the onset of menses and other reproductive functions including pregnancy:

> During menstruation women's crime rate increases.
>
> Of course the onset of mensus is a physiological function through which the lining of the womb is expelled within five days or so, but if we hypothesize that menstruation were to continue every day, and calculate the criminal danger of that menstrual cycle, we would find that the female crime rate would near that of the male crime rate. From this fact we can deduce that sexual desire and crime are related.[30]

Hormonal imbalances and menstrual flows—what Otto Pollak referred to as "the generative phases of women"—invite (the specialists allege) deviant female behavior.

Nozoe's study *Women and Crime* opens with the claim that any hormonal alteration such as that caused during pregnancy and menopause can cause the subject to debilitate into a criminal. On puberty Nozoe writes: "The onset of puberty signaled by menstruation tends to be taken lightly but it is a very serious event. Wishful impulses to experience adventure are born from dreams that should shame. Wild fancies and sexual desires are awakened and there is a more pronounced tendency toward lying. Women make false accusations of having been a victim of kidnapping and rape. As a result they develop tendencies to insult others or commit arson."[31] Nozoe cites the Italian criminologist Cesare Lombroso to argue that with the onset of menses women commit the crimes of shoplifting, murder, poisoning, and arson with much more frequency.[32] The production of estrogen during another moment of hormonal imbalance—pregnancy—is said to stimulate a tendency toward the crimes of abortion, infanticide, and involuntary manslaughter. (Here abortion is considered homicide): "Pregnancy has a tremendous influence on the woman's mental life. Perverse desires, impulsive behavior, and cruel impulses occur and appear as thievery, shoplifting, and violent behavior. It may feel as though the new life in the pregnant woman threatens to take over her being and it causes changes in the female's sense of reason and emotional life."[33] Menopause is another hormonal tidal shift that causes mental instability:

> The fifty-year old woman fights against various criminal temptations and sometimes she gives in to them. Not only that but during periods of intense sexual desire, she is more likely to commit crime. Her expression appears

irreverent and takes on the look of a witch. This old woman who has sexually deteriorated suddenly exhibits a tendency toward cold egoism or illustrates revolting greed and cruel and malicious intent.[34]

The female body is defined primarily as a hormonal body. This physicality causes irrational behavior in woman, which leads to crime.[35] Sexual desire is a marker of possible erratic behavior since, as Nozoe writes, "Women's sexual instinct is on the average weak and female sexual needs are weak."[36] Possible transgressive behavior, therefore, is marked in reproductive changes and signs of sexual desire.

Nozoe argues that crime by heterosexual men is not hormonal but intellectual in origin. Men commit crimes as a result of their protracted struggle in the social world. The extreme pressures of nation-building and modernization in which they actively participate lead them to commit crimes because they are progressive, mentally charged. Women, on the other hand, follow their instincts uncontrollably: "Women's relationship to nature is more primitive than that of men. They have a less developed constitution, consequently, their innate instincts operate more freely. Just as the instinct for cruelty is common in the animal world, this erupts more easily and more dramatically than in men."[37] Evolutionary theory is the basis of this characterization of female deviance. The woman's belated development on the evolutionary scale makes her more sensitive, more excitable. Her inability to make decisions is cited as proof of her susceptibility to bodily drives and instinct:

> As signalled by the process of menstruation woman has retained a very intimate connection with organic nature *[shintai kikan]*. . . . Woman is much more strongly dependent on her innate instincts than man. Just as the animal is guided by the extremely purposeful instincts, and can dispense with the power of judgment within the animal sphere so also is it the case with the animal of the human sphere. Women are provided with a number of instincts which safely pave the way for her through life. These instincts, including sexual instincts, steer her emotions in a purposeful direction with less need for reflection than in the case of the man.
>
> P. T. Mobius expresses the same thought: ". . . Instinct is nothing to be afraid of. . . . Instinct makes woman animal-like, independent, secure and cheerful. In this instinct is the original strength of woman.". . . In good as well as in evil, woman lets instinct decide for her.
>
> We thus perceive that the female criminal is a victim of her bad instincts. She shows greater hate, jealousy, revenge, anger, blind rage and the

highest cruelty. . . . The female criminal not only appears to us more terrible than the male but is so in reality.

Woman's subjection to her emotions is thus explained. It follows from this, that the development of abstract thought is excluded. However, since we have the opposite relation in the male, the two sexes compliment each other perfectly.

Just as with animals, if it were a world of only women, this human race would be unchanged, halted in its primitive stage. All progress issues from men.

Women do not need judgment. For that reason, their development of judgment is much narrower than men's and their world sentimental.[38]

Nozoe goes to great lengths to prove, first, that woman is a sexual criminal and, second, that she is driven by hormones and instinct, which inhibit her ability to think rationally or abstractly. He carries his conclusions quite far. Women's tendency to follow their instinct and their need for immediate gratification make them susceptible to outside influence. They are—and we might remember the story of Omatsu here—unable to handle the independent thinking that progress requires.

This criminological discourse, which links crime with an innate inability to postpone gratification, asserts man's ascendancy over woman on the evolutionary scale. The female body is linked with nature insofar as nature is conceived as that which is less civilized. This criminological view places woman in the paradoxical situation of being both aggressive and passive. Woman's inability to show restraint, which is the precondition of the progress of the species, turns her at any moment into a predator. She transgresses social morality but only out of primitive uncontrollable instinct. She is sexually passive, but it is that lack of aggression that makes her react so readily to outside influence. In other words, all women are potentially victims of their own instincts. All women are potentially disruptive. Nature makes few exceptions. Nozoe's findings are strikingly similar to arguments made by Erich Wulffen, a medical doctor, in 1920s Germany. The long passage from *Women and Crime,* above, corresponds almost exactly to a passage in Wulffen's book *Woman as Sexual Criminal.*[39] *Woman as Sexual Criminal* takes as its primary premise that "the male criminal [is] a type and the female . . . a born sexual criminal in relation to that type. Most of woman's criminal tendencies, on account of close lying psycho-physiological causes, stand in some fixed relation to her sex life. In this sense then, the female thief, swindler, extortionist, incendiary, robber, murderer, may be regarded as a sexual criminal. This imputation is so lucid and so easy to understand that its adoption bids fair to become current."[40] Wulffren further argues, "Woman's primordial character, so intimately tied up with her bodily organization, like that of the child, demonstrates this disposition to crime so simply and emphatically that it was, perhaps, this very simplicity that prevented its discovery till now."[41] In this statement, woman is phylogenetically "primordial" and ontogenetically childlike. The female criminal is dangerous not because she wields power but because she wields power without control or intention. This is not the portrayal of a wily, conniving poison woman that we see in tales of Takahashi. The women in Nozoe's and Wulffen's discussions of the female criminal are not in control of their bodies and minds. Scientific rationalization proves them to be ever at the mercy of their instinctual and bodily drives. It discounts them as rational subjects.

In this model of crime, natural drives, which inhibit the evolution of the human race, are primarily exhibited in the female body. It is particularly woman's sexual instinct that contributes to her behavior. Wulffen follows Lombroso in arguing that "the born female criminal possesses a heightened sexuality and is inclined to prostitution which is a natural atavism with her inasmuch as she is more or less of a prostitute in the primitive state. In the born female criminal the other traits are grouped around this 'need of erotism': in most cases motherly love is absent in her, for the maternal sentiment in woman counteracts her criminal impulses."[42] Specialists in England further reported a link between sexuality, sexual practice, and crime among women. A study published only a few years after Nozoe's *Women and Crime* reported that while only seventy-one of one thousand college graduates had indulged in sexual relations prior to marriage, 74.1 percent of girls of a reformatory studied by the authors had engaged in "illicit sexual indulgence" before marriage; 98.2 percent were found to have been "sexually immoral prior to entering the Reformatory." A close relationship was found to exist between the age at the first illicit sex experience and the onset of other delinquent conduct.[43] "Illicit sexual behavior" included professional prostitution, occasional prostitution, "one-man" prostitution, promiscuous adultery, adultery with one man, promiscuity, unconventionality in sex life, and having a "doubtful" sex life.[44] It is only too clear when deviation from conventional morality is cited as the source of delinquency that criminal diagnosis works to shore up conventional morality as normative.

In a book in the same criminology series as Nozoe's, Takada Giichirō, in a chapter entitled "The Characteristics of Crime by Women," agrees that crime by women involves sexual desire. There he states that regardless of the crime ("whether we are speaking of lese majesty or shoplifting"), and regardless of the woman ("whether we are speaking of the modern woman, women of the past, or women of the future"), without exception, crimes by women will always be related to the sexual.[45] Takada's first proof of the relationship of sex and crime involves Kaneko Fumiko, the anarchist who, with her Korean lover (whom Takada refers to as Bokuretsu) attempted to assassinate the emperor. Takada finds it impossible to imagine that Kaneko could have wished to murder the emperor on her own. Certainly Bokuretsu would have committed the crime without Kaneko, but would it have occurred the other way around? Certainly not, he argues. He makes a similar argument regarding Kanno Suga's involvement in the High Treason Incident suggesting that it was surely her feelings for Kōtoku Shūsui rather than her political beliefs that motivated Kanno to become involved in the attempted assassination of the Meiji emperor.[46] The language of criminological science is deployed to depoliticize her politics and lodge her motivations squarely within the realm of desire.

In Takada's mind, women cannot be political criminals. They do not commit crime out of reason but out of desire. Two other examples that Takada draws on to prove the relationship of sexual desire and crime engage Meiji poison women Takahashi Oden and Hanai Oume. Reaching even further into the past, he finds another example of what he considers to be the inevitable relationship between sexual desire and crime by women: the greengrocer's daughter Oshichi, who committed arson in order to meet her lover again in the temple where they had fled after an earlier fire and met for the first time.[47] In Takada's eyes, women never act alone. They are always accomplices and their partner in crime is always a male lover. Even abortion, he argues, would not be committed without the encouragement of the male partner.

One grim consequence of this understanding of the female body as a bundle of instinctual drives propelled by her reproductive nature and uncontrolled desire is that the potential for a mature sexuality is deemed practically irrelevant due to its unattainability. Female desire is no more than a sign of the inherent uncontrollable animalistic drive bubbling beneath the surface of civilized rationality. It is metonym for the natural laws that civilization seeks to extinguish in human society. By definition, female sexuality and self-control are mutually exclusive. Female sexuality had to be managed because woman was not always in control of herself. She was irrational. Effectively the coherent, rational, and consequently more highly evolved body in this criminological writing was male. The problem with this model that I refer to here as an "evolutionary model of female criminality" is that it relegates woman to an inferior position in a regulated hierarchical system of power on the basis of physiology. When the raw material of the female body is made to substantiate claims to privilege, the social and political history that relegates women to a position of inferiority is left uninterrogated. These claims based on sex, which fetishized the scientific "reason" of evolutionary theory, named rationality a specifically male trait at the expense of female bodies.

The Medical Reports: Crooked Teeth, Flaring Hormones and a Killer

Just as with Takahashi Oden, physiognomy continued to be an important semiotic index for explaining why Abe committed the crime. The connection between Abe's murderous act and her physical and mental health was buttressed by a battery of tests she had to undergo. Extended physical and psychological analyses—especially as related to her sexual behavior—were first performed on Abe for the court. Abe was ordered by the Tokyo Police Regional Courts (Tokyo keiji chihō saibansho) to undergo a full examination. The exams took seventeen days, from 10 September to 26 September 1936. According to the *Japan Psychological Examinations* (Nihon no seishin kantei, 1973), these medical exams were led by Muramatsu Tsuneo, a professor at the Tokyo Imperial University Medical School.[48] For his report, Muramatsu examined the records of testimony by Abe and her clients, her genetic history *(idenreki),* her current state of physical health *(shintai-teki genzai shō),* and her current state of mental health *(seishin-teki genzai shō).* An almost voyeuristic attention centered on how Abe regarded the male body and how she touched it. Witnesses, presumably former clients of hers, were even brought in to testify. Among the topics discussed in the findings were why Abe considered the penis and the testicles to be "one set," the many men she had been with and what they had to say about her, such as how she was usually more interested in the satisfaction of her own pleasure, how she would lick or suck the penis, how she would lose her breath after orgasm, and how she was "ten times" more sensitive than usual women, to the degree that her eyes would even change color when she was sexually excited. Another witness had said that he feared she was ill because she was wet before sex, but she had replied that she had seen a doctor about it and was diagnosed as merely easily excitable.

The state of Abe's current health was deemed part of the evidence as well. Muramatsu's physical exam found Abe to be physically and nutritionally below the norm—her teeth were crooked, and her pupil reaction slow; he was not sure whether she had syphilis (she had been diagnosed with syphilis earlier) but her cerebrospinal fluid appeared "normal." His conclusions regarding her mental state were that while she had tendencies toward sadism and fetishism, she was not necrophilic. She did not gain a sense of pleasure in the act of murder. Surprisingly, he did not find her to be pathologically sexually perverse. Her sexual life was unusually active and her orgasms "were unusually long and deep but otherwise qualitatively she does not exhibit perversion that would become pathological."[49] He found that though she was born not breathing and did not speak until the age of four, this had not made her mentally weak. She grew at a normal rate, her teeth came in at the normal time, her reflexes were good. Her problem was that she had not been in an environment in which she could correct or reflect upon her immorality and low ethics as a juvenile; rather she had continued to reside in places that encouraged them. Syphilis, drug addiction, and alcohol addiction (the amount she consumed before the murder is measured in bottles consumed per day) were found not to have contributed to the incident. However, Muramatsu revised his opinion in view of the court judgment to later assert that Abe exhibited mental and physical hysteria, which he called nymphomania.[50]

The police tried to find a connection between Abe's female functions and criminality. Abe's interrogator addressed precisely this point in asking her whether her period was regular, to which she replied: "I started my period toward the end of my sixteenth year. It's always regular and is over in about four days. Sometimes I get a headache during my period which makes me crabby but not bad enough that I have to lie down."[51] The police were also apparently interested to learn that near the age of seventeen Abe experienced an inflammation of the ovaries for which she was treated at Hamada hospital.

The police report reflected a belief that menstruation might lead to bad behavior: "She began to menstruate at about age fifteen and from that time she continuously quarreled with members of her household." It further stated in a longer section specifically entitled "Menstrual Period" that

the defendant's menses began at age fifteen, and while she has experienced some irregularities, she still is experiencing them. Her flow tends toward the heavy side and continues for three or four and up to five days in duration. From two or three days before her menses begin, she often experiences irritability and insomnia, and stays that way until two or three days after they cease. Although her condition might not be so severe as to require bed rest, she often takes "Teerin" or other medications for headaches. She experiences no abdominal pain, and says that she does not quarrel with people or act impulsively during her period. In addition, she said that at the time she committed the crime, she was between periods. She said that she has not been pregnant.[52]

These studies of criminological physiology reignited interest in Takahashi Oden. Nozoe argued for the inextricable relationship of sexual desire and crime in women in suggesting that the Takahashi case was a prime example of the way in which susceptibility to orgiastic pleasure (signified by the size of Takahashi's sexual and generative organs) indicated a propensity toward crime.[53] Perhaps the most bizarre link between Takahashi and Abe was the resubmission of Takahashi's formaldehyde-soaked organs for analysis a year before Ishida's murder—an analysis that resulted in the publication of detailed measurements of her sexual and reproductive organs following Abe's arrest by an army surgeon from Keiō University's medical school. The findings published in 1937 were discussed in chapter 1. In December of 1936, one of the original attendants at the autopsy of Takahashi gave an interview to the *Miyako* newspaper. Takada Chūryō, a wizened old man by 1936, compared the treatment of Takahashi and Abe in the press: "Kanagaki Robun and folks like him excitedly wrote [about Takahashi]—the public was even more stirred up than now with Osada!"[54] Takada's remarks that he was disappointed that Takahashi's headless body looked so much like a man's sustained the link between crime, the female body, and female sexual desire: "Oden's body looked just like a man's body. You didn't get the sense from her body that she was a very good-looking woman. She was dark, you know. We all thought that since she was a wanton woman that she would have polyps but we checked for them and there were none."[55]

The Psychoanalytic Diagnosis of Abe Sada: A Case Study

Because the crime occurred at the height of romantic passion, the murder by Abe Sada proved an ideal case for substantiating the link between female sexual desire and transgression. This was true for those who sought not only a physiological explanation but a psychological aberrance that might explain why Abe committed the crime. Prominent sexologists and psychologists in Japan including Takahashi Tetsu and Ōtsuki Kenji joined specialists from the Tokyo Psychoanalysis Research Institute and a forensics psychologist from the Tokyo Municipal Police Department to diagnose Abe's behavior in *The Psychoanalytic Analysis of Abe Sada* (Abe Sada no seishin bunsekiteki shindan, 1937).[56] The contributors gleaned much of their information from discussions about Abe run in the widely read *Ladies'*

Journal (Fujin Kōron). The Tokyo Psychoanalysis Research Institute's purported motivation in publishing the medium-length book was to illustrate what normal female sexual development looks like and to promote psychoanalysis as the best model for understanding the impetus to social and sexual deviancy. As the introduction put it: "There were various hypotheses concerning the psychology of the criminal in the strange murder that created a sensation in Japanese society in 1936. Many of these were within the limits of common sense but few deserved the designation 'scientific diagnosis.' We find this to be true because we believe that in researching sexual or female psychology of this kind of mentality, only the psychoanalytic method is sufficient and suitable."[57] In these prefatory remarks, the authors state their primary goal to be a truth that can be revealed only through the science of psychoanalysis. They are disdainful of various hypotheses published in newspapers regarding Abe and are determined to correct the misinformed public. The included essays were "From the Perspective of Forensics" (Kaneko Junji), "Abe Sada's Psychoanalysis" (Nagasaki Bunji), "On Osada's Unconscious Motivation" (Takahashi Tetsu), "A Consideration of Abe Sada's 'Sada-ism'" (Takahashi), "A Tendency within Everyone that We Should Fear" (Morooka Tamotsu), "The Osada Incident as a Case of Sexual Frustration" (Ōtsuki Kenji), and "The Wave of Crimes Modeling the Osada Incident" (Ōtsuki).

The Psychoanalytic Diagnosis of Abe Sada, though focused on deviancy, purported to expand contemporaneous ideas of what constituted normal female desire. The fact that it did not repeat judgmental platitudes of the press and offered competing diagnoses at least encouraged the questioning of the categories of deviancy. The primary focus of the study was to uncover Abe's impetus to criminal intent through an analysis of her sexual instinct (in the psychoanalytic sense of drive). These studies of Abe Sada at first appeared not to replicate the findings of Nozoe's *Women and Crime,* given their emphasis on the psychological over the biological. Within the larger discourse of criminology at this time, this emphasis on the psychological over the biological could be liberatory. In earlier discussions of female sexuality in criminological discourse, the body was considered a primary influence on behavioral patterns. In the psychological model, the female subject was potentially freed from her body. The hormonal and the hereditary were not longer inherent determinants of behavior. Rather, an attempt was made to draw a distinction between sexual instinct as a specific aim localized in the excitation of the genital apparatus (the earlier biological model) and sexual instinct as represented in the mind as drive (the psychoanalytic model).[58]

Like other criminological discourse, however, *The Psychoanalytic Diagnosis of Abe Sada* is concerned primarily with the abnormal or perverse in creating a model of normativity. The transgressive woman is symbolic of *all* women. Anyone, under the right conditions, may gravitate toward the perverse (and homicidal) behavior exemplified by Abe. Abnormal behavior is argued to be the result of a regression. The authors consistently, though not explicitly, follow Freud in regarding "sexual perversities" to have developed out of a normal constitution. Freud's usefulness for the contributors of this study lay in the fact that he used the existence of perversion as a weapon for rethinking "normal sexuality." The persistence of perverse tendencies "whether these underpin neurotic symptoms or are integrated into the normal sexual act in the guise of 'forepleasure' led to the idea that perversions are no great rarity but persist or re-emerge as a component part of sexuality such that perversion becomes a regression to an earlier fixation of libido. Thus so-called normal sexuality cannot be seen as a prior aspect of human nature."[59] Unlike the theories of perversity pursued by Krafft-Ebing in which the kind of sexual behavior exhibited by Abe would fit into the category of the psychopathic, the sick, Freud moves perversions into the realm of the "normal," defining them as a persistent re-emerging part of (an unrepressed) sexuality.[60] Abe's behavior as described in the study is similarly found to illustrate not a psychopathic *vita sexualis* but a deviation from normal human behavior produced by an immature sexuality with limited access to a normal sexual object—features that were determined by Freud to lead to sexual perversity.[61] The authors seek to prove the general thesis that sexual perversions constitute underlying components of normal human sexuality, which emerge under particular circumstances and mark a regression to an earlier libidinal phase: "We have reached the conclusion that Abe Sada's psychology is undoubtedly abnormal but not pathological and not unrelated to the psychology of the ordinary person. In her case we discern a caricature, an exaggeration, an amplification or primitive form of the human, especially the female, sexual psychology."[62]

The study as a whole expresses two intertwining points regarding Abe's deviancy.[63] The first emphasis regards repression. Abe is described as wholly unrepressed. She is unable to resist satisfying her instinct. Interestingly, Takahashi argues that because she is unable to repress, she is a hysterical personality. She primarily exhibited a hysterical personality, he argues, for her strong ego, lack of restraint, and propensity to take immediate action.[64] This is an unusual interpretation of hysteria, which is usually found to occur *within* the mechanism of repression. Furthermore, hysteria is found primarily in the phallic and oral libidinal spheres,[65] and the contributors question whether Abe even entered the phallic stage, in part for her interest in sexual acts beyond copulation.

The second point highlighted in the study is that Abe is found to have regressed to the infantile stages of pre-Oedipalized sexuality. Perversions Abe allegedly exhibited are considered by the authors to express the pre-genital organization of the subject. They are the nonrepressed manifestation of her infantile sexuality. Precocity is also included as proof of her undeveloped self. Abe has not managed to pass through the excruciating test of infantile sexuality. She has not graduated to accept the phallocentric sexual norm. Abe is both unrepressed (operating at the level of instinct) and undeveloped (exhibiting a regression to earlier libinal stage). The authors implicitly follow Freud here, particularly his argument in his *Totem and Taboo* that the neurotic (as opposed to hysteric) patient exhibits behavior that bears a striking resemblance to the horror of incest by "savages." The boy, for example, liberates himself from the incestuous attraction when he matures: "A neurotic, on the other hand, invariably exhibits some degree of psychical infantilism. He has either failed to get free from the psycho-sexual conditions that prevailed in his childhood or he has returned to them—to possibilities which may be summed up as developmental inhibition and regression."[66] Primitive people reveal undesirable behavior that has been rejected and overtaken by repression in the mental life of modern man. This "primitive" evoked in *Totem and Taboo* has been equated with marginalized figures. Diana Fuss writes that Frantz Fanon's remarks on homosexuality, "while failing to challenge some of Freud's most conventional and dangerous typologies of sexuality, simultaneously question, at least implicitly, the ethnological component of psychoanalysis that has long equated 'the homosexual' with 'the primitive.'"[67]

In the *Psychoanalytic Diagnosis of Abe Sada,* it is the sexual woman who is the primitive. She is not a hypersexualized racialized body in the way that the savage man is in *Totem and Taboo,* but she is similarly depicted as voracious, unable to maintain sexual decorum, and unable to keep desires in check. This psychological infantilism is said to represent an earlier stage in humanity. Abe is the ontogenetic form of the uncivilized past of human civilization. She is unrepressed (instinctually immature) and exhibits regression (ontogenetically immature). Therefore, while there is a concerted effort to move beyond a somatic understanding of Abe's crime, what we see in this study is not so far removed from the earlier evolutionary biological understandings of criminality. Despite his attempt to distinguish his analysis from biologizing ones, the psychologist Ōtsuki Kenji, for example, ends up replicating arguments made in evolutionary theoretical arguments about deviancy. Animalistic sexual drive is interpreted as the impetus for Abe's criminal behavior:

> A lustful person is simple but not evil. Just as an animal is guiltless *[tsumi ga nai]*, she may also be guiltless. What she did was animalistic. Or rather, insect-like. She is more animal than human, more organism *[seibutsu]* than animal, more insect than organism. . . . the unconscious rooted in a psyche *[shinri]* transmitted from animals. Furthermore, that psyche is deeply embedded from the experiences of primitive times *[yabanjin jidai]* and the infant years are accumulated in the deep layer of the psyche *[shinri shinzō]*. Osada's act was an unconscious act and insect-like because . . . insects act similarly. As many know, [female] scorpions and like insects often eat the heads of the male after copulation.[68]

In this analysis of entomological mating rituals, Abe is described metaphorically as closer to insect or animal. She is shown to experience not an erotic but an animal sexual drive. Another contributor to the volume believed that through her desire we can see how love operates in "the animal world."[69] Her sexuality is primitive. It is prefigured as primary, ontologically discrete, prior to language and culture. The use of insect metaphors may be the author's attempt to simplify the content for the general reader. However, since this is a part of numerous publications on psychoanalysis by the Tokyo Psychoanalysis Research Institute and appears not to have been circulated widely, it is unclear whether the general reader was of concern.

Nagasaki Bunji's analysis perpetuates the image of Abe as primitive. He argues that Abe is unable to sublimate and those who cannot sublimate are operating on a primitive level.[70] She "acted primitively by trying to possess him [Ishida]."[71] In that sense, Abe is not only classified as primitive on the continuum from primitive to civilized but she is also classified as immature on the continuum between child and adult. She is immature and childlike, though precocious.[72] Nagasaki describes the sadistic behavior Abe testified to in court as similar to that of animals after sex. While he believes that Ishida, as masochist, contributed to their particular brand of lovemaking, he specifically describes Abe as sadistic in the way that "animals bite each other after copulation."[73] A normal sexuality, he argues, is not instinctual or animalistic. It is one that represses. The emphasis in the analysis of Abe, is to show that her violent behavior, which is unrepressed, is "uncivilized." Abe is "primitive" *(yaban-na)*, "animalistic" *(yasei-teki, dōbutsu-teki)*, and "primal" *(genshi-teki)* just as uninhibited "primitive" men in *Totem and Taboo* acted immediately upon their desires such that their acts were deemed "substitute for thought."[74]

This notion of the inability to postpone satisfaction of desire represented predominantly in terms of a struggle between instinct and culture in early psychoanalysis is not free from evolutionary theoretical underpinnings. Freud's *Civilization and Its Discontents* is the clearest example in early psychoanalysis of the link that is made between civilization and the repression of instinct (versus the uncivilized and the unrepressed instinctual drive). It is a link manifest in *The Psychoanalytic Diagnosis of Abe Sada*. The heroic sign of health is the ability to postpone satisfaction. Uncontrolled erotic feelings are fatal and the search for gratification is destructive. Rather than turning to the self for gratification, contributing to the social community and "with the help of a technique guided by science, going over to the attack against nature and subjecting her to the human will" is working for the good of all.[75] One conquers suffering through sublimation of instinctual aims: "One gains the most if one can sufficiently heighten the yield of pleasure from the sources of psychical and intellectual work."[76]

The evolution of humanity is mirrored in the experience of each individual. It is something that each individual must enter into and overcome through sublimation and repression:

> We cannot fail to be struck by the similarity between the process of civilization and the libidinal development of the individual. . . . Sublimation of instinct is an especially conspicuous feature of cultural development; it is what makes it possible for higher psychical activities, scientific, artistic or ideological, to play such an important part in civilized life. . . . it is impossible to overlook the extent to which civilization is built up upon a renunciation of instinct, how much it presupposes precisely the non-satisfaction (by suppression, repression or some other means?) of powerful instincts.[77]

The development of the individual is akin to the development of civilization. The value system from the instinctual to the civilized (from the pleasure principle to the reality principle) aligns such that immediate satisfaction is delayed, pleasure is restrained, joy is replaced by work, security is valued over the absence of repression, and the self is productive.[78]

To describe one of the processes of civilization, Freud on at least two occasions in *Civilization and Its Discontents* turns to menstruation. The taboo on menstruation in modernity is a defense against a phase of development that has been surmounted in human history. The olfactory stimulation of the menses was devalued (Freud's term) and civilization progressed. In other words, the devaluation of female sexuality encourages civilized behavior. But Freud explains in much more explicit terms how women stand in opposition to civilization and "display their retarding and restraining influence": "Women represent the interests of the family and of sexual life. The work of civilization has become increasingly the business of men, it confronts them with ever more difficult tasks and compels them to carry out instinctual sublimations of which women are little capable."[79] Freud gestures toward women's role in the social symbolic. They stand for family, they represent family. In the second half of this statement, however, woman is constitutionally incapable of sublimation. She has been moved from the realm of the symbolic to the realm of the biologic or genital.

Here the framework of psychoanalysis coincides with the developmental model of evolutionary biology. On the evolutionary criminological scale, woman is less civilized than man for her inability to put off immediate gratification for the greater good. The case study seems influenced by the early works of Freud. Abe is described as less evolved in psychoanalytic terms. She has an immature sexuality; she not healthy because she is unable to repress, not civilized enough. In this psychoanalytic framework, her inability to repress is the sign of degenerative or at least unhealthy development. This attunement to her own instinct leaves her intellectually wanting in the modern world, to which she is unable to adjust given her inability to postpone the fulfillment of her desires. She cannot think abstractly or atemporally.

Nagasaki goes further to say that Abe's inability to repress meant that her instinctual drives have veritably been revealed for us to see: in her we can see raw instinctual drive. Nagasaki describes Abe and Ishida's prolonged lovemaking in the single six-mat room as the death instinct, the desire to return to the womb. Referring directly to Freud's *Beyond the Pleasure Principle,* he describes Abe as lacking that state which is civilized in Freudian psychoanalysis—shame, the shame to mask her sexual desire. She is no longer "red-faced" as a new prepubescent suppressing her newly felt sexual desire.[80]

Abe is consistently framed in terms of underdevelopment, immaturity, infantilism. This conception of the murderous woman marks a fairly significant shift in the representation of the poison woman. She is not overly developed sexually but underdeveloped for not having accepted her Oedipal castration, and consequently she suffers and causes suffering. Various aspects are deemed revealing of Abe's lack of development: how she remains stuck in a pregenital phase, how she has not transcended the Oedipus complex, or assumed the castration complex, and has not accepted the prohibition on incest. Her sexual "perversions" (sadism, masochism, nymphomania, and fetishism were all identified by Kaneko Junji as exhibited in Abe) are considered as the nonrepressed manifestation of infantile sexuality that also reveals an undeveloped sexuality.[81] A structural economy of desire through which female sexual desire is pathologized on a universal scale is staged via Abe. The copy on the book jacket for *The Psychoanalytic Diagnosis of Abe Sada* claims, "The study is not merely a description of Abe's disorders but a diagnosis." This is a partial truth. It was not a diagnosis of Abe but of the entire female sex in the alarmist albeit colorful depictions of Abe that turn her into an example of a "bizarre but real" sexual fiend despite claims to the contrary in the text.

How this psychoanalytic study contributed to contemporary notions of femininity is suggested by Jane Flax's point that psychoanalysis has played "an important part in generating categories of identity and standards of normalcy and health, especially for practices of sexuality, child rearing, and gender. The normalizing veils of scientific language and claims to the objective discovery of 'natural' forces, identities, or drives disguise the operation of these standards. More critical examination reveals the congruence of these identities and standards, especially those of femininity/masculinity, good/bad mother, healthy/deviant, and homosexuality/heterosexuality, with the practices and commitments of other dominant power/knowledge configurations."[82] In short, psychoanalysis can function as a form of biopower through which governing moralities maintain their legitimacy. The psychoanalytic model in the *The Psychoanalytic Diagnosis of Abe Sada* that treats female sexuality as exhibiting ontogenetic and phylogenetic regression works to the advantage of the contemporaneous Japanese *ie* system that proscriptively channeled all behavior by woman toward the good of the patriarchal family—the husband, the son, the father-in-law, the nation. The psychosexual discourse in the case study is bounded to the epistemology of male heterosexual freedom contra the female heterosexual under the guise of scientific reason, which argues that woman is constitutionally incapable of managing her own desires. This implicit rhetoric of management and control is ironic considering that one of its main contributors, Takahashi Tetsu, generally imagined and presented himself as a proponent of female sexuality—as one who enabled the expression of female desire and promoted the subversion of gender and sexuality norms.

The image introducing this case study, with the appended German subtitle "Psychoanalytische Studien über einen Fall (Sada Abe) von Salome-Komplex" (Psychoanalytic Study of a Case [Abe Sada] of Salome Complex), exacerbates the treatment of the female criminal as both sexual and dangerous. The illustration is by Aubrey Beardsley, from the 1893 French edition of Oscar Wilde's play *Salome,* of a masculine-looking Salome, her hair angrily streaming out from her face. She stares into the face of a beheaded John the Baptist, who curiously looks like a feminized Medusa, with snake-like hair. The lettering beneath Salome's bent knees reads, "I kissed your mouth, John. I kissed your mouth." The image in this context is a compli-cated one. Is the severed head the consequence of an immature or primitive or desirous woman? Or is it the revenge exacted by the castrated woman face to face with her enemy?[83] The terrorizing head recurs later in the *The Psychoanalytic Diagnosis of Abe Sada* when Takahashi diagnoses Abe as suf-fering from a Salome complex, though he is one of the only contributors to make this assertion. He, like Nagasaki, cites Freud's discussion of the "red face" at puberty, which is the result of the suppression of a young libido. As the subject is increasingly sexually involved, she is no longer red-faced as the blood stays in the genitals. In a rare reference to the victim of the mur-der, Nagasaki goes on to assert that Ishida and Abe, so practiced in love, were far beyond the stage of the red-faced girl and clearly had internalized the antipodal distinction between the head and the genitals.[84]

The Psychoanalytic Diagnosis of Abe Sada places Abe in another cultur-ally specific group of mythologized fatal women by comparing her with Takahashi Oden. By being aligned with Takahashi, Abe becomes a leg-endary figure in history. This comparative inclusion of the myth of the poison woman and analysis of a female criminal is defended by Takahashi Tetsu, who argues that the similarities between myths and women's lives reveal elements of a universal human nature, just as Freud argued when he appealed to the familiarity of the Oedipal myth as something we might recognize within our personal histories. This combination of psychiatric hermeneutics with novelistic detail might be described as "pathographic," a term employed by Emily Apter following Freud in describing literature that fuses medical observation with "the literary chronicle of behavioral aberration":

> As the broad parameters of what constituted medical discourse in the nine-teenth century gave way to the more specialized disciplines of psychiatry and psychoanalysis by the century's end, nosological realism was joined with case-history narrative conventions, thus constituting a new kind of writing, one that, following Freud and Sander Gilman, I have called pathography. From P. L. Jacob's *Curiosités de l'Histoire de France* (1858) to Richard von Krafft-Ebing's *Psychopathia Sexualis* (1886); from Oskar Panizza's *Psychopathia Criminalis* (1898) to Dr. Augustin Cabanès' *Le Cabinet secret de l'histoire* (1900); and from Havelock Ellis's *Studies in the Psychology of Sex* (1936) to Magnus Hirshfeld's *Geschlechts Anomalien und*

阿部定の精神分析的診断

東京精神分析學研究所編

PSYCHOANALYTISCHE STUDIEN
ÜBER EINEN FALL (SADA ABE)
VON SALOME-KOMPLEX,
Verfasst vom Tokio Institut für Psychoanalyse, 1937

J'AI BAISÉ TA BOUCHE
IOKANAAN
J'AI BAISÉ TA BOUCHE

東京精神分析學研究所出版部發行

Figure 9. Cover of *Abe Sada no seishin bunseki teki shindan* (The psychoanalytic diagnosis of Abe Sada) (Tokyo Seishin Bunsekigaku Kenkyōjo, 1937).

Perversionen (1957), legendary biographies were pathologized; that is, they were built up as medical dossiers and collected like so many rare specimens. Each case study was exhibited, as in a psychohistorical museum, demonstrating individually the determinative traits of a given perversion, obsession, or paranormal *idée fixe,* and exemplifying as a totality the taxonomy of criminal anomaly.[85]

The Western examples Apter uses to illustrate the genre of "pathography" generally include as part of their narrative makeup "grotesque details," "social panorama high and low," and "the darker side of desire," among other qualities.[86] Like Freud, Takahashi exploits wordplay and ambiguity, but knowledge, myth, social institution, and status converge to promote a particular family drama through which a "healthy" female sexuality can be produced. Takahashi's enthusiasm for the rehabilitative effects of psychoanalysis is quite clear. Transmission of this model of psychoanalysis is important to Takahashi, who seeks to legitimate psychoanalysis as scientific practice through the repetition of particular psychoanalytic rhetoric and concepts. Nevertheless, the primary concern of the contributors in *The Psychoanalytic Diagnosis of Abe Sada* to establish a coherent model of psychoanalysis does not come to fruition in this study and is illustrative of the status of psychoanalysis in Japan, which Jonathan Hall describes as never managing to assume the full mantle of science, becoming a form of literary criticism and, increasingly in the 1930s, a mode of popular national characterization.[87]

Furthermore, the challenge to codes of normativity is absent in this analysis, which seeks to promote a particular type of *normal* female sexuality. This study may not present "woman as sexual criminal" in the way that evolutionary theory-based criminology did, but it did promote the importance of the repressive machinery of civilizing science. As the authors succinctly put it:

> We must pursue foremost this particular woman's psychology with scientific accuracy as it stands, without prejudice, without enmity, and without eulogy to serve as an admonishment, education, and foundation for the normal individual. . . . Sada is a caricature of female psychology, a close-up. To scientifically analyze her is to become more self-aware. To educate oneself. To be cautious. The secret notebook of sexual psychology has been laid open.[88]

This particular psychoanalytic account does not relieve Abe of the position of deviant, excluded other. Further, it actually burdens *all* women with this

positionality by framing the study as a warning, as an educational document by "privileging" female characters as exemplars of the degenerative
forms sexuality can take at the hands of our unconscious, no matter what
our subjective purpose or motive might be. The reader must be cautious,
must carefully internalize what constitutes an inappropriate love object and
inappropriately "unhealthy" sexual behavior. Indeed, one of the dangers of
this study is that its meaning is structured by certain people who are sanctioned as able intepreters of truth.[89] The study is framed as an educational
one based in neutral, objective scientific thought that will reveal the truths
of female sexuality. The faculty of reason is something the study claims
Abe does not have as a "primitive," "animalistic," and "infantile" or "undeveloped" woman. Rather, it is the specialists who create logic out of the
mayhem produced by Abe. This work encodes a presumed interior world
of Abe with the language of the science of psychology, which reiterates the
status quo. The language of science is deployed to construct an internal
female desire that needs to be repressed for a diagnosis that is remarkably,
coincidentally suitable for maintaining the familial state order. This appropriation of the Oedipal law proposed by the *Psychoanalytic Diagnosis of Abe
Sada* encourages a gender hierarchy that inscribes female desire as inherently pathological and thereby colludes with the social order for which the
suppression of female desire is useful, even necessary.

It is clear that while *The Psychoanalytic Diagnosis of Abe Sada* does not
replicate the language of *Modern Criminology* texts, it does replicate certain notions related to female deviancy including ideas of regression and
infantilism. We might remember that Nozoe referred to female criminals
as primarily "sexual" criminals. In curious distinction to the examination
by Muramatsu for the courts, the essays in this text find sexual behavior
to be the symptom through which we can understand the motive for the
crime. We can understand Abe's behavior through her sexuality. Within
this structured order of civilization and crime, sexual difference and psychopathology, sexuality is again pressured to explain deviance. By linking discussions of *normal* female sexuality with a criminal figure (who enjoyed sex), and by simultaneously introducing within *The Psychoanalytic
Diagnosis of Abe Sada* other immortalized mythological deadly women,
female sexuality gets pathologized. Abe's sexuality is attached to the crime
of homicide so that the sexual woman is imbued with the homicidal. The
result is a scientifically sanctioned cultural paranoia that both pathologizes
female sexuality and naturalizes that pathology.

5. How to Be a Masochist and Not Get Castrated in the Attempt

Most pre–World War II texts about Abe Sada describe the generic female criminal as uncivilized, antithetical to social progress, and an example of the disaster that uncontrolled female desire can wreak. However, nearly all texts about Abe Sada in the *post*–World War II era treat her implicitly as a heroine. She is an eroticized icon of emancipation, ideal for having achieved sincerity of the flesh and for being unencumbered by ideological pressures. In this newly emerging depiction of Abe Sada in the postwar period, female self-assertion and especially sexual assertion still remained dangerous to the public good. That part of the discourse of the transgressive woman did not change. What did change is that this capacity for disrupture was recuperated and strategically engaged to critique prewar totalitarianism and to proffer a new mode of masculinity—one that is masochistic, admiring of the powerful woman, and therefore framed as *critical*. If the female criminal had previously been put to work to outlaw certain sexual behaviors and ultimately female sexual desire itself, in the postwar period she works in the service of producing a new counterdiscourse of masculinity through which masculine totalitarian politics and cultural values are explored and critiqued. Through a discussion of a diverse set of postwar films and literature on the celebrated criminal Abe Sada, this chapter shows that the contentious subject that emerges out of these works is a masochistic male obsessively dependent on the transgressive woman for his countervalent position.

Heroines of Pulp and Their Adoring Devotees: The Cult of the Female Deviant in Occupation Japan

Narratives of Sada in postwar literature and popular pulp magazines (*kasutori*) exhibit a new construction of female gender and sexuality that retains a dual tendency to fetishize and to promote the free expression of female desire, thereby forming a provocative alternative or addition to the frequently invoked models of domestic femininity.[1] The case studies of sexual perversion of the prewar era were joined by new types of case studies that employed anecdotes and interviews to prove not the perversity but rather the normalcy of female sexual desire. These new images included the domestic woman, and not just the transgressive woman, as sexual being. Stories and magazines purporting to express an enlightened view of female sexuality presented these ideas in sensational representations of the sexual woman, which worked conversely to undermine the idea that female sexual desire could be unremarkable. Furthermore, it should be recalled from the previous chapter that criminological discourse of the 1930s deemed every woman a potential criminal, implicitly including the domestic woman. In this way every woman was a potentially fetishizable object and delinquent citizen.

What was the reason for this new focus on female sexual desire in the postwar period and to what ends was it put? In elaborating on this point it is useful to describe one type of print culture through which discussions of female sexuality were perpetuated in the occupation period—the *kasutori zasshi* or "pulp magazine" press. Pulp magazines were peddled as the literature of a new postwar liberalism and later considered a representative medium of the era. Along with sensationalist pulp newspapers *(kasutori shinbun)*, pulp magazines were a main staple of the immediate postwar era, along with jeeps, the black market, *pan-pan* girls, and a kind of Japansese version of "moonshine" *(kasutori)*, all of which were symbolic of the chaotic nature of this "burned ruins period" *(yakeato jidai)* of the occupation.[2] The erotic stories and revealing images of deviant women in these pulpy pages represented the felicitous crumbling of oppressive social taboos of wartime and repressive wartime publishing laws.[3]

Writing on erotic literature in postwar Japan, the literary critic Kōno Kensuke proposes that the deluge onto the reading market of *kasutori* was to some degree a response to new entrepreneurial editors taking advantage of the relaxed censorship laws of the Allied Occupation Press Code.[4] The new code was aimed more at eliminating unpropitious political material than titillating stories whose "obscenity" would have been found injurious to public morals by the Japanese government during the war years. Censors mainly limited themselves to the eradication of material involving relations between occupying forces and prostitutes. As old censorship codes were repealed, new ones took their place and were designed to limit the publication of dissent toward the occupying forces. In order to draw critical attention away from the activities of the U.S. occupying forces, the Yoshida cabinet cooperated with the new government to create the "3-S" strategy, which allowed and even promoted what were called the three S's of sports, screen, and sex. With this new policy of funneling popular attention away from politics and into popular sexual and sports media, the shoestring pulp industry blossomed.[5]

Pulp magazines, which constituted a main source of reading material in the early years of the U.S. military's occupation of Japan, were presumably named for the poor quality of paper on which they were printed (the print was often hardly legible), though one etymology suggests that they were named for their short life span, which equaled the number of glasses of rubbing alcohol (often the only affordable alcohol after the war—also called *kasutori* or "from the dregs") a body could endure (only three).[6] Pulp magazines had short runs or would change their name either to avoid censors or to start new magazines that might garner fresh interest. Some of the pulp magazines had long runs, and those that did not were passed along from friend to friend to be read by many despite their brief period of publication. Among the pulps offering provocatively illustrated true tales were *Romance* (Romansu), *Perversion Posse* (Hentai Shūdan), *In Repose* (Danran), *Cabaret* (Kyabare), *Sex Culture* (Sei Bunka), *Thrill* (Suriru), *Strange Lust* (Kyōen), and *Gem* (Hōseki) to name only a few of the hundreds of titles containing thrilling stories of love, lust, and mystery.[7] Pulp encompassed the "pleasure" *(gōraku)* and "exposure" *(bakurō)* magazines as well as the "true tale" stories *(jitsuwa yomimono)* featuring mysteries of voyeurism and seduction.

While the few literary historians writing on the subject restrict their classifications of the "pulp" to the two main categories of the (1) titillating and bizarre tabloid and the (2) true-story or detective magazine, I propose a third category: (3) the sensational sexological magazine. This category includes such mental science magazines as *Red and Black* (Aka to kuro) founded by Takahashi Tetsu, featuring psychological studies, the use of psychoanalytic terminology, and case studies, along with the late 1940s and early 1950s "conjugal life" magazines inaugurated with the publication of the eponymous *Conjugal Life* (Fūfu Seikatsu). The "conjugal life" magazine also included medical topics but focused more directly on offering advice and knowledge regarding issues of reproduction and sexual desire to women in sexual relationships. Thus much in the pulp magazines reproduced elements common to the prewar erotic-grotesque culture in the form of a cultlike devotion to bodily experience.[8] The pulp magazines, produced in much greater numbers, unflinchingly extolled sexual, nonconventional behavior through a kind of visual and literary popular romanticization of the postwar *nikutai* or "carnal" ideology.

A cursory glance at a few pulp magazines reveals a continuing interest in female criminality, including Meiji poison women. The thin 1947 founding issue of *Crime Stories* (Hanzai Yomimono) ran a story on Meiji poison women Harada Okinu and Takahashi Oden. It began with a sympathetic rendering of the actual circumstances under which Harada gave birth in prison and nursed her baby for months before her beheading, and it concluded with the familiar details of Takahashi's execution, the autopsy, and the preservation of her reproductive organs:

> [Executioner] Asaemon, flustered, brought down the blade but the sword missed the neck and plunged into her chin, the gash spraying blood. The blindfold slipped, and half of her face was dyed in blood. Each time she moved her neck, the wound opened its red mouth.
>
> "Oh mercy! Oh give me mercy!"
>
> As she continued to cry out, the fierce pupils in her white eyes stared at Asaemon with hate when he began a Buddhist chant, "Namu . . ." and swung down the blade. Oden's head dropped. It was a merciless and cruel beheading. Oden was twenty-nine years old. Her corpse was autopsied at the Asakusa Metropolitan Police Fifth Hospital. The private parts were preserved in alcohol and today are kept at the Imperial University.[9]

Both women are shown as devoted lovers to the end, thinking only of the men for whom they had killed as the blade dropped. Other poison woman stories that appeared in pulps were less sympathetic, including the popular author Matsumura Shōfū's story about one of the only poison women popular in Meiji to have lived during the Tokugawa reign—O'hyaku. The story's preface describes her as a physically insatiable *(nikutai wa aku koto o shiranu)* woman who seeks men to fulfill her desires.[10] A few years later, in 1954, a short story of Meiji's poison woman Oshin ran in the *Nightly Read Newpaper* (Yoru Yomu Shinbun). In "Egg of the Poison Woman: A Strange Tale of Pickpocketing," Oshin was compared with poison woman Takahashi Oden: "So, what happened to Oshin after that? If she'd lived at least thirty years then she would have without a doubt become an even greater rare poison woman than Takahashi Oden, but for better or for worse, at twenty-one a cold suddenly turned to pneumonia and she passed away."[11] These few examples illustrate a continued popular curiosity about the female criminal, but as a stereotypical figure of the past that deflates her cultural power. This is not the case for Abe Sada in the postwar period, who was still alive, visible, and of deep interest to postwar Japanese authors and made symbolic in postwar male discourses of liberation expressed through the female body. The Japanese literature scholar Douglas Slaymaker has examined how, in postwar fiction by writers who rely on the sexualized female body to articulate their own postwar hopes, "a woman's body serves as an object, a means, via sex, for male characters to achieve a variety of goals: utopia of communality, connection with fellow human beings, a guide for the path to another level of existence, or liberation from current oppressions. Tamura [Taijirō's] idea of a 'liberation from the body by the body,' shared to some extent by all the flesh writers I discuss proves to be a liberation of male bodies (rather than all bodies, as they seem to assume) towards, via, or from, a woman's body."[12] After the war, Abe was plucked from the field of poison women and made heroine by many liberal writers of pulp during this period in literary history. She was portrayed as a transgressive heroine for those espousing postwar liberation and freedom from empire building and totalitarian nationalism. A photo of Abe in the 1949 June edition of the *Monthly Reader* (Gekkan Yomiuri) appears in a four-page photo section called "Heroines of That Time" (Ano koro no hiroin). Depicted is Abe at the age of forty-five, whipping green tea in a traditional tea ceremony. Abe is not a "heroine" for having attempted to clear her name after it had been sullied in "a mountain of erotic books" and retired to Kyoto to learn the traditional art of tea but rather a bold heroine of *that time* who followed her desires during a period of oppressive militarism and oppressively "false" moralities.

In postwar literature, the sexualized, antisocial, and even treacherous Abe Sada represented a hopeful possibility for a break from the past repressive strictures of prewar and wartime morality. Stimulated by the philosophy expressed in the new "decadent" and (existentialist) "carnal" literature *(nikutai bungaku)* appearing in both high-brow and low-brow literary magazines, competing editors of the pulp magazines appealed to a new postwar sensibility or spirit that posited the body and sensation as the basis for meaning, and the female criminal became the ideal figure for representing these ideological claims. The enigmatic lady, Abe, who had spoken of her pleasure publicly before the war with the same kind of conviction of postwar decadent "idealists," intrigued proponents of the new postwar ideology of the body, becoming the darling of postwar writers like Sakaguchi Ango, Oda Sakunosuke, Nagata Mikihiko, and others whose writing was devoted to establishing a new postwar subjectivity.[13]

The addressed reader of the pulp and "carnal" literature was identified (usually by the magazines themselves) as liberated from the oppressive

Figure 10. Photograph of Abe Sada performing a tea ceremony. From the magazine *Gekkan Yomiuri* (June 1949).

morality of the past. Maruyama Masao, in his "From Carnal Literature to Carnal Politics" (Nikutai bungaku kara nikutai seiji made, 1949), uses the loose format of a "dialogue" *(taidan)* in exploring the significance of the development in the postwar period of "carnal literature"—a category that for him encompassed both existentialist literature of the body (*nikutai bungaku* associated most frequently with Tamura Taijirō) and the pulp medium. This fiction of the body became a springboard for discussing the possibility of a successful democracy comprising social organizations that would be governed by citizens invested in their own governmental body. This flippant but imaginative equation of participation in the new government with "carnal" literature would not have been lost on *kasutori* editors who peddled their magazines as not only entertaining but also educational to readers charged with founding a new democratic society.

This purposeful postwar erasure of prewar philosophies in a "return to the body" was expressed most succinctly by Tamura Taijirō, who tenaciously dedicated himself to the portrayal of the sexual and criminal in chaotic, dystopian worlds of the underclass. Tamura's works not only critique prewar and wartime morality but create a utopian vision of a better world, conveyed in his celebrated *Gate of the Flesh* (Nikutai no mon, 1946) but equally in his other literary works. Tamura's disdain for the prevailing stifling moralities, to which, to his chagrin, people clung even in the postwar years, is expressed in his groundbreaking essay "The Flesh Is Human" (Nikutai ga ningen de aru, 1947): "[T]he fundamental element forming the human must be freed. We must undo the various restrictions that squeeze the flesh, to let it breathe naturally like a baby. We must strive for this, and in doing so, we will no doubt learn what a real human is."[14] In this essay, Tamura challenges his fellow citizens to reject social habits and disturb public order: "The people have to evolve and even dare to destroy ready-made morals and regulations. The resulting temporary chaos is not a problem."[15] It is this movement within literature that the historian Victor Koschmann draws on in examining the complicated formation of postwar subjectivity. He describes the role of the fleshly and bodily in the postwar period as connected with a "loss of faith in values, philosophies, and ideologies. . . . For many writers, it was only in the lowest common denominator of human existence that some glimmer of hope for the future could be perceived, and this often meant emphasizing the flesh rather than the spirit."[16] Quoting the cultural critic Tsurumi Shunsuke, Koschmann describes a skeptical postwar generation who believed that "only when the self hurls forth with passion will the world respond with meaning."[17]

The sexual and criminal were portrayed as idealized subjects who had rejected common values and ideologies from even before the postwar years. The marginal, the deviant, and the outcast were described as paragons of the new possibilities for Japan for having hurled themselves into the world of flesh. They now occupied the position of the utopic and became the agents through which the conformist could imagine transforming himself. This romanticization of the marginal symbolized the possibility for the rejection of cultural and ideological encumbrances for even those men in positions of authority during this time of radical national transition from an aggressive, imperial nation to a subordinated national body within the global political sphere. The disintegration of the culturally and ideologically produced masculine ego of the empire is encouraged in the name of the body, especially the deviant female body.

It was in this context, as the "body" and the "transgressive" were celebrated in a burgeoning popular culture, that Abe Sada was treated as an authority on sexual matters and enlightened living. In 1946 a prominent author, Sakaguchi Ango, interviewed Abe for her opinions about female desire, heterosexual love, and the media and followed the interview with an essay praising Abe as a "tender, warm figure of salvation for future generations" for her sincere passion.[18] She embodied for Ango the possibility of a new "morality" that would be based in the logic of the flesh. A fellow "decadent school" *(buraiha)* writer, Oda Sakunosuke, wrote two stories about Abe—"The State of the Times" (Sesō, 1946), and "The Seductress" (Yōfu, 1947). A number of less literary novels about Abe were published the same year. Fuyuki Takeshi wrote *Woman Tearstained in Passion—The Life Led by Abe Sada* (Aiyoku ni nakinureta onna—Abe Sada no tadotta hansei, March 1947) while Funabashi Seiichi penned *A Record of Abe Sada's Behavior* (Abe Sada gyōjō-ki, August 1947). The leading article for the founding edition of the magazine *True Story* (Jitsuwa) in January 1948 featured a number of previously unseen photographs taken at the time of the discovery of Kichi's corpse, with the eye-catching headline "Ero-guro of the century! First Public Release. Pictorial of the Abe Sada Incident." One story about Abe Sada in a pulp magazine, was "Abe Sada no hansei" (Abe Sada's Memoirs of her Youth, September 1947) by Kimura Ichirō, composed of police records and testimony that provided excellent publicity for the inaugural edition of the pioneering pulp magazine *All Bizarre Hunt* (Ōru Ryōki, September 1947). Nagata Mikihiko serialized a novel *True Story: Abe Sada* (Jitsuroku: Abe Osada), the title later changed to *Impassioned Woman of Love* (Jōen ichidai onna), from September 1950 to August 1951. He followed this story with another serial poison woman story about Meiji poison woman Night Storm Okinu, beginning in October 1951.

In *Impassioned Woman,* "Sada" urges women readers to give up their bourgeois attitudes toward love. The novel begins with Sada not as object of storytelling—confessing woman, patient, criminal on trial, and prostitute—but as reader and critic. This inclusion of text claimed to have been written by Abe interrupts the fetishistic gaze of an objectifying narrator common in earlier stories of poison women. In a letter to "Nagata," Sada compares Ihara Saikaku's celebrated fictional work *The Amorous Woman* (Kōshoku ichidai onna, 1684), about the travails of the prostitute Oharu, with the recent plethora of erotic novels in the pulp magazines. Praising Saikaku's portrayal of a woman's sexual life as a wife, secret mistress, and streetwalker, her letter reads, "The genius of that novel pierced me to the bone. Unlike today's vulgar erotic novels, that kind of novel is strikingly moving. It stayed with me for three or four days. . . . You're responsible for making me read that kind of book when, in the style of Sagano's 'Kōshoku-an,'

Figure 11. Cover of pulp *(kasutori)* magazine *All Bizarre Hunt* (O-ru Ryōki) that includes an article about Abe Sada taking Kimura Ichirō to court for libel as well as an advertisement for Kimura's book that ignited her anger, *Sada's Confessions of Love* (Osada irozange), touting it as a "secret history of love and passion" (October 1947).

I was cleansing my soul in Izu's 'Fukiya' while listening to the sound of the wind whistling through the pines from morning till night."[19] Sada makes her own poetic allusions to the similarity of her situation with that of the protagonist in the seventeenth-century *Amorous Woman* while being careful to draw the line between Oharu's experience and her own. Sada empathizes and is moved by Oharu's plight while distinguishing herself from Oharu to remain, in the context of Nagata's story, reader and critic. Unlike most stories about Abe, the narrative does not rely on the trope of revealing the neuroses of the criminal woman or on the idealization of erotic deviance to forward the narrative.

The "Carnality Adrift" chapter of the novel is reflexively introduced with a description of the narrative framework employed: "From here [the story] is written as autobiography." Here Sada controls the narrative and in it she attempts to normalize sex and even so-called perverse sexual behavior by women. Sada states matter-of-factly that she only appeared to be as lascivious as Saikaku's Oharu because most women are not honest about their sexual activities: "I don't think that I'm that different from other women. Most of the women I've known don't confess the truth because they're liars. I still don't know what they mean when they say that I was perverted until about twenty-four or twenty-five. After thirty, I may have done some frightening things with Ishida, but are they really not part of a normal married lifestyle?"[20] Here Sada accuses women of wrongly condemning sexual play as perverse. References to sexual play as a normal part of a couple's existence, couched in the framework of the ambiguous term "conjugal life" (fūfu seikatsu), run throughout the novel with a dramatic conclusion addressed directly to the Conjugal Life reader. Sada admonishes women for being too restrained and circumspect in their relationships:

The relationship between a man and a woman is not something you can read about in a book. It's not that simple. . . . Perhaps I should call it a merging of the spirit and the flesh, though it's absolutely impossible to explain it in words. I know that I won't meet that kind of person again so you won't see me putting on iron sandals to go out searching for him; but in the one in a million chance that a man like Ishida were in this world, I would gladly throw myself into the inferno, risking even becoming a female devil or being turned into a witch. Attempts to delve into the spirit and the flesh by ordinary women, even in relationships as a married couple, have been too timid. I may sound presumptuous but it seems to me that women don't savor even half the joys of the body. Men and women can be in love enough to want to die together. The life most worth living lies in the arduously researched life of passion, and the discovery of a pleasure, which can be two or three times the intensity of what you've ever experienced before. People often laugh that what I did was too extreme. But for the sake of love [aijō], for the love between a couple, and for building a harmonious society, isn't it necessary to grapple earnestly with problems of love and desire? With that, Professor Nagata and readers, I bid you good-bye.[21]

Sada exhorts couples to dedicate themselves to the pursuit of sexual pleasure, encouraging women to recognize and express their desire as a normal part of life. The reward for a woman's free expression of her desire is nothing less than a "harmonious society." Nagata forwards the concerns of liberal postwar thinkers through the voice of Sada. The female criminal is successfully deployed in romanticizing the rejection of cultural and ideological encumbrances. This is only one of many examples of the way in which Abe's crime of passion emerged as a popular touchstone for exploring a new postwar subjectivity and its concomitant celebration of the body and the flesh as a response to the prewar repressive morality and government. Oda Sakunosuke parodies this popular interest in the criminal woman in his second story of Abe, "The Times."

Satire of the Fetishizing Writer: Oda Sakunosuke's "The Times"

Oda Sakunosuke's "The Times" (Sesō) satirizes the frenzied attention to the amoral, sexual woman of so many pulp stories. The reportage-inflected story by a bedraggled writer, "Oda," infatuated with the idea of writing about a sexual and criminal woman, Sada, takes place among the panoply of prostitutes and black marketeers of wartime and postwar Osaka. The unsuccessful attempts of a wandering "Oda" to capture in language the amorous woman bind together various vignettes of misfits inhabiting the Osaka underworld. Early in the story "Oda" recalls his first experience with a sexually aggressive woman named Shizuko. Student "Oda" recalls lying quietly with his back to Shizuko when "a white arm twined around my neck, and suddenly my ear was being kissed. What followed was all a dream: the distinctive odor of bodies, the moist sensations, breathless warmth, squirming, the arms and legs going every which way, the rhythm that drove me senseless . . . how could I have been so stupid as to think that a woman merely lies there grudgingly and lets herself be manipulated!"[22] "Oda" becomes hopelessly infatuated with Shizuko but is disconcerted to find that she has other lovers. In order to control his jealousy he denigrates Shizuko by comparing her to Sada. His solution for getting over Shizuko is to freeze in language the metonym for female sexual desire—Sada: "I had been astounded at the wild, abandoned sex life of Terui Shizuko. But compared to the sex life of this woman Sada, Shizuko's was like a cheap little pair of pajamas displayed alongside a long slinky undergarment. And here I thought I saw a way to free myself from my jealousy over Shizuko's escapades. I thought I could do it by writing the story of Sada."[23] A frustrated "Oda," however, soon finds that not only is he unable to write Sada's story but the female body and psychology are hard to master, impossible to represent in balanced form: "You can take a round egg and trim it until it's square, but the parts you trimmed off still remain. . . . [E]ach time you are surprised all over again at the secrets of a woman's physical makeup."[24]

"Oda" again tries to capture Sada in writing but is left with mere cliché: "I thought that if I could write the story of Sada's youthful wanderings and the trick that fate had played on her, I could give expression to the pity that surrounds a woman's existence."[25] "Oda" eventually turns from his failed attempt at portraying Sada to a different woman—this time a geisha at a bar he frequents. In the final paragraphs of the story, "Oda's" gaze alights on a quiet young woman, the sister of the madam of Dice café, who elicits "Oda's" sympathy as he stares at her from across the bar: "As she disappeared behind the partition, her figure dressed in a chilly-looking garment of purple *meisen* silk, I thought to myself that if I wrote about anyone, it would surely be about her."[26] Each fanciful fantasy of a sexual woman ends in disappointment and self-dissatisfaction with his inability to capture the demure woman in writing.

Oda's fictional reportage about the lives of impoverished urban denizens of Osaka has led people like Sakaguchi Ango to identify within his work a drive to write a "language of the body." Addressing Oda directly, Ango writes: "I am certain that future literature rests upon the discovery of the language *[kotoba]* of the thinking body and that with this discovery of truth, for the first time, it will be possible to have new truthful morals. But this should not be an easy road. Oda, it shouldn't be easy."[27] For Ango, writing literature of a "bodily logic"—the "truth of flesh and blood"—means ridding oneself of desire for "pragmatic expedience" or the "wholesome." It requires understanding the logic of the physical.[28] In "The Times," the desire to write a "logic of the body" becomes the object of commentary within the story itself. The author's interest in writing about female sexuality is born of a desire to reject the philosophical. However, through the whimsical combination of fictional anecdote and first-person narration, "Oda" becomes uncomfortably aware that this desire to write about the female body is not necessarily related to a conscious intellectualized rejection of "ideas." In a playful dialogue between "Oda" and his wife, the writer questions his own interest in the miserable world of the criminal and prostitute:

"Another murder story?" said my wife with a look of disgust.

"What do you mean—another? Oh yes—'Ten-sen Geisha' ends with a murder, doesn't it."

"And you're always saying you want to write something about that awful Abe Sada case too. How *grorotic*!"

My wife described my writings by the English words "grotesque" and "erotic." "Grorotic" was a word she had coined by combining the two. It was meant to emphasize the fact that she found my stories highly unsavory.

"Yes, and I still want to write it! I'm thinking of calling it 'The Enchantress.' It will probably be the greatest thing I've ever written!"

With a scornful laugh, my wife went downstairs. That was just as well. If she had asked me why I wanted to write about Abe Sada, I'd have been hard put for an answer.[29]

While Oda did write a story entitled "The Enchantress" (Yōfu, 1947), in this satirical depiction, the details of a writer who is himself the most pitiful character in the story make explicit the fetishistic and obtrusive nature of the contemporary discourse of the flesh *(nikutai)*.

A useful example of the type of fetishistic writing that Oda was parodying is Kimura Ichirō's *The Amorous Woman of Shōwa: Confessions of Sada* (Shōwa kōshoku ichidai onna: Osada irozange, 1947). In an article run in the pulp magazine *All Bizarre,* Kimura portrayed Abe as a vixen who produced a sexual terror that made her infinitely desirable. Kimura was a frequent contributor to pulp magazines with articles on "sexual perversion" *(hentai seiyoku)* describing sadomasochistic practices in Europe, treatises on "free love," and serialized modern versions of classical erotic stories. Presumably he was attracted to the Abe Sada incident for its associations with sadomasochistic practices. The novel is based on courtroom testimonies and postwar stories about the incident. Written in the form of an autobiography with intervening commentary by people who had been romantically involved with Abe or subpoenaed for her trial, the novel also includes a rare glimpse of Abe's father, who had abandoned Abe at a brothel when she was young so that she might mend her lascivious ways or at least get paid for her sexual activity. The novel moves chronologically through her various sex-related jobs working as a waitress, escort, and *jokyū,* intermittently employing the same medical logic of the 1930s in enticing statements promising that the "truth" of her life could be gleaned through careful attention to the physical body and its drives. The epigraph to chapter 2 begins, "Is she wildly sexual, oversexed, or perverted? What is the nature of the human instinct?" A later question introduces the problem of nature versus nurture: "Did the environment control her or was she born to be a flirtatious girl?" The author, posing as confessor and analyst, commented on his position in the writing of the story as an observer who "didn't want to despise or distort raw human instinct of even homicidal feelings. . . . [or] deliberately glorify the protagonist who exhausted the limits of romantic infatuation *[jōchi]*."[30]

In furthering an image of Abe as vixen, *Confessions of Sada* introduced the "testimony" of a past lover: "She wasn't satisfied with less than three or four times a night. She couldn't rest if my hand wasn't moving all night long. . . . When I was with her, she wouldn't wave knives around or toy with poison, saying that she would kill me or let me live, or that I would live or die. She was a greatly oversexed, seductive type of woman—the kind of terrifying woman men love."[31] In this expression of masochistic love the speaker willingly, happily, encourages a fantasy of sexual fright that he projects onto the desiring woman, and his description of Sada's arousing, indeed inspiring, frightfulness portrayed through negation ("she wouldn't wave knives around," "she wouldn't toy with poison," "she wouldn't threaten") suggests more strongly the very possibility of those acts. It is this excitable masochistic desire expressed cursorily here in *Confessions of Sada* that is at the core of later films and plays about Abe written in the 1970s and discussed below.

The occupation-era novel *Confessions of Sada* so incensed its heroine that it brought Abe out of hiding to level a defamation case against its author. Abe shocked the public by giving up her pseudonym and new identity provided by the authorities upon her release from jail to take the author and its publishing company to court for character defamation. In the interview with Sakaguchi Ango, Abe revealed her feelings toward her reemergence in the postwar media:

> About two months after the war, in a discussion of . . . the year 1936, the February 26 incident was brought up and then me. Then the newspapers picked up the story again. . . . I was really upset that they were still talking about me, but I could have put up with it if the story hadn't shown up in *Liberal* [Liberaru] and other magazines and been discussed on the radio that summer. Then it came out in hardback and got me really angry. If they had written about my real feelings I wouldn't have minded, but all they write about is how I flirted with men.[32]

Abe's ire was also raised by the fact that she had never "repented" of her crime, nor had she "confessed" (which hints at a mood of "repentance") as the title and use of first-person narrative in the story suggested. She had merely talked openly and freely about the circumstances leading up to the crime.

Oda's satirical "The Times" formalistically undoes this kind of fetishizing narrative by eradicating the "voice" of the femme fatale or any authoritative narrative voice. The story is devoid of a mastering narrative. A number of anecdotes are only loosely tied together by the narrating "Oda"—a writer in postwar Japan flashing back to the prewar and war years for fictional material. The murder of a dance hall girl, the antics of an impoverished gambler, and the misplaced sexual advances of the older madam of the Dice café are woven together for the plural experience of the sexual and criminal, not just that of the femme fatale. The reader can wander among the narratives much like the characters and their narrator, slowly picking their way through postwar rubble. Masao Miyoshi makes the intriguing proposition that the café's name, "Dice," suggests Oda's own philosophy of composition, "namely that the narrative ought to remain without closure, with all its elements left to chance and accident. . . . Oda believes in the chance form, rejecting the authorial interpretive will that imposes its control on the work."[33] The author is no longer the authority. He no longer knows what is at the core of the female criminal by looking at appearances. He cannot be a valid source of evidential knowledge. Rather he is exposed as an obsessive admirer. "Oda's" failure to write the story of Sada produces in the story a lack of closure that effectively interrupts the narrative fixated on the sexual woman common to pulp magazines in which the desirous, transgressive woman is the undemanding object of narrative pleasure. The voyeuristic fascination with Sada is decentered with the duplicating presence not only of other sex workers but especially with the comical narrator, whose gloomy experience functions as a critique of the drive to fantasize and idolize the imagined impassioned female criminal. Author Oda effectively takes the literary spotlight off of the female criminal and shines it on the fetishistic, self-marginalizing male.

Why Perversion Is Not Subversion:
Tanaka Noboru's *The True Story of Abe Sada* and Ōshima Nagisa's *In the Realm of the Senses*

The impassioned male who submits himself to the sexual and dangerous woman is at the core of Ōshima Nagisa's film *In the Realm of the Senses* (Ai no koriida, 1976), which continues the practice of featuring the admiring masochistic male, though more explicitly. The focus of this feature-length film is Ishida Kichizō, the masochistic victim of Abe who unwittingly carried the logic of devotion to a sexually powerful woman to its bitter end. Surprisingly little attention was paid to Ishida in the trial or early stories about Abe despite the interest in sadomasochism at the time in psychoanalytic studies. *In the Realm of the Senses,* however, like so many postwar texts based on the Abe Sada incident, introduces the male masochist who serves an allegorizing function in the narrative. Male masochism is cultivated as symbolic of the complete rejection of political and imperial power through the juxtapositioning of two types of men—the imperial soldier of the February 26 incident, which was an armed uprising in Tokyo organized by members of the Imperial Army's First Division by 1,400 soldiers who called for direct imperial rule, and the devoted lover. Abe herself, in discussion with Ango, recalled hearing a radio show declaring her arrest in May of 1936 and the February 26 incident of the same year as important for understanding the era. Sekine Hiroshi's poem "Abe Sada" (1971) begins with a reference to this attempted military coup, which occurred three months before Kichi's murder. The first-person voice of Sada introduces the surprisingly subdued poem: "The February 26 incident / gave rise to war / the year of my incident / gave rise to a love not yet over."[34] In citing the February 26 incident in conjunction with the Abe Sada incident, Sekine draws a contrast between the men who have devoted themselves to the imperial state and the man who devoted himself to the free pursuit of pleasure in the boudoir.

The two incidents are juxtaposed even more explicitly in two films about Abe Sada: *The True Story of Abe Sada* (Jitsuroku Abe Sada, 1975), directed by Tanaka Noboru, and the aforementioned *In the Realm of the Senses*. Both clearly develop the image of Ishida as social and political rebel. In an early scene in *The True Story of Abe Sada,* Sada watches military soldiers march by and then closes the shutters. When a maid tries to open them, Sada forbids her, saying, "The outside light disturbs us." The devotion of Kichizō to Sada (and not to the burgeoning empire) is illustrated in his dress. Throughout the film, he wears only Sada's red undergarment. Even in outdoor scenes, Kichizō wears only her red robe. He has so withdrawn from society that he needs only the lingerie she provides him in her absence. Otherwise he is nearly always half-naked in the film. As illustrated in figure 12, especially in comparison to Ōshima's shot of a similar scene, in Tanaka's film the outside political world of imperial Japan remains distant. The imperial nation is symbolically marked in a long shot when Sada looks down upon the soldiers marching down the street. In contrast, medium and close-up shots of the couple in the first half of Tanaka's film predominate. The two exist in a private, exclusive world of sexual play that becomes an irresistible web for Kichizō, symbolized grotesquely in a scene in which, lonely for Sada (who has gone out to retrieve money from a patron) he pulls apart a clump of Sada's combed-out strands of hair from a tissue, stretches it out like a spider's web, and licks it. The perpetrator of the murder in this film is less the jealous lover than Kichizō, who is resentful of any time that Sada spends with other patrons, even if it is to procure money for their extravagances. When Sada erupts in anger at Kichizo's

Figure 12. Soldiers seen from the boudoir. From Tanaka Noboru (director), *Jitsuroku Abe Sada* (The true story of Abe Sada) (1975).

Figure 13. Watching the soldiers. From *Jitsuroku Abe Sada*.

suggestion that he go home to his wife, Kichizō quickly backs down. He gives himself over to Sada completely, seemingly aware that she plans to murder him. In this way, Kichizō is portrayed as a submissive man wearing the robes of a woman against a backdrop of masculine soldiers in starched uniforms dedicated to the state and the emperor.

Nevertheless, while Tanaka's film, which predated Ōshima's, juxtaposes the devoted lover with the imperial soldier, it is ultimately interested in Sada's biography. Close-ups and medium shots of the couple are replaced, in the second half of the film, with flashbacks of Sada's childhood accompanied with a voice-over of "Sada" describing her past, and long shots of Sada eluding police in cars and on foot. Thus, while Tanaka earlier than Ōshima juxtaposed Kichizō with the military in his film, and gives some attention to Kichizō as masochistic lover, Tanaka ultimately rejects Kichizō as central figure in the film. The romantic, sexually explicit film *In the Realm of the Senses* dramatically affirms the pursuit of masochistic pleasure and complete withdrawal from society as a laudable response to a country on the brink of war. The masochistic lover Kichizō is politicized as an anti-authoritarian rebel for his rejection of male privilege and power. His devotion to a domineering mistress is most clearly expressed in a scene in

Figure 14. Wearing Sada's robes. From *Jitsuroku Abe Sada*.

Figure 15. Kichizō examining Sada's web of hair. From *Jitsuroku Abe Sada*.

which Kichizō in *yukata* robe and sandals, saunters down a narrow street opposite but in very close proximity to a stream of soldiers in starched uniforms parading before cheering crowds waving the Japanese imperial flag. Kichizō represents a challenge to the rigorous social order for his rejection of male privilege and selfless devotion in serving a woman's every desire. "Perversion" is privileged to critique a military economy that makes no room for pleasure, though another narrative depicting both incidents by Satō Makoto (discussed later) suggests that the imperialist militarist machine itself produces a kind of masochistic pleasure.

The spectacle of male masochistic pleasure featured throughout this film enables an implicit critique of normative codes in imperial Japan of the 1930s when the incident took place. Through the figure of the male masochistic lover who willingly sacrifices himself to the fancies of his sadistic lover outside the institution of marriage and reproduction in a colonialist era, the film *In the Realm of the Senses* celebrates the man who rejects the bourgeois system, which ensures its own survival through sexual repression and familial ideology. He happily wraps himself in Sada's clothes. The scene in which a nearly nude Kichizō appears to chase after a train carrying Sada is a romantic depiction of a man liberated by the erotic love of a sexually aggressive woman.

Critique of Japanese politics is not foreign to Ōshima. The inclusion in his *Cruel Story of Youth* (Seishun zankoku monogatari, 1960) of actual and staged documentary footage of anti–U.S.–Japan security treaty demonstrations in 1960 and his criticism of the treatment of Koreans in Japan and the death penalty in *Death by Hanging* (Kōshikei, 1968) are only two examples of Ōshima's filmic critiques of Japanese political agendas. In his films, the romantic portraits of the pursuit of pleasure constitute a filmic critique of imperialist and capitalist systems. The problem with many of Ōshima's early films, however, is that they attempt to criticize social and political authority through an uncritical romanticized, oppressive, and even

Figure 16. Kichizō walking against soldiers. From Ōshima Nagisa (director), *Ai no koriida* (In the realm of the senses) (1976).

Figure 17. Kichizō and soldiers. From *Ai no koriida*.

Figure 18. Kichizō wrapped in kimono. From *Ai no koriida*.

Figure 19. Sada next to train window. From *Ai no koriida*.

Figure 20. Kichizō running after Sada's train. From *Ai no koriida*.

violent male who possesses, violates, and ultimately annihilates his object of desire in the assertion of an anti-authoritarian position. This uncritical tendency is most apparent in *Cruel Story of Youth,* a film that is surprisingly unselfconscious in its celebration of a particular kind of sadistic masculinity that is rebellious and resourceful in its denial of authority. *Cruel Story of Youth* opens with its hero Kiyoshi waving at a friend participating in an anti–U.S.–Japan security treaty demonstration. This delinquent student later that evening saves a young woman, Makoto, from the unwanted sexual advances of an older man. This would-be hero undoes his good deed by driving Makoto out to a lonely location to rape her on a wide log floating amid thousands of others in an aquatic lumberyard—an industrial floating world. After rushing her out to this lonely location in a motorboat, prominent in so many "sun-tribe" *(taiyōzoku)* films of disaffected youth, Kiyoshi pushes Makoto into the water, aware that she cannot swim, until she "agrees" to have sex with him. The critical sting is submerged in this abusive scene of physical power when she turns to him afterward to ask in a wistful tone whether he likes her or not. Greeted with the affirming grunts of this affected youth, she closes her eyes peacefully, happy in her new romance.

Social revolt in this early Ōshima film seems to require compulsive misogynistic behavior. The expression of youthful rebellion through the rape of a sexually inexperienced girl by a playboy was not new to cinema in 1960 when *Cruel Story of Youth* was filmed. The sun-tribe films of the 1950s had also used the scene of a rape to illustrate the angst of disaffected youths. The narrative effect of Ōshima's rape scene in *Cruel Story of Youth* as representative of youthful alienation and rebellion of a culture within a culture—the world of the decadent versus bourgeois living—is undermined by the hokey sentimentality of the girl who can hardly wait to cohabit with her abuser. In an otherwise quiet scene in which he watches over his girlfriend while she is under anesthesia after an abortion he demands she undergo, Kiyoshi contemplates their situation while crunching noisily on a green apple in a very long take. He appears sentimental in this scene, though this brief moment of contemplation contrasts sharply with previous scenes of reckless and violent abandon. That Makoto underwent the abortion while he attempted sex with a rival's girlfriend who was kicked down the stairs by her jealous boyfriend is depicted as another sign of the youth's resistance to the kind of domestic love his girlfriend seeks.

The heroically sadistic males in Ōshima's films have been defanged through a number of interpretive strategies. Maureen Turim's strategy in writing about violence against women in Ōshima is to recuperate the multiple interpretations she finds in these scenes of violence. While she recognizes that Ōshima films are not free of exploitative representations of women, she holds that because they offer multiple readings, and because they are framed through modernist filmmaking practices, we should accord them value. In *Cruel Story of Youth* the rape scene is considered one of many scenes of violence, some perpetuated by Makoto herself in the form of pyrotechnic play, that punctuate the film with sensual, visual explosions symbolizing the couple's sense of alienation. Turim, along with Joan Mellen, also asserts that the depiction of violence against women is an inspired critique of patriarchy. Certainly the depiction of violence against women is a common mode for critiquing unequal social relations, but in this film violence and cruelty as a metaphor for alienation does not wholly explain Makoto's emotion. The pain inflicted by Kiyoshi, perhaps because it is so "real" in a corrupt world, inspires within her deep, romantic feelings. Violence oddly inspires feelings of romantic love and the desire to create a family. Furthermore, the perpetrator of that abuse is a handsome rebel—a romanticized masculine ideal whose rejection of romantic love increases his desirability. In this sense, Ōshima's early film is surprisingly unself-conscious in its celebration of a particular kind of sadistic masculinity even while it may be using that sadistic masculinity to critique violence against women. *Cruel Story of Youth,* much as it tries to illustrate the "awakening" of a girl to a nontraditional lifestyle, is unsuccessful. Ōshima's early encodings of women are uncourageous and unambitiously standard. They are bearers of a lost love ideal.

Ōshima's contribution to gender politics is not as a feminist filmmaker but rather as an astute reader of the postwar male ego in an increasingly wealthy, bureaucratic world in which Japan is a pawn of global American power. His early films embody not the spirit of the age but the spirit of the male youth of the age and the sort of violence that this emasculated state can perpetuate. Though the films seem interested in romanticizing the rejection of cultural and ideological encumbrances, Ōshima unwittingly illustrates the misogynistic rebel as primarily concerned with self-cohesion. The rejection of the maternal—a repudiation out of a fear that feminine warmth and sensuality will disintegrate the self—typifies the rebellious male youth mentality in his films.

This discussion of Ōshima's *Cruel Story of Youth* serves as comparative prelude to an alternative vision of masculinity in his *In the Realm of the Senses* in which the rebel is not angry or misogynistic but self-effacing and generous. Lover Kichizō gives himself over fully to women's desires—not only Sada's but those of other women in the film, such as an old woman Sada tells Kichizō to make love to, and who urinates on him from the pleasure she experiences. In comparison to *Cruel Story of Youth*, which does not alter usual gender relations in which woman is subordinate within the power structure, *In the Realm of the Senses* flips the usual gender power structure. The male masochist undermines the socializing functions that are in service to a masculinist, totalitarian culture.

Ōshima depicts the perversion of male masochism as a critical force much in the way that Marcuse celebrated sexual transgression as a challenge to the foundation of a repressive society, which equates and enforces the normal, the socially useful, and the good:

> Against a society that employs sexuality as means for a useful end, the perversions uphold sexuality as an end in itself; they thus place themselves outside the dominion of the performance principle and challenge its very foundation. They establish libidinal relationships which society must ostracize because they threatened to reverse the process of civilization which turned the organism into an instrument of work.[35]

In Marcusean fashion, *In the Realm of the Senses* capitalizes on the Abe Sada incident to critique imperial Japanese society by showing "perversion" to be that romantic thing that society wrongly rejects as emasculating and therefore disruptive to patriarchal society. One well-known theorist of masochism, Gilles Deleuze, elaborates on the anti-patriarchal nature of the male masochist as one who does not seek to be integrated into the phallic order. In his highly provocative essay on the subject, he defines the masochistic psychology as the rejection of the paternal for the maternal ego, which produces a pleasurable discontinuity of the ego through having an incestuous relationship with the mother, whose castration is disavowed. By disavowing the castration of the mother, the male refuses to mature in the way the Oedipal subject is supposed to. He enters into a contractual alliance with a cruel woman and thereby ensures that the father will be exiled from his fantasy since he (the "son") has not entered into the usual "healthy" patriarchal relationship: "Finally, he ensures that he will be beaten; we have seen that what is beaten, humiliated and ridiculed in him is the image and the likeness of the father, and the possibility of the father's aggressive return. . . . The masochist thus liberates himself in preparation for a rebirth in which the father will have no part."[36] To become a man, for the masochist, does not mean to take the father's place or to assume the father's symbolic mandate: instead, "it consists in obliterating his role and his likeness in order to generate the new man."[37] The ego is "liberated" from Oedipal maturation as long as it is tied to the pre-Oedipal mother. In this Deleuzean model, masochism, which marks the failure by the son to respond to the paternal symbolic mandate, is explicitly performed and "flaunted" so that the failure of this mandate is rehearsed to become a "critical practice."[38] Ōshima's masochism of *In the Realm of the Senses* is very similar to Deleuze's model of masochism. Kichizō relinquishes the masculine subject position in his disinclination to support the imperial army. More important, he abases himself by performing tasks given to him by Sada, which are literally performed before others, such as making love to an elderly geisha or making love to Sada in the garden while a housekeeper sweeps nearby. These indulgent acts directed by Sada are presented as a private challenge to the "health" of the imperial body. While Ōshima's film is not an explicit philosophical working out of masochistic psychology, the masochist is deployed to critique usual gender and sexual relations by inverting them: by placing man on the bottom rather than the top, by making Sada the "breadwinner," and by showing Kichizō to be out of the capitalist loop, gaining access to capital only through marriage. The premise is that patriarchal Oedipal relations are the norm and a man's rejection of these usual relations makes him subversive. The male masochist becomes a primary site for critiquing the totalitarian system of imperialism and bourgeois puritanical sexuality because it affirms a radical inversion of that sexual morality in which heterosexuality with man "on top" is the norm.

By unveiling the penis in a very literal fashion in this sexually explicit film, and doing it within the context of a critique of militaristic masculinity, Ōshima purports to be unveiling the phallus. But in rewriting the violence of Sada's act and turning her sadistic lovemaking into a story of romantic love, *In the Realm of the Senses* ultimately denies the inversion of usual patriarchal relations by presenting Kichizō as allowing Sada to expel paternal law—exactly the role that the masochist plays in Deleuze's articulation of the libidinal psychology. I am inclined to agree with Mandy Merck that this comforting type of masochism is a result of romantic expulsion of sadism by the woman from the discussion.[39] Treating the top girl as the recipient of a green light undoes the (terrifying) power that the sadistic woman can represent, as the earlier manifestations of the hysteria-provoking poison woman could. Ōshima's Sada cannot be identified with a usurpation of the law (Oedipal, social, or otherwise)—despite any subverting of the usual Oedipalized relations in sex—because she still resides in the position of unempowered woman earning her keep through one of the only lines of work available to her at this point in her life, prostitution. Sex in the bedroom does not alleviate the lack of economic and social power outside the bedroom, which manifests itself in Kichizō's suggestion that he return home for a while and set Sada up as his mistress in an apartment. Peter Lehman has claimed that Ōshima's filming of the penis/phallus in this film is contradictory. While Ōshima avoids the spectacle of the penis, in the final scene the "visual spectacle associated with the penis, so carefully avoided by Ōshima, returns with a vengeance at a critical moment of sexual tension. . . . and ultimately *In the Realm of the Senses* remains caught in a contradictory critique of the phallus. Could a man's desire that a woman would want a penis as a keepsake lie entirely outside a phallocentric order?"[40] Lehman suggests that the film finally does not avoid the usual spectacularity of male power through erection scenes found in sex films. Despite Kichizō's presumed escape from the phallic order, it is reasserted for him.[41] I would suggest that whether the penis or the phallus, the Deleuzian argument, which would champion masochism as the realm of matriarchal law through the disavowal of the female castration, does not work here because Sada is homicidally invested in owning the physical, material penis, which she can only achieve through a sadistic act.

A Paradise Lost: Watanabe Jun'ichi's Portrait of a Masochist

Another masochist modeled explicitly after Ishida appeared in Watanabe Jun'ichi's *Paradise Lost* (Shitsurakuen, 1997). Originally serialized in the *Economic Newspaper* (Nikkei Shinbun) *Paradise Lost* treats the Abe Sada incident as a love story through the tale of an affair of two entwined lovers, Kūki and Rinko, who model their lovemaking after Sada and Kichizō. The couple in this drama, especially successful Kūki, is depicted as nothing short of heroic for cutting themselves off from the day-to-day routine of work and home and eventually life itself. The first mention of the Abe Sada incident occurs during the couple's adulterous tryst at Lake Chuzenji:

> Rinko turned toward him nestling close. "My God, that was incredible."
> For Kūki it had been no less so. "I almost died," he said. "Just a little more. . ."
> She nodded. "Now you know what I mean, when I say I'm scared."
> Yes, she did sometimes say that. So this is what she meant. He retraced the contours of the experience in his mind, then thought of something else. "Kichizō said the same thing."

"Who?"

"The man strangled by Abe Sada." Images of the two lovers floated through his mind, based on what he'd read.

Rinko's interest was caught. Her voice still sounding exhausted, she repeated, "Abe Sada? The woman who did that grotesque thing?"

"It wasn't especially grotesque."

"She mutilated her lover and then killed him, didn't she?"

She knew only the sensational aspects of the case. Kūki, having read up on it in some detail, saw it rather as a deeply human incident between a man and a woman hopelessly in love. "She was misrepresented in the media." He nudged away the lantern, and added quietly in the half-light, "She did cut it off, but that was after she strangled him, not before."

"A woman strangling a man?"

"She'd done it often enough before, during sex. Like you, just now."

Rinko immediately shook her head and clung to his chest. "I only did it because I love you, I love you so much I can't stand it, I almost hate you."[42]

As the couple's relationship deepens, Rinko becomes more sadistic in lovemaking while her lover Kūki submits himself increasingly to her wishes. The couple withdraws further and further from normal society. Kūki abandons his job and wife and Rinko leaves her husband. Feeling that this world has little to offer, they determine to leave it.

This popular serial's initial primary readership, since it was run in the *Economic Newspaper,* was likely businessmen who read it on the train to and from work. Certainly it can be read as a male fantasy of romantic submission based on the Abe Sada incident in which a man who rejects social position, prestige, and wealth is deeply loved and heroic. Kūki gradually becomes delinquent in his work and inattentive to his family. Demoted at work, he finally quits his company and married life to devote himself fully to Rinko and her desires. This series of decisions is portrayed romantically as an impressive act of rebellion. The woman he loves, Rinko, is transgressively dominant in sex, but now he is a rebel in his own right on an ideological level for giving up power and privilege to succumb to the wishes of his sadistic lover. Both heroically reside in a liminal space at the margins of society. Watanabe's novel, like Ōshima's film, pits sexuality and male masochistic desire against political and social privilege. In both reinterpretations of the Abe Sada incident, male masochism is the romanticized rejection of patriarchal privilege.

The dominant woman Rinko who models herself after Abe is heroic because she enables the male to assume a countervalent position. She is essentially used in the narrative for this very purpose; that is, to create an oppositional, antisocial position for her male lover. The sexual dominatrix who convinces Kūki to commit suicide becomes heroine to the aspiring bad boy because she has enabled him to reject patriarchal privilege even while he is the fantastical lover of her dreams. This familiar unconscious fetishization of the transgressive woman defangs any disruptive potential of the sadistic woman. The deaths of Kūki and Kichizō are the deaths of men who have specifically accepted this position, making them potent actors rather than subordinated victims. This kind of portrayal of the Abe Sada incident makes the murder of a man by a woman much easier to take culturally because she is considered to have been driven by love and he a willing participant.

Both of these texts of the Abe Sada incident replicate occupation-era fetishization of the sexually transgressive, violent woman "of the flesh" who became representative of the desire to renounce the patriarchal power of imperial Japan and who provided an alternative masculine identity. The male masochist and worshipper of the violent woman has been motivated to articulate a kind of celebratory critique of dominant ideologies informing masculinity and patriarchy. This romantic idealization of dominant womanhood, which had no basis in reality, enabled the fantasy of an anti-authoritarian, anti-imperialist Japanese masculinity and perpetuated a fantastical ideal that the sexualized woman herself could resist dominant forms of power. An alternative reading of masochism within a framework that is not limited to maintaining the fetishized woman as other might disable this fetishization of the sexual woman as subversive other (rather than objectified fantasy), and it is with this idea that I turn to Satō Makoto's *Abe Sada's Dogs*. In *Dogs*, male masochism is not the other to dominant patriarchal structures but the very source of it.

Abe Sada's Dogs and Taking It Like a Man: Abe Sada vs. the Emperor

Satō Makoto's unromantic parody of masochistic love, *Abe Sada's Dogs*, is one of at least four major works about Abe Sada to be published, filmed, or performed in the years between 1968 and 1976 and to refer directly to the February 26 incident.[43] This avant-garde play enables a different conceptualization of masochism. In *Dogs*, masochism is the libidinal fantasmatic *supporting* the phallic order, not disrupting it. Masochism does not compromise masculine power. Rather, it is shown to *perpetuate* forms of patriarchal dominance. Within a Deleuzean conceptualization that treats masochism as anti-Oedipal, this would be an impossibility. Nevertheless, in

Dogs, masochistic psychology and behavior are shown to support the hierarchy girding fascistic social and political relations. This conflation of male masochism with imperial power in *Dogs* suggests that patriarchal relations are supported by and evolve out of a desire to be dominated (and guilty).[44] The play counters any notion that masochistic desire displaces patriarchal relations, suggesting rather that it is fundamental to such a structure, especially in its exaggerated form in militarism.

The masochistic male subjectivity, which Ōshima used to animate social noncomformity, Satō uses to animate military conformity. The masochist is portrayed as *perpetuating* totalizing systems of war rather than being exterior to them. It is not the depraved dilettante but the rabidly devoted imperial soldier who experiences the pleasures of the debauched in his position as servant to the imperial sovereign—his beloved imperial "dominatrix" on whom he bestows the ritual cry of love in death: *Tennō heika banzai!*—Long Live the Emperor! The masochistic male submits to another, but not counterhegemonically. This new portrayal of masochism takes "perversion" out of the realm of the nonhegemonic (or that which subverts the hegemonic) and places "perversion" at the heart of fascistic hegemony. The usual understanding of perversion—that it subverts order— that "it puts the body and the world of objects to uses that have nothing whatever to do with any kind of 'immanent' design or purpose"—is undermined.[45] In *Dogs,* perversion is at the heart of empire.

Dogs is one play of a trilogy spanning Shōwa era (1926–89) colonialist history entitled *The World of Comedic Shōwa* (Kigeki Shōwa no sekai), the early part of which represented the most violent colonialist activity in Japan's modern history. The play was performed by Satō's Black Tent (Kuro Tento) troupe, which broached political and intellectual questions in imaginative experimental theater.[46] It is perhaps easiest to describe this complicated avant-garde play via an interpretation offered by the Japanese theater scholar of the underground or "little" theater (*angura* or *shōgeki*) movement, David Goodman, who worked with the Black Tent troupe that performed this play. Goodman finds the play's core to reside with the "Photographer" *(Shashinshi)* who acts as protector of "Safety Razor Township." The two dangerous and intervening forces who threaten to challenge the Photographer are a suicidal young man, Chitose Shōchikubai (a name that contains within it the Sino-Japanese characters for millennium and pine-bamboo-plum, which in Japanese tradition signify longevity), and "I" *(Atashi),* who is revealed early in the play to be "Abe Sada." Sada and Shōchikubai each carry a bundle wrapped in a purple fabric scarf. Sada's bundle initially holds Kichizō's penis while Shōchikubai's carries a pistol. Goodman argues that Kichizō's penis signifies the (Photographer's) fear of castration and the gun signifies the (Photographer's) fear of revolt.[47] The play broadly revolves around how these two scarves get exchanged—how a woman gets armed and the Photographer can disarm menacing sources of rebellion with an awkward assemblage of ragtag troops.

If *Dogs* is concerned with the question of hegemony and personal power, the epigraph, from Walter Benjamin's "Thesis on the Philosophy of History," reveals Satō's impetus to rewrite Japan's imperial history: "A historical materialist cannot do without the notion of a present which is not a transition, but in which time stands still and has come to a stop. For this notion defines the present in which he himself is writing history. Historicism gives the 'eternal' image of the past; historical materialism supplies a unique experience with the past."[48] A timeless history disregards its author; an author who ignores his subjective engagement with history risks writing myth. *Dogs* perverts the historical perspective of the Japanese empire by distorting this monumental imperial history signified by the imperial era name Shōwa through absurdist theater. Satō's characters are not merely symbolic. He creates a linguistic space permeated by multidimensionality, which was part of a new temporal and linguistic philosophy he developed in the 1960s. Just as other avant-garde playwrights were using absurdist language and action as an alternative to social realism, which they found to be ineffectual, Satō was developing his own theatrical aesthetic, stating, "I painfully felt the sensitivity *[binkonsa]* of leftist language. I felt that it was no better than conservative language or tradition. Thus, I willed the construction of a theatre of linguistic art *[gengo geijutsu]*." Satō uses the term *jūsōteki hyōgen* to describe a sort of expression that is "multilayered" in order to write a history that is multidimensional.[49]

The new little theater movement of the late 1960s and 1970s *(shōgekijō undō)* was a movement to replace the realist new theater *(shingeki)* that featured tragedy as a common narrative form. The movement grew out of a response to the failure of modern political movements to provide forms for action and being. It also represented a shift away from theater practices that perpetuated orthodox Marxist politics tied to prewar modern realist theater. Influenced by Brecht, who felt that the task of theater was not only to spread ideas but to entertain, the playwrights of this movement broke with the realist narrative form of the modern theater through which the viewer could fully lose herself in the action on stage. Like other post-*shingeki* playwrights, Satō rejected the social realism and orthodox

Marxist theater of *shingeki* for a comedic but elucidating restaging of history through nonromantic narratives and erasure of the dichotomous pairing of performing subject and viewing subject common to new theater. The Brechtian-style post–new theater of the late 1960s and 1970s sought to disable such mechanisms of identification through various processes of distanciation. A moving theater—the tent—was created to offer a new physical space through which to rewrite failed leftists' struggles in theater and politics.[50] Politically, the members distanced themselves from any institutional narratives, and the new theater form and space had become just that—a national institution. As Kazama Ken points out, the little theater movement provided a path for students who no longer had a direction after the fizzling of the 1960s student movements and struggle against the U.S.–Japan security treaty. In reference to the little theater movement in general and Kara Jūrō's Red Tent (Aka Tento) troupe in particular, Kazama quotes Ōzasa Yoshio on the "time" *(jikan)* of the revolutionary sixties: "The 'time' of the young people became muddled, they lost their way, and they couldn't help but step into *[fumikomu]* a maze. . . .The Red Tent overcame the limits of theatre, to be a visceral *[kannō teki na]* avant garde theatre that could lead even a society that had lost its way."[51] The little theater troupes proposed a new theatrical form that instilled a hope that although political and social change may not be possible, there is still a place for reflection and the rewriting of history.

Dogs perverts the monumental history of empire by introducing soldiers as the perverse bodies of the empire, taking "perversion" out of the margins and placing it at the heart of hegemony. The masochistic soldier in *Dogs* burns, to borrow a phrase from Kaja Silverman, "with an exalted ardor for the rigors of the super-ego."[52] He yearns to surrender himself to authority and act out his fantasies of self-dissolution in the name of the imperial mister-ess. Throughout the play an endless superimposition of dog and soldier on the level of wordplay, photograph, and image enables this portrayal of the soldier as masochistic. The play opens with Safety Razor Township under martial law. The Photographer snaps pictures, proclaiming, "To forget is not to remember." The insistent presence of the photographic image in the play shows history not to belong to the realm of succession or causality but to be a historical act of representation in which images hold iconographic power.[53] Seeking buyers for his images, the Photographer detects someone: "Hey! Hey you over there! Listen you! Huh? It's just a dog."[54] Immediately following this identification of "a dog," a photographic image is projected of a first-class army officer. This shift from dog to soldier initiates countless conflations of the two. In another scene, three pregnant women *(ninshin-tachi)* carry in mourning the framed photographs of dead soldiers while the Photographer sings the imperial anthem "Kimi ga yo." But instead of carrying photographs of human husbands, they carry photographs of dogs in uniform. Photographs and the Photographer are at the center of this critique of the imperial order to which these soldier dogs abase themselves because they represent a perversion of what is in so many empires an idealized image of the hegemonic system—the portrait of a soldier in uniform. The investment that the subject has made in the imperial system is sustained in the idealized portrait of a first-class soldier. The investment of that soldier in the empire is shown to be a libidinal one through the symbol of the epitome of loyalty and dogged devotion, a dog.

The Photographer announces Shōchikubai as the "leader of the indolent." He is to form an army using his buried bones as feed and to incite lost, homeless souls to devote themselves, which they do all too easily, to a larger cause—the colonialist state: "You must take those indolent shits of the imperial city who are dozing and form a well-controlled group. . . . You must swiftly organize thirty-four miscreant dogs into a unit. . . . From tomorrow you are a decorated sergeant." Shōchikubai is soon subsumed by military duties. He is readily integrated into this ragtag military, and Sada has been left behind. In radical contradistinction to Ōshima's and Tanaka's films, the hero of the play, Shōchikubai, is not interested in devoting himself to Sada but chooses the military instead as the object of his devotion.

Meanwhile, in another part of Safety Razor Township Sada unsuccessfully seeks a submissive sex partner. In the contractual style reminiscent of Wanda and Severin in Leopold von Sacher-Masoch's *Venus in Furs* in which Wanda writes a contract for Severin to sign in which he promises to be her faithful servant, Sada asks an intellectual referred to as "the school Principal" to be her devoted lover.

The Principal is the primary figure through which we see the rejection of the feminine and acceptance of the imperial as fetishized object of desire. Initially he is devoted to Sada. He licks her face, he will become anything if she will sing for him. The Principal quickly transforms into a willing devotee stealing around after her. The old Photographer shoots pictures of Sada riding the Principal, who wears a chain around his neck, like a horse. The commodification of this relationship of submission and dominance occurs when the Photographer offers to sell photographs of Sada riding the Principal: "Sure. I'm happy with these." Sada generously invites the Principal to look them over. Asked whether he likes them, the Principal can only answer that his brain his turning to water: "I have a will. What is a will? That's the question." Sada: "Principal, do you love me?" "Woof!" "A lot?" (He nods). "If that's the case then stop with your gibberish."

The Principal competes with younger men at being doggedly devoted but experiences grave self-doubt, concerned with his ineptitude at being a credible dog. When dog-sergeant Shōchikubai comes bounding in with a banana tail tied to his rear, performing the nearly perfected movements of a dog, the Principal is emotionally moved: "The young folks are really working at it. They force me to consider my own actions. How unkind." Depressed at his inability to act the nonthinker, the Principal feels as if he is being passed up by the younger generation. This disturbing satire shows the Principal worried that he is not passive enough, and consequently a failure. To overcome his questioning nature—to prove his devotion to the new social and political order protected by other dog-soldiers—the Principal praises the emperor in his final death throes after he is fatally wounded by the cork of a pop-gun fired by a dog-soldier. Atashi looks on in horror as the Principal, with blood oozing out of his wounds, whispers, "The Emperor . . . Long live the Emperor . . ." Sada is betrayed by the Principal, who honors the imperial leader of his murderers. In the hierarchy of adoration, her position of "top dog" is usurped.

The Principal is killed by Matsushima, Itsukushima, and Ama-no-hashidate—the three soldiers wearing, in an amusing pun, black armbands labeled *kenpei* and usually meaning "military police" but written with the homophonic characters "dog-soldier." After the Principal's death the three hungry dog-soldiers pry open their *hinomaru* lunchbox named for the red rising-sun flag. They find bones in their boxes. They happily gnaw on their "calcium and protein," fantasizing about pleasing "Tenteru Daijin," which is an inauspiciously diminutive reading of Amaterasu Ōmikami, the sun goddess of the Japanese archipelago. Sada wields no power in this libidinal economy that requires identification with the imperial.

Sada also propositions the leader of the dog-soldier army, Shōchikubai: "Will you lap up my urine? Will you wear a collar and go where I go? And when I feel the urge, will you adhere to my whims?" Shōchikubai drops his head: "Is that what the Principal did?" She nods affirmatively. "Was he a dog?" "Mm hmm," she nods. In the course of their conversation, Sada pats Shōchikubai lovingly on the rear and is horrified to find that he has grown a real tail! Performance has become reality. Shōchikubai once merely performing the duties of a dog-soldier with a fake banana-tail has metamorphosed into a real dog. Horrified that another lover has metamorphosed into a dog, Atashi grabs handfuls of mud and begins to pelt Shōchikubai, crying, "You fool! You fool!" Shōchikubai's performed devotion is replaced by a deeper devotion, which is symbolized as a physical transformation. This new imperial subject who embraces that masochistic position as devotee of the emperor frightens and angers Sada.

Shōchikubai dreads sexual bondage to woman. He chooses the military. Safety Razor Township is Kafka's world of assistants—a symbolic structure of power constructed on the postulation of the phallus that does not really exist but which nevertheless founds this order. Power, in this new, dispersed, and discursive form is disciplinary practice. The male characters transform into dogs who serve not a woman but the emperor honored in their death with praises of "Long live the Emperor!" Proudly singing the name of the emperor while in the throes of death is the result of a pedagogical principle implemented by the imperial training and disciplinary system. In a farcical moment, the dog-soldiers named for the nationally sanctioned most beautiful views in Japan *(Nihon sankei)*, Matsushima, Itsukushima, and Ama-no-Hashidate, are called to attention. The Photographer cries, "Announce to the sergeant that tonight you will howl at the moon for us. Tenor, baritone, and bass—if your three voices are coordinated, we can use you in the Singapore ship's concert." The dogs reply in rhythm: "The artists will be put out" (Itsukushima). "I want to die for the townspeople" (Matsushima). "It is an emergency" (Ama-no-Hashidate). They are encouraged to declare publicly that they are following their own desires. Their desires are consistent with the sovereign's, which they identify with a coherent (unfragmented) self.

In comparing two games of submission—the desire of the Principal to serve Sada in a game of erotic domination and the dog-soldiers' desire to serve the emperor—*Dogs* turns the "noble" act of altruistic men dedicated to the cause of the nation to a politically charged farce. These faithful dog-servants who achieve a mystical and even salacious joy in self-sacrifice, deprivation, and dependence are the perverse legs on which the totalitarian structure stands. The so-called perverse enables the successful integration of an authoritarian system. The masochist does not transgress the system but enables its success—as long as the object of desire is not a woman. The depiction of soldiers who find titillating pleasure serving the imperial master is not subversive but dangerously fanatical.

In other words, if *In the Realm of the Senses* suggests that the masochistic position is romantically subversive, Satō's play illustrates that the frenetically obedient male is also dangerous. The play shows that phallic identification requires homosocial (male-male) subordination. The "unhealthy," "perverse" subject is now the one who happily submits to the imperial system, suggesting the radical notion that it is not the perverse subject who disables the successful integration of an authoritarian system. The masochist does not transgress the system but represents its success. Assimilation into the phallic system requires self-subordination, and the more fanatical that subordination, the more dangerous the system. The play is critical of conventional masculinity and does not romanticize masochism as a libidinal psychical experience that could undermine it. *In the Realm of the Senses* romanticizes the passionate masochistic self that rejects the social world. Furthermore, it rejects the separation of "outside" history and the individual internal world that frames Ōshima's film. No internal "passion" exists for the individual that is not related to the system. What makes Satō's text so perilous is that he challenges the binary between the austere imperial and the corporeal libidinal.

Ultimately, even Satō can't resist placing the destruction of phallic power in the hands of a sexual woman. Sada, who appears to have the round belly of a pregnant woman, pulls out from under her kimono a purple bundle, which was assumed to hold Kichizō's penis. In fact, it holds a gun, and Sada shoots the Photographer. By shooting the Photographer she erases any possibility of fixing Shōwa imperial history. She murders the support of the imperial system: she puts an end to its photographic representation and thereby its memory. Even in this deconstructive avant-garde theater, the femme fatale still holds power in the cultural imagination as the ultimate transgressor. Like other postwar reconstructions of Sada, she remains a heroine. David Goodman writes that the search for immortalizing symbols "in a world where traditional symbols had been discredited was a major preoccupation in Japanese culture in the 1960s."[55] In *Dogs*, the transgressive woman is again immortalized as the desirable, heroically unreproductive woman. Ultimately, she most successfully perverts imperial history, although in this portrayal of Sada as an anti-imperialist agent, she is not the fetishized feminine contra the masculine or the handmaiden to male anti-authoritarianism. Rather, she is a cruel woman who is nobody's mistress. She is not the fetishized dominatrix enabling a new return to premodern erotics (Ōshima) or the fetishized dominant maternal enabling a unique Japanese modernity found in writing by intellectuals of the Nihon Romanha or Japanese Romantic School.[56] Nevertheless, in *Dogs* the historically grounded transgressive woman still holds power in the cultural imagination as a provocative source of anti-authoritarian power. The usual gender politic in which the perverse woman is a transhistorical figure prevails albeit in a much more politicized, metamorphosed form. The perverse woman is emblematic of transhistorical meaning because she herself destroys history.

Epilogue: By Way of Antidote

The poison woman was brought into being through the new discourses of enlightenment thought. Stories about her promoted normalizing visions of sexuality and gender that conformed to the promises of modernity, though the stories implicitly articulated the failure of those promises to include women. Poison woman stories, as popular serials, needed obstacles and conflict, and enlightenment discourse provided a convoluted backdrop for the contest of meaning over women's role during this time when absolutist modes of control were ostensibly being replaced by a society of "equals." Crimes, especially by women, contributed to the discursive struggle for meaning with regard to sovereign power but also a woman's right to resist. In other words, the subject of women's crime carried with it an implied concern with sexual difference and the role it should play in a purported new "society of individuals." Sexuality was an essential part of the representation of this struggle—sexuality and sexual desire came to suggestively symbolize the struggle to define woman's place in society.

Perhaps it is not surprising that the detective's eye appears only infrequently in poison woman stories. It is the detective's eye that has "the essential qualities of the unseen seer, who stands at the center of the social panopticon and employs his science to make all things visible on behalf of the forces of order." The detective, according to Franco Moretti, "discovers the causal links between events: to unravel the mystery, is to trace them back to a *law*."[1] Sherlock Holmes, for example, is "the great doctor of the Victorians, who convinces them that society is still a great organism: a unitary and knowable body."[2] If the classic detective story embodies an aspiration toward a transparent society, then it stands to reason that the lack of

such a controlling, peering, logical "spectatorial subjectivity capable of establishing epistemological and aesthetic control over an environment commonly perceived to be threatening and opaque" signals an absence (consciously created or otherwise) of the imagination of such a possibility. The
writer of poison woman serials reasserted for himself a place in Meiji-era
reforms through writing on crime. He became the newspaperman-cum-
detective who asserted epistemological and aesthetic control through tying
together new discourses of science and politics to claim authority to speak
about the criminal woman who was proved by him to be perversely sexual
and gender deviant.

The poison woman stories of the Meiji period were narratives that threw
into relief the contests for the meaning of gender and, not inconsequentially, class, even while they reveal the limited range of meanings provided
to woman in fiction—fiction that in the process of producing itself was
also in the process of producing female subjectivity. Catherine Belsey has
spoken to the role of fiction in articulating problems of the subject, which
are "often only implicit in other modes of writing":

> the range of meanings it is possible to give at a particular historical mo-
> ment is determined outside the subject. The subject is not the origin of
> meanings, not even the meanings of subjectivity itself. Fiction . . . is about
> what it is to be a subject—in the process of making decisions, taking ac-
> tion, falling in love, being a parent. . . . Fictional texts also address them-
> selves to readers or audiences, offering them specific subject-positions from
> which the texts most readily make sense. In that it both defines subjectivity
> and addresses the subject, fiction is a primary location of the production of
> meanings of and for the subject. The fiction of the past, intelligible in its
> period to the extent that it participates in the meanings in circulation in
> that period, constitutes, therefore, a starting-point for the construction of a
> history of the subject.[3]

Fiction does not emerge in a vacuum but is intimately tied to nonfictional
texts and popular cultural texts, as illustrated in discussions of the conditions
under which poison woman literature and repentance tales emerged. In them
the gendered subject—the subject of gender difference—was a centerpiece of
the poison woman story. The very term "poison *woman*" made it so.

As discussed in chapters 1 and 2, the poison woman was enlisted in producing an idealized narrative of woman in the new nation: the masculine,
overdeveloped body of the poison woman was the *antithesis* to the healthy,
feminine reproductive body; the woman of the *hinin* class was incapable

of controlling her new freedoms and autonomy; and the repentant speaker transmitted and reproduced the conservatism of mid-Meiji government. Criminological texts of the early twentieth century implicitly argued the need to control all women whose behavior could not be anticipated because of their physiological volatility as the female sex. Texts about female criminals essentially argued the justice of paternal power except inasmuch as narratives occasionally suggested the continued need to depend on old traditions over the new, especially in the realm of law. As argued in chapter 2, the autonomy of woman, as expressed in the *Kanayomi* serials, poison woman fiction, and other small newspapers, is conditional on conformity to standards by which she can be measured, classified, ranked, and disciplined. Women were shown to be free to choose to the extent that they were free to acquiesce.[4] Those who did not acquiesce were not the subjects of political or social inquiry but the sensationalized subjects in stories of grotesquery and bizarre behavior.

The actual ex-convict's difficulties in contesting the poison woman image that had been constructed for her illustrate the powerful cultural attachment to the criminal body that had been produced through enlightenment ideology. The narrative that emerged in repentance tales, as discussed in chapter 3, reveals instabilities in the subject produced by ex-convicts. The narrators speak with conviction to conflicting subject positions— positions that define a positive relationship to authorial power while defying the claims of that power. A struggle to speak as a subject is articulated in them, but in most cases they provide no clearly delineated sense of an autonomous subject, with the exception of narratives by Kaneko Fumiko and Kanno Suga, who wrote anticipating their death and not their survival as an ex-convict in society. Evident in the narrative convolutions of the text, the ex-convict spoke of acquiescence in order to articulate the *desire* to speak or make demands.

In later writing by those considering the poison woman retrospectively she is imagined as dazzling and dangerous. Hanada Kiyoteru once fantasized that Takahashi Oden was Japan's own Belle Starr, the Oklahoman outlaw who dressed and rode horses like a man and killed her male enemies with a single gunshot before galloping off into the distance.[5] Belsey has argued that "the demonization of women who are portrayed as subverting the meaning of femininity is contradictory in its implications. It places them beyond meaning, beyond the limits of what is intelligible. At the same time it endows them with a (supernatural) power which it is precisely the project of patriarchy to deny."[6] While poison woman figures in literature and newspaper are primary figments of a patriarchal imagination and the product of patriarchal anxiety if not hysteria, they are not, in pre–World War II texts, the magical creatures of legend, the modern interpretations of romantically alluring vessels of mystery that the modern literature scholar Nina Cornyetz has identified in her provocative discussion of the fictive "dangerous woman" archetype in Japanese canonical fiction.[7]

The poison woman was coterminous with the production of the modern state and the question of woman's role within it. She is not archetypal nor endowed with erotic agency or empowerment in her inception but a distinctly perverse character, curious but undesirable. Nevertheless, the poison woman figure was flexible enough to be an agent of new gender discourses in later eras. That is, the poison woman narrative is starkly different in the postwar era, when heroines began to resemble the Western femme fatale as a powerful cultural symbolic of the unknowable secrets of woman—as provocative, enigmatic other, to even the curious existentialist, as illustrated in chapter 5. One pulp novel about Takahashi Oden published in 1950 begins, "Who turned her into this kind of woman?—so goes the pan-pan girls' song so popular in this age of Sartre. Turn back the clocks and that same type of voluptuous beauty, that fleshly body walks the dark alleys of life. This is the Meiji poison woman's story." In the postwar period, the poison woman becomes an unknowable other, the pursuit of whom leads to an understanding of the (masculine) self—a Laplanchean "enigmatic signifier": "the presence of an unknown and unknowable question from the other that is central to and constitutive of subjectivity. . . . the other [who] is constantly inaccessible, a subjectivity that is recognized . . . but whose meaning remains illegible and enigmatic."[8]

The postwar poisonous body in its fantastical form expressed the notion of a surplus existence, one that may be caught up in the positivity of the social but that ultimately exceeds it. The figure of the mythical Turkish poisonous damsel illustrates corporeally the way in which this fatal woman exceeds herself. Turkish lore tells of "poisonous damsels" who were fed small amounts of poison as infants. By their teenage years, these young women were immune to the toxic drug and fully prepared to be used as powerful political pawns. An intimate embrace allowed the drug to seep from the damsel's pores into those of her enemy. Their venom was invisible, odorless, and without form. This same inviolable, invisible power was associated with the postwar poison woman. She was codified as erotic, alluring, and eminently female though often in the service of a devoted male admirer, present in the text. She resembles, as illustrated in chapter 5, a figurative handmaiden to a male discourse of liberation, much in the way that Douglas Slaymaker has described the postwar heroine of "carnal literature" writers: "The sexual body of a woman becomes Other in every sense, a paradisiacal locale where the quest for comfort, solace, nurture, and peace culminates, a place of [carnal] liberation."[9] While early poison woman stories tended to argue that authority, and even state authority, was not such a bad thing because it provided a structure for installing women as subjects in society, postwar stories of female criminals made no such claims. In prewar criminal literature, sexually desirous women were created as "unnatural" subjects—made unnatural through bizarre claims about their physiology and psyche in criminological literature of the 1920s and 1930s, as introduced in chapter 4.

In the postwar years, the mysterious, sexual, alluring woman is a heroine to an idealized masculine identity that articulates the fantasy of a counterhegemonic masculinity through the spectacularized, sexually available criminal woman. In these postwar texts (films, novels, and theater discussed in chapter 5), the prevailing fantasy of the criminal woman is clearly shaped by the preoccupations of masculine fantasy rather than fear, likely because by this point, the question of whether society as a paternal entity will succeed is no longer of concern, as it has stabilized. The male subject can imagine being counterhegemonic through the dominant woman while assured of his power as a social and sexual subject.

The novelist and feminist Tomioka Taeko, however, undermines the erotic fantasy of the fatal woman in her short story "Another Dream" (1979) by joining "Sada's" tale with the more banal one of a quiet young woman who had many of the same experiences as Sada. Tomioka is an experimental novelist, poet, playwright, and essayist belonging to a generation of Japanese writers whose works are celebrated for their acute representations of female identities and radical feminist voices. Her writing generally portrays powerful characters who challenge mores subordinating women's social and sexual freedom in postwar Japan. The strategy that Tomioka as a writer takes in "Another Dream" is to concentrate on the everyday, ever mundane obstacles to a woman's pursuit of her sexual pleasure. This care not to eroticize the female subject, often by making the sexual ever banal, is not an anomaly in Tomioka's work. "Another Dream" begins by quoting verbatim Abe Sada's testimony for several pages and then describing it as honest, open, and romantic. But the testimony is "interrupted" in the narrative numerous times by the gloomy portrayal of "Aunt Asa," who refuses to speak, whose life comprises pregnant silences that signal the emotional pain of a bad marriage. Asa had a parallel life to Sada's though she had only vague notions of Abe Sada's murder of Ishida Kichizō, according to the narrator, since she had been so preoccupied with work and family. Like Sada, Asa was from a working family and was forced to earn a living as an entertainer for a few years. Her second marriage was to a man who continued to treat her as an entertainer even after she had given birth to five children, while he also kept a mistress. The husband within the story desperately tries to maintain his fantasy of living with a sexually provocative entertainer. Disgusted by his sing-songy voice when he returns home from being with his mistress, Asa withholds sex from him, though she experiences sexual yearnings for him.

This juxtaposition of Sada's spectacular story of love and gore with the quiet fortitude of the much more subdued and stoic Asa, who experienced a very similar young adulthood, suggestively critiques the active suppression of the banal realities of domestic life in stories of the female criminal. Most poison woman stories are not interested in the mundane details of a woman's life, despite the fact that these tales are ostensibly based on the lives of real women. At the heart of "Another Dream" is an implicit critique of the prominence of the titillating sexual in stories of female criminals because it contrastingly does pay close attention to the mundane details of an unhappy housewife. "Another Dream" draws critical attention to that desire expressed in narratives of the female criminal by male writers for an alluring "excess" or an existence or entity that is unabsorbable—a "surplus existence that cannot be caught up in the positivity of the social."[10] Instead of a spectacular scene of execution by beheading (Robun), the bloody castration of her victim (Ōshima), a dramatic love suicide (Watanabe), or the shooting of the Photographer of imperial Japanese history (Satō), Tomioka concludes her story anticlimactically with a depiction of Asa and her children visiting the home of her husband's mistress to tell her husband of his father's illness:

> A light seeped out from the sliding paper door.
>
> "Umm, your father is ill," Asa repeated again.
>
> The sliding paper door suddenly opened and Asa's husband was standing there.
>
> "Umm, your father is ill," Asa said.
>
> "Daddy!," the four-year-old said. Hearing that, the six-year-old also called out "Daddy."
>
> The sliding door snapped shut in front of Asa and the children. After just a few moments, it opened.
>
> "Ma'am, bringing your children!" Wearing a short coat over her nightgown, Yoshi poked her head out from the sliding paper door and looked at the three of them.

"Because they say that father has fallen ill," said Asa.

"Still, there was no reason to wake up these little ones and bring them along! . . ." she said patting the six-year-old on the head.

"You go first without me!" the husband said from behind the sliding door.

"Sorry to bother you in the middle of the night," Asa said.

"Bringing the kids along . . ." Yoshi repeated.

Asa descended the stairs almost dragging her six-year-old. The four-year-old had dropped his head on Asa's shoulder and was already asleep.

If she had gone alone without the children to call her husband out to tell him that his father was ill, he wouldn't have believed her, Asa thought to herself as she walked the night streets.[11]

In a story shared by the intriguing details of a murderess and the banal life of an impoverished woman, it is the latter who takes center stage. Tomioka extinguishes the tabloidlike spectacle of the deviant woman with the banality of an unsatisfied woman's life and a man's crude infidelities. In other words, by intertwining the life a criminal woman with that of a common housewife only to drop the former from the narrative so that the housewife becomes the central figure in the story, the structure of narrative fundamentally critiques the instrumentalization and reduction of the transgressive woman to sexual spectacle and marker of male subjectivity. In this way, Tomioka strategically challenges the preceding figurations of the criminal woman in modern Japanese culture.

Notes

Introduction

1. See Bruno Latour, *We Have Never Been Modern,* trans. Catherine Porter (Cambridge, Mass.: Harvard University Press, 1993), for a discussion of how moderns have worked to ignore hybridity, especially modern "quasi-objects" that blur the line between the natural and the human.

2. Avital Ronell, *Crack Wars: Literature, Addiction, Mania* (Lincoln: University of Nebraska Press, 1993).

3. *Kanayomi Shinbun [Fukkoku],* vol. 1, ed. Yamamoto Taketoshi, Tsuchiya Reiko (Akashi Shoten, 1992), 6.

4. The Seinan war is the backdrop for a number of poison woman novels including Kubota Hikosaku's *Torioi Omatsu kaijō shinwa* (1878) and Okamoto Kisen's *Sono na mo Takahashi: Dokufu no Oden: Tokyo kibun* (1879).

5. See Paul Heng-Chao Ch'en, *The Formation of the Early Meiji Legal Order: The Japanese Code of 1871 and Its Chinese Foundation* (Oxford: Oxford University Press, 1981), 58–60.

6. Mary Poovey, *Uneven Developments: The Ideological Work of Gender in Mid-Victorian England* (London: Virago Press, 1989), 2.

7. Ann-Louise Shapiro, *Breaking the Codes: Female Criminality in Fin-de-Siècle Paris* (Stanford, Calif.: Stanford University Press, 1996), 9–10.

8. Lisa Duggan, *Sapphic Slashers: Sex, Violence, and American Modernity* (Durham, N.C.: Duke University Press, 2001).

9. Sharon Sievers, *Flowers in Salt: The Beginnings of Feminist Consciousness in Modern Japan* (Stanford, Calif.: Stanford University Press, 1983), 10.

10. Avital Ronell, *Crack Wars,* 62–63.

11. Quoted in Lynda Hart, *Fatal Women: Lesbian Sexuality and the Mark of Aggression* (Princeton, N.J.: Princeton University Press, 1994), ix.

12. Peter Stallybrass and Allon White, *The Politics and Poetics of Transgression* (Ithaca, N.Y.: Cornell University Press, 1986).

13. Asakura Kyōji, *Dokufu no tanjō: Warui onna to seiyoku no yurai* (Yōsensha, 2002), 15–18.

14. Stallybrass and White's discussion of class relations and the "high" and the "low" was influential in thinking about the transgressive for *Poison Woman*. For example, Stallybrass and White write that "a fundamental rule seems to be that what is excluded at the overt level of identity-formation is productive of new objects of desire. As new classificatory sets emerge with new forms of production and new social relations, so the carnivalesque and transgressive anti-structure of the emergent classical body will also change, marking out new sites of symbolic and metaphorical intensity in the ideological field. In class society where social conflict is always present these sites do not necessarily coincide with the 'objective' conflict boundaries of antagonistic classes but will nevertheless function to the advantage of one social group rather than another"; *Politics and Poetics,* 25.

15. Stallybrass and White write, "If we can grasp the system of extremes which encode the body, the social order, psychic form and spatial location, we thereby lay bare a major framework of discourse within which any further 'redress of balance' or judicious qualification must take place"; ibid., 3.

16. Ibid., 5, italics in original. It should be noted that I do not specifically adopt the authors' Bakhtinian perspective in my discussion of transgression.

17. *Kafū zenshū,* vol. 13 (Iwanami Shoten, 1963), 125.

18. Kafū's romantic reading of the poison woman's transgressive nature as representative of the angst and revolutionary struggle of an underclass shares commonalities with Terry Eagleton's reading of the carnivalesque, which he describes as the "lowbrow" transgression of "highbrow" morality. To Eagleton, the abased, the vulgar, and the criminal reveal the hypocrisies of the empowered. They provide a "temporary retextualizing of the social formation that exposes its 'fictive' foundations," allowing a glimpse of the dominant ideological constructs. See Stallybrass and White, *Politics and Poetics,* 18.

19. Judith Butler and Joan Scott, eds., *Feminists Theorize the Political* (New York: Routledge, 1992).

20. Judith Butler, *Bodies That Matter: On the Discursive Limits of "Sex"* (New York: Routledge, 1993), 3.

21. Here I am thinking of Jean-Francois Lyotard's concept of the *différend*: "The *différend* is the unstable state and instant of language in which something which ought to be able to be phrased cannot yet be phrased. This state involves silence which is a negative sentence, but it also appeals to sentences possible in principle. . . . In the *différend,* something 'asks' to be phrased, and suffers the wrong of not being able to be phrased." *Le Différend* (Paris: Minuit, 1984), 22–23, quoted in Geoffrey Bennington, *Lyotard: Writing the Event* (New York: Columbia University Press, 1988), 147.

1. Anatomy of a Poison Woman

1. Maeda Ai, "Kaika-ki no hanzai jitsuwa—*Takahashi Oden yasha monogatari* no baai," *Kokubungaku kaishaku to kyōzai no kenkyū* 20, no. 4 (March 1975): 106.

2. Lisa Duggan, *Sapphic Slashers*, 2.

3. Statistically there was no shortage of crime. From the years between 1876 and 1879 the government reported that more than 340,000 crimes were committed. In the years from 1873 to 1881 at least eighty-one women were executed. Statistics are from Paul Heng-Chao Ch'en, *The Formation of the Early Meiji Legal Order: The Japanese Code of 1871 and Its Chinese Foundation* (New York: Oxford University Press, 1981), 60–61.

4. For a discussion of late Tokugawa *gesaku* literature in Japanese, see Okitsu Kaname, *Tenkanki no bungaku: Edo kara Meiji e* (Waseda Daigaku Shuppanbu, 1960); Okitsu, *Kanagaki Robun: Bunmei kaika no gesakusha* (Yokohama: Yūrindō, 1993); Okitsu, *Saigo no Edo no gesakusha-tachi* (Jitsugyō no Nihonsha, 1976); *Edo Gesaku* Shinchō koten bungaku arubamu 24, edited by Jinbo Kazuya and Sugiura Hinako (Shinchōsha, 1991). In English, see Andrew Lawrence Markus, *The Willow in Autumn: Ryūtei Tanehiko, 1783–1842* (Cambridge, Mass.: Council on East Asian Studies, Harvard University, 1992).

5. Atsuko Ueda makes this point in "Meiji Literary Historiography: The Production of 'Modern Japanese Literature'" (Ph.D. diss., University of Michigan, 1999), 23.

6. Markus, *Willow in Autumn*, 61.

7. Mitamura Engyo, "Meiji jidai gōkan-mono no gaiken," *Waseda Bungaku* (April 1927), 153.

8. Markus, *Willow in Autumn*, 68–69.

9. Mitamura, "Meiji jidai gōkan-mono," 154.

10. Shinoda Kōzō, *Bakumatsu Meiji Onna hyakuwa* Kadokawa Sensho 42 (Kadokawa Shoten, 1971); and Hirata Yumi, "Monogatari no onna—Onna no monogatari," in *Jenda no Nihonshi*, vol. 2, ed. Wakita Haruko and S. B. Hanley (Tokyo Daigaku Shuppan Kai, 1995), 229–57.

11. *Tokyo Akebono*, 9 August 1877.

12. See the *Chōya Shinbun*, 24 October 1878, and the *Yūbin Hōchi Shinbun* of the same date.

13. Seven years earlier another convicted woman, only later referred to in the press and story as a poison woman, Harada "Night Storm" Okinu, was decapitated and her severed head put on display. Harada's case likely followed the Ming-influenced penal code promulgated in 1871, the Shinritsu kōryō (Outline of the New Code), which had changed little from the preceding penal code, the Kari keiritsu, which was a temporary penal code until the Shinritsu kōryō was put into effect in 1871. Oden's case came before court after the Kaitei ritsurei (Revised Code) had been promulgated to be effective from 10 July 1873 to handle cases in the new social setting not addressed by the Shinritsu kōryō. The later codes

did not alter very drastically the recommended punishments of the Kari keiritsu. Crimes for which execution by beheading was a usual punishment in the Kari keiritsu were thievery and murder. Under this code, robbery with weapons, intentional homicide, arson, rioting in jail, counterfeiting, and theft by guards were all punishable by death. For more on the early Meiji legal system, see Paul Heng-Chao Ch'en, *The Formation of the Early Meiji Legal Order: The Japanese Code of 1871 and its Chinese Foundation* (New York: Oxford University Press, 1981).

14. Georges Canguilhem, *The Normal and the Pathological* (New York: Zone Books, 1989), 242.

15. Ibid., 282–83.

16. The removal of class distinctions began in 1869 and the government formally reclassified the populace in 1872. Equal treatment did not prevail, however. In practice distinctions were maintained in modern family registers in which a family's status was recorded either as *kazoku* (members of peerage), *shizoku* (samurai descendants), *heimin* (commoners), or *shin-heimin* (new commoners, a term used to denote that the family was formerly of untouchable status). See Ian Neary's *Political Protest and Social Control in Pre-War Japan: The Origins of Buraku Liberation* (Manchester: Manchester University Press, 1989), 33.

17. See Hirota Masaki for a further discussion of the invocation of the discourses of heredity to perpetuate previous class divisions, in *Sabetsu no shosō* Nihon kindai shisō taikei, vol. 22 (Iwanami Shoten, 1990), 458–70.

18. Hirota, "Bunmei kaika-ki no jenda—'Takahashi Oden o megutte,'" *Edo no Shisō* 6 (June 1997): 84, 89.

19. *Meiji kaika-ki bungaku shū 2* Meiji bungaku zenshū, vol. 2 (Chikuma Shobō, 1966), 4.

20. Ibid., 11. Yamabuki and Tomoe were the lovers of General Kiso Yoshinaka. They were both considered brave in wartime, especially Tomoe, who was legendary as attractive and equally as excellent in military arts as men.

21. *The Physical Life of Woman* was so popular among Western readers that it was already in its fourth edition within a year of its first publication in 1869. Hirota Masaki makes this insightful connection between Robun and Napheys in his "Bunmei kaika no jenda."

22. *Meiji kaika-ki bungaku shū*, vol. 2, 59.

23. Napheys, *The Physical Life of Woman: Advice to the Maiden, Wife, and Mother* (Philadelphia: Maclean, 1870), 29.

24. For a century, the corpses of criminals had been used in autopsies not to prove their guilt through forensics study but as a convenient source for medical study. It was believed that spirits left the body in dissection, making families reticent to donate the corpses of loved ones to medical science. I have not found any evidence in this period that male crime was considered to be body-based. However, as illustrated in this chapter, books of nature, especially the earliest ones, devoted substantial discussion to male reproductive functions.

25. *Tokyo Nichi Nichi Shinbun*, 5 February 1879.

26. *Tokyo Akebono,* 12 February 1879.

27. *Meiji kaika-ki bungaku shū,* vol. 2, 61.

28. See the documented evidence in Matsumoto Kappei, *Watashi no furuhon daigaku* (Seieisha, 1981), 288–95. I thank Ayako Kano for introducing me to this book.

29. Yoshida Yoshikazu, *Takahashi Oden* (Tōhō Tosho-shinsha, 1966), 10–11.

30. Anne McLaren, *The Chinese Femme Fatale: Stories from the Ming Period* (Sydney: Wild Peony, 1994), 1.

31. No illustrations of the autopsy accompany Kisen's much more sympathetic rendering of Oden's biography and the autopsy, which is reported in a few short lines based on the newspaper article about the autopsy. See his *Sono na mo Takahashi Dokufu Oden: Tokyo kibun* (1879). No movable-type version of this *gōkan* is available.

32. Bruno Latour has shown how the reification of the fact is a strategy for producing order in modernity: "[W]e live in communities whose social bond comes from objects fabricated in laboratories; ideas have been replaced by practices, apodeictic reasoning by a controlled doxa, and universal agreement by groups of colleagues. The lovely order that Hobbes was trying to recover is annihilated by the multiplication of private spaces where the transcendental origin of facts is proclaimed—facts that have been fabricated by man yet are no one's handiwork, facts that have no causality yet can be explained." *We Have Never Been Modern,* 21–22.

33. Sander Gilman, *Difference and Pathology: Stereotypes of Sexuality, Race, and Madness* (Ithaca: Cornell University Press, 1985), 76–108.

34. The Japanese cultural studies field recently has enjoyed a small "boom" of its own with a number of essays on Meiji sexology, including books of nature sexology. Ueno Chizuko writes of them in her explanatory notes in *Fūzoku Sei:* Kindai Nihon shisō taikei. See also Oda Makoto, *Sei* (Sanseidō, 1996); Kawamura Kunimitsu, *Sekushuariti no kindai* (Kōdansha, 1996); Kawamura Kunimitsu, "Onna no yamai, otoko no yamai: Jenda- to sekushuariti o meguru 'Fūkō no hensō,'" *Gendai Shisō* (July 1993), 88–109; Kimoto Itaru, *Onani- to Nihonjin* (Subaru Shobō, 1976); Gregory Pflugfelder, *Cartographies of Desire: Male-Male Sexuality in Japanese Discourse, 1600–1950* (Berkeley: University of California Press, 1999), among others, for discussion of *zōkakiron.*

35. Ishii Kendō, *Meiji jibun kigen,* vol. 4 (Chikuma gakugei bunko, 1997), 218–19.

36. *Kanayomi Shinbun,* 4 January 1977.

37. While the "science" of the *zōkakiron* may seem naive from our point of view, I use this term here (rather than "pseudo-science" or "naive" science) because at that time, the sexological information was viewed as progressive, informative knowledge; and because I do not wish to valorize our science today as being more objective, though it is more technologically advanced.

38. Ueno Chizuko's list in *Fūzoku Sei* is less extensive. Some but not all the

titles that have been consulted for this discussion are *(Tsūzoku) Zōkakiron* (1876), translated from Ashton's *Book of Nature*; *(Tsūzoku) Nannyo jiei ron* (1878); *Zōkakiron* (1879), translated from Edward Foote; *Zōka seizei shinron* (1879); *Nannyo kōgō tokushitsu mondō hashigaki* (1886); *Shinsen: Nannyo kōgō shinpen* (1888); and a later *Danjo jiei: Zōkaki shinron* (1907).

39. I would like to thank Furukawa Makoto for sharing the results of his close reading of the entirety of the *Kanayomi* and dates of the appearances of books of nature-related journalistic stories and advertisements.

40. *Kanayomi Shinbun*, 31 July 1878.

41. Medical jurisprudence books, which were translated from or based on Western European and American law books and concerned with such topics as paternity suits, the definition and punishment of "rape" or "violation of women," and other sexual activities including pederasty, sodomy, incest, adultery, and polygamy, were also newly available to the general reader. Two examples of this kind of medical jurisprudence book are Matsui Junji's *Wakan kensatsu hō* (Izumiya, 1879) and *Eibei hankan ritsu* (Izumiya, 1879). This medical jurisprudence literature provided explanations on how to examine and prosecute paternity, legitimacy, and the concealment of birth suits. A hybrid form of literature also emerged in which premodern conduct literature was joined with sexological knowledge to provide practical advice on sexual behavior in and outside the home with such titles as *On Male and Female Sex Organs* (Danjo kikai no wake) and *How to Check for Venereal Disease* (Baidoku kensa no wake).

42. *Fūzoku Sei*, Nihon Kindai shishō taikei 23 (Iwanami shoten, 1990), 529.

43. Ueno Chizuko, *Sei'ai ron—Taidan shū* (Kawada Bunko, 1994), 48. A more substantial essay by Ueno on sex at the turn of the century is her aforementioned essay in *Fūzoku Sei*.

44. Pflugfelder, *Cartographies of Desire*, 242.

45. James Ashton, *Tsūzoku Zōkakiron*, translated by Chiba Shigeru (Inada Sahei, 1876), 3–4.

46. In a bizarre contribution to poison woman cultural history, Watatani Kiyoshi traces the path of the jar of these organs up through the war in his book *Kinsei akujo kibun* (Seiabo, 1990), 20–22.

47. See Matsumoto Kappei, *Watashi no furuhon daigaku* (Sei'eisha, 1981), 288–94, for the data.

48. Duggan, *Sapphic Slashers*, 6.

49. "Claiming to speak the truth, it stirred up people's fears; to the least oscillations of sexuality, it ascribed an imaginary dynasty of evils destined to be passed on for generations; it declared the furtive customs of the timid, and the most solitary of petty manias, dangerous for the whole society; strange pleasures, it warned would eventually result in nothing short of death: that of individuals, generations, the species itself." Michel Foucault, *History of Sexuality*, vol. 1, trans. Robert Hurley (New York: Vintage Books, 1992), 53–54.

50. See the letter in *Meiji kaika-ki bungakushū*, Meiji bungaku zenshū, vol. 1,

410. For an English translation excerpt, see Mark Silver, "The Lies and Connivances of an Evil Woman: Early Meiji Realism and *The Tale of Takahashi Oden the She-Devil,*" *Harvard Journal of Asiatic Studies* 63, no. 1 (2003): 11.

51. Maeda Ai, "Meiji ishin to kindai bungaku," in *Gendai bungaku kōza, Meiji no bungaku,* vol. 1, ed. Kōno Toshio et al. (Chibundō, 1975), 16.

52. Yamamoto Yoshiaki, "Keimō-ki no shisō to bungaku," in *Nihon bungaku shinshi Kindai-hen,* ed. Maeda Ai, *Kokubungaku Kaishaku to Kanshō Bessatsu* (1986), 38–39. The Ransen essay was originally published in "Bunmei kaika wa shōsetsu-an o gai su," *Hōtan Zasshi* 137 (May 1880).

53. Tsubouchi Shōyō, "Shōsetsu shinzui" from *Tsubouchi Shōyō shū,* vol. 3 of *Nihon kindai bungaku taikei* (Tokyo: Kadokawa Shoten, 1974), 40–41; trans. Nanette Twine, *The Essence of the Novel: Occasional Papers* 11 (Department of Japanese, University of Queensland, 1981), 1–2; quoted with slight revision in Ueda, "Meiji Literary Historiography," 49–50. Along with *jitsurokumono* (true-tales), *haishi* is a term used by narrators in referring to the story as a novel. *Haishi* is also used with *shōsetsu* (novel) as in *haishi shōsetsu.* For further discussion of *haishi,* see Ueda, 41–45.

54. See select chapters of Ueda, "Meiji Literary Historiography," for a discussion of the category of *gesaku* in Shōyō's *Shōsetsu Shinzui.*

55. See Yamamoto Yoshiaki, "Keimō-ki no shisō to bungaku," 41, for this quote from the preface of Itō Kyōtō's *Na ni tatsunami ryujin Otama* (Kingyoku Shuppan, 1885) on *jitsugaku* and *gesaku* literature.

56. One notable exception to this exasperation with the "true-story" form is the Meiji literary historian Yanagida Izumi, who is less alarmist regarding the adoption of a new "true-story" style, which he interprets as a survival strategy that revitalized *gesaku* literature. See his *Meiji shoki no bungaku shisō,* vol. 1 (Shunshusha, 1965), 33–86.

57. *Shinpen kokon dokufu-den,* ed. Nomura Ginjirō (Genkadō, 1887), 1.

58. Ibid., 14. Students of my Meiji literature graduate seminar at Princeton deftly translated the body of this story (without the preface), which I then edited. The participating students were Anna-Marie Farrier, Reggie Jackson, Dylan McGee, and Lianying Shan.

59. Ibid., 15.

60. Ibid., 17–18.

61. Ibid., 67.

62. Ibid.

63. Reproduced in Takahashi Katsuhiko, *Shinbun nishiki-e no sekai* (Kadokawa Bunko, 1992), 88–89.

64. *Meiji kaika-ki bungaku shū,* vol. 2, 4.

65. Hirata Yumi, *Josei hyōgen no Meiji shi* (Iwanami Shoten, 1999), 6.

66. See Hirata, "'Onna no monogatari' to iu seidō," *Nashonariti no datsukōchiku,* ed. Naoki Sakai et al. (Kashiwa Shobō, 1997), 161–82, and Christine Marran, "'Poison Woman' Takahashi Oden and the Spectacle of Female

Deviance in Early Meiji," *U.S.–Japan Women's Journal,* no. 9 (December 1995): 93–110.

67. Ino Kenji, *Meiji bungaku shi* (Kōdansha, 1985): 77–78.

68. Hirata, "'Onna no monogatari' to iu seidō," 180.

69. Nancy Armstrong discusses the "monstrous woman" in a chapter entitled "History in the House of Culture," in her *Desire and Domestic Fiction: A Political History of the Novel* (New York: Oxford University Press, 1987), 161–76.

70. One extreme example is Okuno Takeo, *Nihon bungaku-shi: Kindai kara gendai e* (Chūōkōronsha, 1970), 10–11, translated in Silver, "Lies and Connivances," 7: "They are nothing more than the specters of a dead-end Edo literature grotesquely pandering to the times; no matter how much one makes of their treatment of contemporary mores and events, one cannot appraise them as belonging to anything like the era of enlightened literature. Their typically childish puns and clichéd expressions, their shallowness of consciousness, and the vulgarity of their catering to the reader [render them] works of such inanity as to make us today feel toward them a physical revulsion."

71. Ueda, "Meiji Literary Historiography," 25.

72. See Yanagida Izumi's discussion of *jitsugaku*-related literatures in his *Meiji shoki no bungaku shisō,* vol. 1 (Shunshusha, 1965), 82–98.

2. Newspaper Reading as Poison and Cure

1. Ronell, *Crack Wars,* 11.

2. The first Sino-Japanese character of Takahashi's name is *taka,* meaning "high" or "tall," and therefore the title is a play on the degree to which her story has spread. "Shōden" and "Oden" are variant readings in this *gōkan.*

3. Gustave Flaubert, *Madame Bovary,* edited with translation by Paul de Man (New York: Norton, 1965), 233.

4. It should be pointed out here that not everyone promoted reading novels as a cure for barbarity. Fukuzawa Yukichi for one omits fiction from suggested reading for the aspiring student in his *Gakumon no susume* (Encouragement of Learning, 1874). Nakamura Masanao's extraordinarily popular translation of Samuel Smiles's *Self-Help* entitled *Saigoku risshi hen* (Success in the West, 1871) is also critical of popular literature. The Japanese translation reads: "*Haikan shōsetsu* are more harmful to the people—especially to those whose minds are still unformed—than diseases can ever be. It is just like the vermin that infect the water and make sick those who drink it." Translated in Ueda, "Meiji Literary Historiography," 58. The term *haikan shōsetsu* is an older term referring to longer tales. Earlier the word had a more specific meaning and referred to the Chinese practice of recording rumors among the people and reporting them to the imperial ruler.

5. "We know that particular morning and evening editions will overwhelmingly be consumed between this hour and that, only on this day, not that. (Contrast sugar, the use of which proceeds in an unclocked, continuous flow; it may go bad, but it does not go out of date.) . . . It is performed in silent privacy, in the lair

of the skull. Yet each communicant is well aware that the ceremony he performs is being replicated simultaneously by thousands (or millions) of others of whose existence he is confident, yet of whose identity he has not the slightest notion. . . . At the same time, the newspaper reader, observing exact replicas of his own paper being consumed by his subway, barbershop, or residential neighbours, is continually reassured that the imagined world is visibly rooted in everyday life. As with *Noli Me Tangere,* fiction seeps quietly and continuously into reality, creating that remarkable confidence of community in anonymity which is the hallmark of modern nations." Benedict Anderson, *Imagined Communities: Reflections on the Origin and Spread of Nationalism* (London: Verso, 1991), 33.

6. Despite the inclusion in the small newspapers of economic news, political news, and current events, much scholarship describes them as sensational and entertainment-oriented newspapers. Recent scholarship by Tsuchiya Reiko, especially in the preface to the republication of the *Kanayomi* newspaper and her book *Taishū-shi no genryū: Meiji-ki koshinbun no kenkyū* (Kyoto: Sekai Shisōsha, 2002), illustrates that the *koshinbun* medium went far beyond the sensational to be a primary place for modernizing writing in Japanese and voicing political sentiment.

7. Yamamoto Taketoshi, *Shinbun to minshū* (Kinokuniya Shoten, 1973), 36. See charts of the *Yomiuri,* for example, in James L. Huffman, *Creating a Public: People and Press in Meiji Japan* (Honolulu: University of Hawaii Press, 1997), 386–87.

8. Huffman, *Creating a Public,* 60.

9. Yamamoto, *Shinbun to minshū,* 34.

10. See Tsuchiya Reiko, *Taishūshi no genryū,* 54, for these statistics. See also Yamamoto Taketoshi's preface to the *Kanayomi Shinbun,* vol. 1, edited by Tsuchiya Reiko and Yamanoto Taketoshi (Akashi Shoten, 1992), 5, which quotes statistics from the *Tokyo-fu tōkei sho.* Among the small newspapers, the *Kanayomi* surpassed the *Tokyo E-iri* in sales after the Seinan war to become second only to the *Yomiuri* in sales (5). The three main small newspapers of early Meiji—the vastly popular *Yomiuri,* the illustrated *Hiragana E-iri Shinbun* (later the *Tokyo E-iri*), and the *Kanayomi*—along with other large newspaper offices, were located in the prestigious Ginza district of Tokyo (though the *Kanayomi* was founded in Yokohama and later moved to Tokyo). The *Yomiuri* was known as the first major small newspaper, the *Hiragana Illustrated* was known for its elegant illustrations, and the *Kanayomi* for its chic humor. See Nozaki Sabun, *Watakushi no mita Meiji bundan* (Shun'yōdō, 1927), 2–9, for a discussion of small newspapers. The *Kanayomi* was founded on 1 November 1875 and enjoyed tremendous popularity in the years from late 1876 to 1879. The newspaper folded in 1880. According to the newspaper historian Tsuchiya Reiko, it was common for small newspapers to burn brightly and then suddenly collapse, with the exception of the long-standing small newspapers that later became "middle newspapers," such as the *Yomiuri* (8).

11. *Kanayomi Shinbun,* vol. 1, 12.

12. Tsuchiya, *Taishūshi,* 53.

13. In contrast, Yamada Shunji surmises that the difference in literacy according to gender was substantial. *Taishū shinbun ga tsukuru Meiji no "Nihon"* (NHK Books, 2002), 89. These statistics from Tsuchiya, 54–57, elucidate the misogyny of claims in newspapers and stories of the time that women easily constituted that group that needed to be educated.

14. *Kanayomi Shinbun,* 1 November 1875, 1.

15. Ibid., 2 November 1875, 2. As with most articles in the earliest *koshinbun,* this one lacks a headline, as do most of the newspaper articles cited hereafter.

16. Ibid., 24 November 1875, 2.

17. Yamamoto, *Shinbun to minshū,* 65. This piece appeared as a contribution in the 23 January 1879 edition of the *Ukiyo Shinbun* newspaper. The *ōshinbun* became more involved in political commentary and debate, including those about censorship, after 1874 (34).

18. Anderson, *Imagined Communities,* 22–26.

19. *Kanayomi Shinbun,* 2 November 1875, 2.

20. See Makihara Norio, *Kyakubun to kokumin no aida* (Yoshikawa Kobunkan, 1998), esp. 176–229 and 197–201.

21. *Kanayomi Shinbun,* 11 November 1875, 1–2.

22. For analysis of the controversial brands of enlightenment espoused by Meiroku Zasshi intellectuals and especially Fukuzawa Yukichi, see Earl H. Kinmonth, "Fukuzawa Reconsidered: *Gakumon no susume* and Its Audience," *Journal of Asian Studies* 37, no. 4 (August 1978): 677–95; and Michael A. Cusumano's insightful "An Enlightenment Dialogue with Fukuzawa Yukichi: Ogawa Tameji's *Kaika Mondō, 1874–1875,*" *Monumenta Nipponica* 37, no. 3, (Autumn 1982): 375–401.

23. *Kanayomi Shinbun,* 13 November 1875.

24. Ibid., 23 April 1877.

25. Asakura Kyoji, *Dokufu no tanjō: Warui onna to seiyoku no yurai* (Yōsensha, 2002).

26. *Kanayomi Shinbun,* 24 November 1875, 2.

27. Huffman, *Creating a Public,* 76–77.

28. Tsuchiya, *Taishūshi no genryū,* 150.

29. The protagonist was not explicitly called a "poison woman" but the story shared a number of traits with that of Omatsu including allusions to taking on foreign clients as a prostitute and being "released in the fifth year of Meiji from prostitution."

30. *Kanayomi Shinbun,* 5 October 1876, 1.

31. Ibid., 1–3.

32. The serial ran from 10 December 1877 to 11 January of the following year with a total of fourteen installments.

33. *Kanayomi Shinbun,* 20 April 1878, 2.

34. Ibid., 10 May 1878, 4.

35. Michael McKeon, *The Origins of the English Novel, 1600–1740* (Baltimore: Johns Hopkins University Press, 1987), 43.

36. See preface to the *Kanayomi Shinbun,* reprint ed., vol. 1, 13.

37. Jacques Derrida, *Acts of Literature*, ed. Derek Attridge (London: Routledge, 1992), 182.

38. Ibid., 191.

39. Ibid.

40. Ibid., 214.

41. Ibid., 216.

42. Dani Botsman, "Crime, Punishment, and the Making of Modern Japan, 1790–1895" (Ph.D. diss., Princeton University, 1999), 217.

43. Ibid., 245.

44. Ibid., 247.

45. Kamei Hideo, *Meiji bungaku shi* (Iwanami, 2000), 29.

46. Ibid., 25.

47. One sensational manifestation of the linking of travel with danger is found in "The Story of Omasa," a story of a traveling mother and daughter who go to the bustling international city of Yokohama to find their fortune through the prostitution of the daughter. This pair does not fool others as in the serialized "Story of Omatsu" but are themselves fooled, falling victim in Yokohama to a Japanese madame and Chinese man who connive to deflower the daughter, Omasa, without paying the promised fee. The story warns of the dangers of travel, concluding: "Evil isn't perpetuated just by low-class Chinese and Westerners. There are plenty of Yokohama Japanese who would cheat you in this way to make money, so don't let your guard down!" *Kanayomi Shinbun*, 19 January 1879, 1.

48. *Kanayomi Shinbun*, 16 December 1877, 2.

49. Ibid., 21 December 1877, 3, italics mine.

50. Ibid., 4 October 1876.

51. Silver, "Lies and Connivances of an Evil Woman," 56.

52. Kyoko Kurita, "The Semiotics of Drifting: Reflections on a Japanese Political Novel of 1887." Unpublished manuscript. In Japanese see her "Meiji 20-nen no hyōryū: Shonin risshi Kanbai iku—Zeniya Gohei jitsuden kō," *Kōhon Kindai Bungaku* 12 (November 1989): 12–21.

53. Kurita is referring specifically to Iwata Itei's *Kanbai ikun: Zeniya Gohei jitsuden* (Tsujimoto Shō-shodō, 1887), 9.

54. Kurita, "Semiotics of Drifting," 16.

55. Ibid., 19–20.

56. *Kanayomi Shinbun*, 13 December 1877. The term *eta* used in the story is a derogatory term and only used here to show its use in the original text.

57. *Meiji Kaika-ki bungaku shū*, Nihon Kindai Bungaku Taikei, vol. 1, 132.

58. Ibid., 168.

59. Maeda Ai, *Genkei no Meiji* (Asahi Shinbun-sha, 1978), 13.

60. *Meiji Kaika-ki bungaku shū*, vol. 1, 165.

61. Rinbara Sumio, "Kindai bungaku to 'tsuzukimono'—*E-iri Chōya Shinbun* kara no mondai teiki," *Nihon Bungaku* 42, no. 4 (1993): 41, 43–44.

62. The conflicts introduced with modernization (meant here as the embrace of progressivism and the rejection of nativism) had already surfaced a few years

earlier in famous exchange between Fukuzawa Yukichi and Mantei Ōga in which, again, it is woman who is the symbolic object of contention in a tug-of-war over Westernization. In "Deformed Girl" (Katawa musume, 1872) Fukuzawa attempts to convince his female readers (to whom the parable was addressed) of the importance of rejecting the barbaric customs of the Tokugawa period, namely, the blackening of teeth and shaving of eyebrows after marriage. The heroine of the story, a "deformed girl" born with black teeth and shaved eyebrows, is ridiculed until she marries (in Tokugawa Japan all married women blackened their teeth). Once married she looks like all other women. Fukuzawa's "Deformed Girl" was the first of a series of fictional writings that expressly employed female characters to expound on the positive aspects of progressive "enlightenment" ideology. In pushing the adoption of modern Western practices, Fukuzawa took as the subject for his fable a girl who eventually reaches a marriageable age and adopted an entertaining fictional style to appeal to impressionable young female readers. Mantei Ōga promptly responded with "A Woman for Our Times" (Tōsei rikō musume, 1873), written in the voice of a woman who questions the patriotism of the author of "Deformed Girl" and asserts her own right as a Japanese citizen to maintain the traditional practices of a proud wife and mother. There is no question in the protagonist's mind that enlightenment rhetoric has very little to offer her, and this position is uncompromisingly expressed in more sophisticated, less condescending prose. Ōga's "A Woman for Our Times" is one of many early Meiji parodic works that used satire in criticizing the paternal calls for reform. What both sides shared, however, was the use of the female figure in determining lines of power. *Musume* (girl/daughter) has been translated as "woman" both because Ōga used the Sino-Japanese character *onna* and because the story is about a married woman: Ōga has glossed the character *onna* (woman) with *musume* likely to alert readers that the story is a parody of or response to Fukuzawa Yukichi's fable "Katawa musume." Fukuzawa's own use of *musume* is a condescending choice because it infantilizes women.

63. Catherine Belsey, *The Subject of Tragedy: Identity and Difference in Renaissance Drama* (London: Routledge and Kegan Paul), 221.

3. Recollection and Remorse

1. This serial of twenty-five chapters *(kai)* began on 29 July 1904 and concluded on 17 November 1904.

2. *Yomiuri Shinbun,* 29 July 1890, 3.

3. Ibid., 18 March 1903, 4.

4. Tomi Suzuki, *Narrating the Self: Fictions of Japanese Modernity* (Stanford, Calif.: Stanford University Press, 1997), 71.

5. Ibid, 70.

6. *Yomiuri Shinbun Kyōiku Furoku,* 18 January 1907, 1.

7. See chapter 3 of Tayama Katai, *Zangeroku to shōsetsu* (Hakubunkan, 1909).

8. Ibid., 20.

9. Judith Butler, "Contingent Foundations," in *Feminists Theorize the Political,* Judith Butler and Joan Scott (New York: Routledge, 1993), 9.

10. John Beverly, "The Margin at the Center: On Testimonio (Testimonial Narrative)," in *De/Colonizing the Subject: The Politics of Gender in Women's Autobiography,* ed. Sidonie Smith and Julia Watson (Minneapolis: University of Minnesota Press, 2000), 95. While the subject of the *zange* aligns herself with a disenfranchised female collectivity, we cannot say that the form itself, as Beverly says of the *testimonio,* is a nonpatriarchal, democratic epic form.

11. James Fujii, *Complicit Fictions: The Subject in the Modern Japanese Prose Narrative* (Berkeley: University of California Press, 1993), 49.

12. Shingaku is a moral philosophy expounded by Ishida Baigan in the Tokugawa period. See Jennifer Robertson, "The Shingaku Woman: Straight from the Heart," in *Recreating Japanese Women* (Berkeley: University of California Press, 1991), 88–107, for further discussion of women and the Shingaku religion.

13. Omasa's biography, "Shimazu's Past" (Shimazu Masa no rireki), for example, had been serialized in the *Asahi Shinbun* newspaper from 5 June 1888 a few months after her release from prison, which had been publicized in the same newspaper on 11 December 1887.

14. *Bakumatsu Meiji Taishō Yokohama no shibai to gekijo,* ed. Yokohama Kaikō Shiryōkan (Yokohama Kaikō Shiryōkan, 1992), 8.

15. *Yomiuri Shinbun,* 12 December 1891.

16. The inner title page sports the more sensational variant title *A Woman of Unsurpassed Evil: Miss Masa Shimazu's Record of Conversion* (Zessei akufu: Shimazu Masa-jo kaishinroku) (Kinrindō, 1891).

17. *Bakumatsu Meiji Taishō Yokohama no shibai to gekijo,* 8.

18. *Yomiuri Shinbun,* 2 November 1892, 3. These confessions, which are narrated after being released from prison, should be distinguished from repentance statements at the gallows. *Yomiuri Shinbun,* 15 September 1896, 3.

19. Ibid., 15 September 1896.

20. "Gekijo Tsūshin," *Asahi Shinbun,* Osaka, 14 July 1888. The title is then again changed to *Repentence of Evil Deeds: Shimazu Omasa's Personal History* (Akuji kaishun: Shimazu Omasa no rireki) to include "conversion" *(kaishun).*

21. *Shimazu Masa-jo kaishinroku,* 7a.

22. Margaret Helen Childs, *Rethinking Sorrow: Revelatory Tales of Late Medieval Japan* (Ann Arbor: University of Michigan Press, 1991), 1.

23. Ibid., 16–18.

24. *Shimazu Masa-jo kaishinroku,* 2a.

25. Ibid., 2b.

26. Ibid, 4.

27. Ibid., 7a.

28. Maki Isaka Morinaga, in "Women Onnagata in the Porous Labyrinth of

Femininity: On Ichikawa Kumchachi I," *U.S.–Japan Women's Journal* 30 (forthcoming), discusses another Meiji case of gender and performance on stage in which a woman must be as good as a man acting as a woman.

29. An example of the female criminal repenting of her crimes can be found in Okamoto Kisen's *Night Storm Okinu: Scattered Blossoms of Empty Dreams* (Yoarashi Okinu hana no ada-yume, 1878). The poison woman ascends an execution platform, which serves as a stage for announcing her regrets. This theatrical conclusion in which the poison woman speaks tearfully and apologetically differs greatly from the harshly punitive conclusions to poison woman stories by Kanagaki Robun, Kubota Hikosaku, and others.

30. Matsuyama Iwao, *Uwasa no enkinhō* (Seidosha, 1993).

31. J. L. Austin, *How to Do Things with Words* (Cambridge, Mass.: Harvard University Press, 1962), 21–22.

32. Scholars writing on the speech act have interrogated the relationship of drama to speech act theory but often the stage is treated as a metaphorical example of what happens during illocution in real-world situations.

33. *Shibai banzuke mokuroku.* (Yokohama: Yokohama kaikō shiryō-kan, 1991), 165.

34. *Osaka Mainichi,* 22 September 1903.

35. *Yomiuri Shinbun,* 13 July, 1905. The *Jiji Shinpō* reported a similar story five days later on 18 July.

36. Kawaguchi Matsutarō, *Meiji ichidai onna* (Shinshōsetsusha, 1936), 2.

37. Yoshino's film was distributed by Shōchiku and Oka's by Kawai.

38. *Hōchi Shinbun,* 13 November 1902 to 10 April 1903. Throughout the racy depiction of her struggles with stealing and attempted murder, Omasa berates herself for the inability to control her greed. The extended story finally concludes with her capture by the police, when she states: "'I am very sorry. I regret nothing that happens to me. I realize evil acts are not rewarding. Next time I am released into the world, I will turn over a new leaf, so please treat me as you wish.'" And with that she was returned to the courthouse (*Hōchi Shinbun,* 10 April 1903, 3).

39. *Yomiuri Shinbun,* 1 March, 1906.

40. Hirata Yumi, "'Onna no monogatari' to iu seidō," in *Nashonariti no datsukōchiku,* ed. Naoki Sakai and Brett de Bary (Kashiwa Shobō, 1996).

41. The 1977 play *Traveling Actor Oume: The Hanai Oume after Her Release from Prison* (Tabi yakusha Oume: Shutsugoku-go no Hanai Oume) perpetuated earlier stories about her by portraying a hysterical, drunken Oume whose genetic disease made her unstable and irresponsibly violent.

42. Quoted in *Meiji Nihon hakkutsu,* vol. 4, ed. Suzuki Kōichi (Kawade Shobō Shinsha, 1994), 14.

43. 2 September 1897; quoted in ibid., 15.

44. *Chūgai Shogyō Shinpō,* 26 July 1912; quoted in ibid., 17.

45. *Nihon Shinbun,* 14 August 1905.

46. *Hanai Oume zange monogatari,* ed. Asai Masamitsu (Tōkaidō, 1903), preface, 1–2.

47. Karatani Kōjin has postulated in his discussion of confession in the work of Uchimura Kanzō and Shiga Naoya that a "system of confession" *(kokuhaku seidō)* based on a "twisted will to power" in which a confessor seeks authority through a confession that precludes disagreement developed in the 1890s. In this "confessional system," "[b]ehind a facade of weakness, the one who confesses seeks to become a master, to dominate. . . . What this amounts to is an assertion that the reader is hiding truth while 'I,' however inconsequential a person I may be, have exposed it." *The Origins of Modern Japanese Literature,* ed. and trans. Brett de Bary (Durham, N.C.: Duke University Press, 1993), 86.

48. *Hanai Oume zange monogatari,* 15.

49. Ibid., preface, 2.

50. Ibid., 149.

51. Ibid., 35–36.

52. Sharon Sievers, *Flowers in Salt: The Beginnings of Feminist Consciousness in Modern Japan* (Stanford, Calif.: Stanford University Press, 1987), 49.

53. Only a few years after the publication of *Warawa no hanseigai,* Futabatei Shimei wrote a short essay in a similar repentance style entitled "Yo ga hansei no zange" (A Repentance of Half My Life, 1908).

54. Fukuda Hideko, *Warawa no hanseigai* (Iwanami Shoten, 1976), 15–16.

55. The interesting point Judith Butler has made regarding this process of the inhabiting power of disciplinary regimes via Foucault's argument that a prisoner is inhabited and brought into existence by the regulatory principles of disciplinary regimes (of inspection, confession, and so on) is that the process of subjection is simultaneously restrictive and creative. In it "subjection is neither simply the domination of a subject nor its production, but designates a certain kind of restriction in production, a restriction without which the production of the subject cannot take place, a restriction through which that production takes place." Butler clarifies this point in her "Subjection, Resistance, Resignification: Between Freud and Foucault," in *The Identity in Question,* ed. John Rajchman (New York: Routledge, 1995), 230.

56. *Warawa no hanseigai,* 16–17.

57. Ibid., 18–19. This passage and the following are a slightly revised version of a translation by Ronald Loftus from his thoughtful unpublished manuscript on Fukuda and Kinoshita Naoe.

58. Ibid., 72–73.

59. Ibid., 73.

60. Ibid., 98–99.

61. Ibid., 63.

62. Ibid., 65.

63. Ibid.

64. Ibid., 66–67.

65. Ibid., 67.

66. Loftus discusses this point regarding Saeki Shōichi, *Kindai Nihon no jiden* (Kodansha, 1981), 185–207, in his unpublished manuscript on Fukuda Hideko's and Kinoshita Naoe's confessional writing.

67. Seki Reiko, "'Warawa no hanseigai' no katari," *Nihon Kindai Bungaku* 31, no. 10 (October 1984), 43–56.

68. Matsuyama *Uwasa no enkinhō*, 72–73.

69. Yokose Yau, *Kinsei dokufu den* (Shōbunsha, 1928), 77.

70. Watatani Kiyoshi, *Kinsei akujo den* (Seiabō, 1990), 168.

71. Ibid., 169.

72. Much interesting work remains to be done on the various styles of self-narrative that emerged during this period under the guise of *zange*.

73. These terms are used by Suzuki in *Narrating the Self.*

74. See ibid., 1–12, for a useful portrait of *shishōsetsu* discourse.

75. Nakamura Mitsuo wrote in *Essays on the Novel of Manners* (Fūzoku shōsetsu ron, 1950) that the I-novel distorted "the proper development of the genuine modern realistic novel" and developed a "deformed I" instead of the "socialized I" or "true modern individual" found in the modern European novel. According to Suzuki, "Nakamura argues that this 'mistaken path' occurred because early twentieth-century Japanese Naturalist writers—who became the first I-novelists—blindly acted out the role of Western fictional protagonists without really understanding how Western authors treated or created fictional characters." Suzuki, *Narrating the Self*, 4–5.

76. Matthew Fraleigh, "Terms of Understanding: The *Shōsetsu* According to Tayama Katai," *Monumenta Nipponica* (2003), 47.

77. Suzuki, *Narrating the Self*, 1.

78. The serialized version of the novel appeared in the journal *Kaizō* intermittently from January 1921 to April 1937.

79. I have relied on Edwin McClellan's translation of *A Dark Night's Passing* (Kōdansha International, 1976), 182–83. For the original, see the *Shiga Naoya zenshū*, vol. 5 (Iwanami Shoten, 1973), 252–54. In the following notes, the second page numbers refer to the original Japanese text.

80. *A Dark Night's Passing*, 185; 257–58. In this case the term *hakoya* in the original refers to Minekichi's status as Hanai Oume's "assistant" who carried her robes and instruments on her short journeys from venue to venue as a geisha.

81. Slavoj Žižek, *Looking Awry: An Introduction to Jacques Lacan through Popular Culture* (Cambridge, Mass.: MIT Press, 1992), 66.

82. Ibid., 63–66.

83. Here I am alluding to the sometimes fetishistic attention to the vernacular (*genbun'itchi*) in studies of Meiji literature. What sometimes begins as analysis of discursive positions devolves into an analysis of vernacular grammar; discursive positions are analyzed as grammar, as if they were the same thing. For example, a

particular verb form can only retroactively be interpreted in a certain way. Despite the fact that we can't force certain institutionalized forms of reading the first time around, there is a tendency to project their power onto the page.

84. Fujii, *Complicit Fictions*, 50.

85. Jeremy Tambling, *Confession: Sexuality, Sin, the Subject* (Manchester: Manchester University Press, 1990), introduction.

4. How to Be a Woman and Not Kill in the Attempt

1. Helene Bowen Raddeker, *Treacherous Women of Imperial Japan: Patriarchal Fictions, Patricidal Fantasies* (London: Routledge, 1997), 123.

2. Ibid., 24–25.

3. Ibid., 15.

4. Books and magazines that have printed the deposition include but are probably not limited to Awazu Kiyoshi et al., *Abe Sada: Shōwa 11 nen no onna* (Tabatake Shoten, 1976); *Tōgenrō*, vol. 41 (September 1982); Maruyama Yukiko, *Hajimete no ai* (Kanō Shobō, 1987); Isa Chihiro, *Ai suru ga yue ni* (Bungei Shunjū, 1989); *Abe Sada: Jiken chōsho zenbun* (Kosumikku Inta-nashonaru, 1997); *Abe Sada shuki*, ed. Maesaka Toshiyuki (Chūō Kōron, 1998); William Johnston, *Geisha Harlot Strangler Star: A Woman, Sex, and Morality in Modern Japan* (New York: Columbia University Press, 2005).

5. Tomioka Taeko, *Hanmyō* (Kawade Bunko, 1982), 66.

6. I include ages because sexual maturation becomes an issue in the psychoanalytic diagnoses discussed later in the chapter.

7. *Abe Sada "Jiken chōsho zenbun,"* ed. Mori no hon henshū-bu (Kosumikku Intānashonaru, 1997), 48–49.

8. Ibid., 10.

9. Ibid., 78.

10. See also Ozawa Nobuo, *Hanzai hyaku-wa Shōwa-hen* (Chikuma Shobō, 1988), 288–90, for these articles that appeared in the 20 May evening and 21 May 1936 morning editions of the *Tokyo Asahi Shinbun*.

11. See Sekine Hiroshi, *Abe Sada: Sekine Hiroshi shishū* (Dōyōbijutsusha, 1971).

12. Sakaguchi Ango, "Abe Sada-san no inshō," *Zadan* 1, no. 1 (December 1947): 36.

13. "Mesu" does not literally mean "bitch"—as in female dog—but it is a word meaning "female" used for animals, therefore I have translated it as "bitch" to capture the connotations of animality and the primitive suggested by the use of this word.

14. *Abe Sada "Jiken chōsho zenbun,"* 86.

15. Kimura Ichirō, *Shōwa kōshoku ichidai onna—Osada irozange* (Ishigami Shoten, 1947), 164–65.

16. *Abe Sada shuki*, 79–81.

17. Ibid., 164.

18. Quoted in Pflugfelder, *Cartographies of Desire*, 312.

19. To be deemed "sick," a body must be diagnosed using scientific paradigms that are in themselves cultural systems. See Julia Epstein, *Altered Conditions* (New York: Routledge, 1994), for a discussion of how medical narratives are cultural and literary.

20. In erotic grotesque nonsense culture, medicine, media, and sensationalism joined to produce a new sensibility that reveled in sensationalized truths, logic, madness, and sex. Print, music, dance, and popular art were the primary media forms contributing to the erotic grotesque nonsense movement. The dominant form was print and included fiction (such as that by Edogawa Ranpo, Yumeno Kyūsaku, and other detective writers), nonfiction such as journalism, and popular cultural anthropology (developed famously by Umehara Hokumei and Saitō Shōzō among others). Itō Seiu's drawings and prints were also representative of the erotic-perverse culture of that time. The citation of a few representative contributors to this popular cultural phenomenon is not the ideal way to describe it and I resort to mentioning them only because this aspect of Japan's cultural history is rather amorphous and interpreted differently by cultural historians. Film certainly should not be excluded but many of the prints have since been destroyed so it is difficult to gauge the degree to which film contributed to *ero-guro* culture. Various interpretations of why an erotic grotesque nonsense culture developed in Japan have been offered by various scholars. The prolific cultural critic Ōya Sōichi described the increasingly economically repressive and straitened social circumstances of the late 1920s and 1930s as having nurtured a popular appetite for such a culture. Kano Mikio's description of the *ero-guro* era focuses on the relationship of the new sex labor force developed during this economically stagnant time, emphasizing the influence of the contemporary economic and labor situation in producing *ero-guro* culture. In his analysis, *ero* (the erotic) and *guro* (the grotesque) constitute two of three "ro"s including *tero* (the terroristic). *Ero* refers to the replacement of the waning world of flower and willows populated by geisha adept in the traditional arts of entertainment by the huge influx of cafés and bars in the first years of the thirties. According to his figures, 30,000 existed in Japan in 1932 (7,000 in Tokyo with 23,000 workers). Most of the workers were either village teenagers sold by families for 600–700 yen for a four-year contract or 800–1000 yen for a six-year contract. *Guro* is said to refer to the crimes and strange events, of which the Abe Sada incident was one, committed in response to the morally loose atmosphere. And *tero* recalls the number of terrorist incidents between 1930 and 1932. See the chapter "Ero guro nansensu kara shiroi kappochaku e," 35–46, in Kano's *Onna-tachi no "jūgo"* (Chikuma Shobō, 1987). Mark Driscoll has suggested the degree to which this erotic-grotesque culture was an imperial phenomenon. Driscoll's point that the culture was not limited to the boundaries of Japan is an important one. Debatable is his placement of the beginning of the culture erotic grotesque nonsense at the founding year of the popular psychology journal *Hentai Shinri* (1919) edited by Nakamura Kokyō. His periodization of the era

shows the degree to which he finds scientific discourse to have been an integral part of the movement. See his dissertation, "Erotic Empire, Grotesque Empire: Work and Text in Japan's Imperial Modernism" (Cornell University, 2000). I am particularly interested in considering the treatment of the Abe Sada incident as produced out of an erotic grotesque nonsense culture that included the technological, scientific, and bizarre.

21. Quoted in Akita Masami, *Sei no ryōki modan: Nihon hentai kenkyu ōrai* (Seikyūsha, 1994), 148. During the late 1920s Japan's economy weakened. According to the economic historian Takafusa Nakamura, however, Japan did not experience the depression to the degree that the United States did and in fact had already experienced a rather dramatic economic recession ten years earlier. The renewed straitened circumstances, abuses of the impoverished, and communist-driven revolts created a charged atmosphere but the depression of the late twenties was nothing new to the metropolitan areas of Japan. See his *A History of Shōwa Japan, 1926–1989* (University of Tokyo Press, 1998) for an enlightening discussion of the late Taishō and early Shōwa economy.

22. Saitō Yozue, *(Taishō Shōwa) Enpon shiryō no tankyū* (Haga Shoten, 1969), 186. The similarity in titles among works produced by this group or journal titles founded by Hokumei such as *Hentai Shiryō* (Resources on the Perverse) or *Gurotesuku* (Grotesque, 1928) illustrates an affinity between the early Shōwa erotic-grotesque literature produced during the time of high modernism in Japan and the immediate postwar pulp journals (see chapter 5 for further discussion of postwar journals). Hokumei was also increasingly involved in archival activities and, in the style of Walter Benjamin in Paris, would frequently be seen in the library frantically copying Meiji newspaper articles. See Akita Masami, *Sei no ryōki modan: Nihon hentai kenkyū ōrai* (Seikyūsha, 1994), and *Erotica* 5, no. 1 (January 1973).

23. Hokumei gained a following with his translation of Boccacio's *Decameron* (1925) and continued to translate erotic and leftist titles (in continuing his earlier leftist interests) such as *Roshia Daikakumei shi* (History of the Great Russian Revolution). In a slow shift away from leftist politics toward eroticism, in 1926 he founded *Bungei Shijo* (Literary Marketplace), a journal of erotic oddity stories with a leftist bent. Soon thereafter, he formed the Bungei Shiryō Kenkyū-kai (Literary Resource Research Society) responsible for a vast amount of erotic grotesque literature in the 1920s and 1930s. This group produced, among other literature, a translation of *Fanny Hill* in 1927 which is said to have marked Hokumei's shift from "red" (communism) to "pink" (eroticism) (though Hokumei's being "in the red" may have been the impetus for the first "pink" series published by the Society). Late 1920s works by Hokumei's group combined the literary, newsworthy, and archival for "bizarre-truth" stories. For the group, the erotic was an oasis away from the ruling discourses of sexology and scientism. Their stories of libertines, scandalous women, and the "sick"—all associated with periphery sexualities— were employed as a strategy for critiquing authority and in self-parody.

24. Yokose Yau, *Kinsei dokufu den* (Bungei Shiryō Kenkyūkai, 1928), 67.

25. Ibid., 103. Yau states that the Nakamura text he quotes is entitled "Kanojo ga tsumi ni naku made" but gives no reference or date of publication of the story except to say that it had been published near the time of the writing of *Stories of Early Modern Poison Women* (Kinsei dokufu den).

26. Saitō Yozue, *(Taishō Shōwa) Enpon,* 190.

27. Published by Bukyōsha.

28. Habuto Eiji and Sawada Junjirō, *Hanzai no kenkyū* (Hōbundō Shoten, 1916), 356.

29. In Japan, Germany, France, and Italy.

30. Kaneko Junji, *Hanzaisha no shinri,* Kindai Hanzai Kagaku Zenshū (Bukyōsha, 1930), 92, 100–101.

31. Nozoe, *Women and Crime,* 3.

32. Ibid., 3–4.

33. Ibid., 4.

34. Ibid.

35. Elizabeth Grosz suggests, following Julia Kristeva's notion of the abject, that body fluids "attest to a certain irreducible 'dirt' or disgust, a horror of the unknown or the unspecifiable that permeates, lurks, lingers, and at times leaks out of the body, a testimony of the fraudulence or impossibility of the 'clean' and 'proper.'" *Volatile Bodies: Toward a Corporeal Feminism* (Bloomington: Indiana University Press, 1994), 194.

36. Nozoe, *Women and Crime,* 5.

37. Ibid., 12.

38. Ibid., 16–19.

39. For the similar passage, see Erich Wulffen, *Woman as a Sexual Criminal* (North Hollywood, Calif.: Brandon House, 1967), 45–46. Nowhere did Nozoe attribute any of his writing to Wulffen. However, the similarities are so distinct that it is almost impossible that Nozoe did not read and even translate parts of Wulffen's German-language version of *Woman as Sexual Criminal* (Das Weib als Sexualverbrecherin, 1925) for *Josei to hanzai,* although Wulffen's text is not acknowledged.

40. Wulffen, *Woman as a Sexual Criminal,* 18.

41. Ibid., 22.

42. Ibid., 26. Here Wulffen has based his argument on what he calls the Italian Positivist School of Criminology, especially Cesare Lombroso's *The Female Offender.*

43. Sheldon and Eleanor T. Glueck, *Five Hundred Delinquent Women* (New York: Alfred A. Knopf, 1934), 90.

44. Ibid., 89.

45. Takada Giichirō, *Hanzai to jinsei / Hentai seiyoku to hanzai* Kindai Hanzai Kagaku Zenshū (Bukyōsha, 1929), 42.

46. Ibid., 43.

47. Ibid., 43–46.

48. See pages 31–60 of *Nihon no seishin kantei* (Misuzu Shobō, 1973) for the full report.

49. See Horinouchi Masakazu, *Abe Sada seiden* (Jōhō Senta- Shuppan-kyoku, 1998), 224–25.

50. William Johnston, *Geisha, Harlot, Strangler, Star: A Woman, Sex, and Morality in Modern Japan* (New York: Columbia University Press, 2004), 139.

51. *Abe Sada: Shōwa jū-ichi nen no onna*, 35.

52. Translation by William Johnston, unpublished manuscript.

53. Nozoe Atsuyoshi, *Josei to hanzai Kindai Hanzai Kagaku Zenshū* (Bukyōsha, 1930), 7–8.

54. Ibid., 296.

55. Ibid., 296–297.

56. Published by the Tokyo Seishin Bunseki-gaku Kenkyūjo. The main author is listed as the renowned psychologist Ōtsuki Kenji. A similar pathographical publication on the Sada incident was purportedly published as "Abe Sada no aiyoku katto shinri," *Seishin Bunseki* (September/October 1936).

57. *Abe Sada no seishin bunsekiteki shindan*, 1.

58. In his discussion of sexuality and drive in *Three Essays on Sexuality*, Freud overturns the prevailing view of sexuality as that which occurs in maturation, as biological, as resulting from sexual drive on the analogy of the instinct of nutrition (hunger) with the aim as sexual union, i.e., a biologizing image of sexuality. Jean Laplanche, *Life and Death in Psychoanalysis* (Baltimore: Johns Hopkins University Press, 1985), 14.

59. J. Laplanche and J.-B. Pontalis, eds., *The Language of Psychoanalysis*, trans. Donald Nicholson-Smith (New York: W. W. Norton, 1973), 307.

60. To avoid simplifying Krafft-Ebing's analysis of perversions we should also recall a distinction made in his *Psychopathia Sexualis* (1886) in which "perversion" of the sexual instinct is psycho-pathological while perversity in the sexual act "monstrous as it may be, is clinically not decisive. In order to differentiate between disease (perversion) and vice (perversity), one must investigate the whole personality of the individual and the original motive leading to the perverse act." *Psychopathia Sexualis* (New York: Pioneer Publications, 1939), 79.

61. See Freud's comment in his "On Sexuality" (originally published in 1905): "The fact is that we must put sexual repression as an internal factor alongside such external factors as limitation of freedom, inaccessibility of a normal sexual object, the dangers of the normal sexual act, etc., which bring about perversions in persons who might perhaps otherwise have remained normal." *On Sexuality: Three Essays on the Theory of Sexuality and Other Works*, ed. Angela Richards and ed. and trans. James Strachey (Middlesex: Pelican, 1977), 85.

62. *Abe Sada no seishin bunsekiteki shindan*, 2.

63. It should be noted here that the authors hold sometimes conflicting points of view though the individual authors are clearly attempting to establish a fixed

hermeneutics. Since they do not maintain a consistent psychoanalytic herme-neutics for explaining Sada's motives for the crime, this suggests that the law that fixes identification may not be impervious to historical variability and pos-sibility. As Judith Butler writes in *Gender Trouble*: "The alternative perspective on identification that emerges from psychoanalytic theory suggests that multiple and coexisting identifications produce conflicts, convergences, and innovative dis-sonances within gender configurations which contest the fixity of masculine and feminine placements with respect to the paternal law. In effect, the possibility of multiple identifications (which are not . . . fixed within masculine and feminine positions) suggests that the law is not deterministic and that 'the' law may not even be singular." *Gender Trouble* (Routledge, 1989), 67.

64. *Abe Sada no seishinbunseki shindan*, 38.

65. See Laplanche and Pontalis, *Language of Psychoanalysis*, 194–95.

66. Sigmund Freud, *Totem and Taboo: Some Points of Agreement between the Mental Lives of Savages and Neurotics*, trans. James Strachey (New York: W. W. Norton, 1950), 17.

67. Diana Fuss, *Identification Papers* (Routledge, 1995), 155. Quoted in David Eng, *Racial Castration: Managing Masculinity in Asian America* (Durham, N.C.: Duke University Press, 2001), 6.

68. *Abe Sada no seishin bunseki shindan*, 68–69.

69. Ibid., 46.

70. Ibid., 15–16.

71. Ibid., 16.

72. Ibid., 17.

73. Ibid., 13.

74. Freud, *Totem and Taboo*, 161.

75. Freud, *Civilization and Its Discontents*, trans. and ed. James Strachey (New York: W. W. Norton, 1961), 27.

76. Ibid., 29.

77. Ibid., 51–52.

78. Herbert Marcuse, *Eros and Civilization* (Boston: Beacon Press, 1974), 12.

79. Freud, *Civilization and Its Discontents*, 59.

80. *Abe Sada no seishin bunseki teki shindan*, 20.

81. Kaneko Junji's essay on Sada, which was the first of eight in *The Psycho-analytic Diagnosis of Abe Sada*, named her four perversions: "Sexual perversion can basically be divided into four areas [masochism, sadism, fetishism, and nym-phomania] but the fact that 'blood-letter' Osada [literally 'Sada who wrote char-acters in blood' or '*chi-moji* Osada'] exhibits equally all four of them is *alarming*" (4). For emphasis Kaneko writes "alarming" or "osoroshii" in *katakana* syllabary, which is only infrequently used for Japanese words.

82. Jane Flax, *Thinking Fragments: Psychoanalysis, Feminism, and Postmodern-ism in the Contemporary West* (Berkeley: University of California Press, 1991), 55.

83. In Freud, woman threatens castration as nurse, governess, teacher, and mother of boys.

84. *Abe Sada no seishin bunsekiteki shindan,* 24.

85. Emily Apter, *Feminizing the Fetish: Psychoanalysis and Narrative Obsession in Turn-of-the-Century France* (Ithaca, N.Y.: Cornell University Press, 1991), 34–35. Freud critiques this sensational treatment saying, "That they should do this is regrettable, for they thereby sacrifice truth to an illusion, and for the sake of their infantile phantasies abandon the opportunity of penetrating the most fascinating secrets of human nature." "Leonardo da Vinci and a Memory of his Childhood," *Art and Literature,* ed. Albert Dickson, Pelican Freud Library, vol. 14 (Middlesex: Penguin Books, 1985), 223.

86. Ibid., xi.

87. Jonathan Mark Hall, "Unwilling Subjects: Psychoanalysis and Japanese Modernity" (Ph.D. diss., University of California, Santa Cruz, 2003), 3.

88. See book jacket and introduction, *Abe Sada seishin bunseki shindan.*

89. While I am referring to Japanese medical specialists, Elizabeth Grosz discusses this problem especially with regard to Freud in *Jacques Lacan: A Feminist Introduction* (New York: Routledge, 1998), originally published in 1990.

5. How to Be a Masochist and Not Get Castrated in the Attempt

1. Kathleen Uno, in her painstakingly researched discussion of the development and transformations of the *ryōsai kenbo* ("good wife, wise mother") ideology in prewar and postwar Japan, argues that the state-influenced conceptions of motherhood and wifehood of the prewar period persisted into the 1980s with an increasing emphasis on motherhood. While Uno makes a compelling argument for the staying power of the conception, it might also be argued, on the basis of images in popular media, that the early Meiji period and the immediate postwar period are two "windows" in modern Japanese history when the *ryōsai kenbo* ideology was either nonexistent (early Meiji) or played little role ideologically. See her "The Death of 'Good Wife, Wise Mother'?," in *Postwar Japan as History,* ed. Andrew Gordon (Berkeley: University of California Press, 1993), 293–323.

2. See John Dower, *Embracing Defeat: Japan in the Wake of World War II* (New York: W. W. Norton, 2000), for a discussion of occupation culture.

3. Censorship continued but in a different form under the occupation.

4. Kōno Kensuke, "Hihyō to jitsuzon—Sengo hihyō ni okeru sekushuariti," *Kokubungaku Kaishaku to Kyōzai no Kenkyū* 40, no. 8 (July 1996): 44–50.

5. According to a *Yomiuri* newspaper report from 11 February 1948, the combined number of tabloid-style erotic pulp magazines sold each month reached approximately two million. Cited in Ota Jirō, *Apure erochisumu—Taihei sensō to bungaku no kiroku* (Kiku Shobō, 1951), 66.

6. Nosaka Akiyuki finds this to be a far-fetched etymology. See his essay "Torisugiteitta adahana, zuisō, kasutori zasshi," in *Kasutori fukkokuban,* ed. Yazaki Yasuo (Nagahisa Hozon-ban, 1970), 72.

7. Erotic novels published in these magazinese were called *aiyoku shōsetsu* (sexual love novels), *nikutai shōsetsu* (carnal novels), and *jōchi-yomimono* (infatuated lust stories); see Yamamoto Akira, *Kasutori zasshi kenkyū: Shinboru*

ni miru fūzoku shi (Shuppan Nyūsusha, 1976), 34–35. See also Kimoto Itaru, *Zasshi de yomu sengo shi* (Shinchō Sensho, 1985), and *Kasutori shinbun*, ed. Shinbun shiryō raiburari- (Ōzorasha, 1995) for discussions of *kasutori* magazines and newspapers.

8. Some prewar "erotic pulp" titles that bear striking resemblance to postwar pulps are *Jūnetsu Jidai* (Era of Passion), *Ego, Doro to numa* (Mud and Swap), *Hanran* (Deluge), *Radical, Yellow Dog, Cosmopolitan, Kemuri* (Smoke).

9. *Hanzai Yomimono* (March 1947), 17.

10. *Jōen Jitsuwa Tokushū* (August 1949), 26.

11. *Nightly Read Newpaper* (September 1954), 23.

12. Douglas Slaymaker, *The Body in Postwar Japanese Fiction* (London: RoutledgeCurzon, 2004), 14.

13. See Slaymaker, *The Body in Postwar Japanese Fiction,* for a discussion of this new image of the body in literature and philosophy by Noma Hiroshi, Sakaguchi Ango, Tamura Taijirō, and others.

14. Tamura Taijirō, "Nikutai ga ningen de aru," *Gunzō* (March 1947), 14.

15. Quoted in Kuro Hyōsuke, "Nikutai bungaku no seiri," *Shisō no Kagaku* (April 1949), 14.

16. J. Victor Koschmann, *Revolution and Subjectivity in Postwar Japan* (Chicago: University of Chicago Press, 1996), 57.

17. Ibid., 57.

18. See his article "Abe Sada-san no inshō," 36–38, and interview with Abe Sada, "Abe Sada Sakaguchi Ango taidan" (30–35), *Zadan* 1, no. 1 (December 1947).

19. Nagata Mikihiko, *Fūfu Seikatsu* (September 1950), 214–15.

20. Ibid., 220.

21. Nagata, *Fūfu Seikatsu* (August 1951), 192–93.

22. For this discussion of *Sesō,* I have relied on Burton Watson's vivid translations in Oda Sakunosuke, *Stories of Osaka Life* (New York: Columbia University Press, 1990). For this quote, see 152 in Watson; for the original, see *(Teihon) Oda Sakunosuke zenshū,* vol. 5 (Bunsendō Shuppan, 1978), 382. In the following notes, the second page number refers to the original text. I have shortened Watson's translated title from "State of the Times" to "The Times."

23. Ibid., 154; 385.

24. Ibid., 153; 384.

25. Ibid., 164; 397.

26. Ibid., 188; 424.

27. Sakaguchi Ango, "Nikutai jitai ga shikō suru," *Sakaguchi Ango zenshū,* vol. 14 (Chikuma Bunko, 1990), 577–78.

28. For an extensive critique of "wholesome" and "pragmatic" literature, see Ango's discussion of Shimazaki Tōson in his "Dekadan bungaku-ron," *Daraku-ron* (Kadokawa Bunko, 1957), 115–29.

29. Watson, *Stories,* 149–50.

30. *Ōru Ryōki* (October 1947), 33.

31. Kimura Ichirō, *Shōwa Koshoku ichidai onna: Osada Iro-zange* (Ishigámi Shoten, 1947), 10.

32. Sakaguchi Ango, "Abe Sada Sakaguchi Ango taidan," 33–34.

33. Masao Miyoshi, *Off Center: Power and Culture Relations between Japan and the United States* (Cambridge, Mass.: Harvard University Press, 1991), 118.

34. Sekine Hiroshi, *Sekine Hiroshi shi-shū: Abe Sada* (Doyōbigutsusha, 1971), 13.

35. Herbert Marcuse, *Eros and Civilization* (Boston: Beacon Press, 1966), 50.

36. Gilles Deleuze, *Masochism*, trans. Jean McNeil (New York: Zone Books, 1991), 66.

37. Ibid., 99.

38. "Through the category of masochism, the crisis of the subject is refined into a critical practice: the masochist triumphantly flaunts and exhibits the crisis of failed patriarchal symbolization." Suzanne Stewart, *Sublime Surrender* (Ithaca, N.Y.: Cornell University Press, 1998), 4.

39. Referring to the writing of the editor of *m/f,* Mandy Merck writes, "Instead of Adams's utopian exchange of consensual acts and disengendered dildos, Creet's defence of the masochistic daughter from the maternal authority she craves, or Modleski's account of the dominatrix who prepares her daughter for the travails of patriarchy, Sade gives us the top girl. The daughter's position . . . is suddenly rendered untenably cruel. And if daughters can take up torture, they might even embrace its sister vocation and become legislators" (Mandy Merck, *Perversions: Deviant Readings* [New York: Routledge, 1993], 259–61). The contrary argument has been made that the dominatrix is "feminist" insofar as she challenges the gendered character of subordination in the Oedipal and social order. (Lesbian masochism has been championed for reasons not far from Deleuze's.) Merck illustrates in her provocative discussion of the feminist ethics of lesbian S/M how Tania Modleski's argument is closely aligned with Deleuze. Modleski argues that in the lesbian context, patrarchal authority is expelled, the father is dismissed from the symbolic order, and the mother is equated with the law (256–57). In Merck's reading, Parveen Adams's nearly idealized masochism enables the maternal (powerful feminine) and expels the paternal law.

40. Peter Lehman, *Running Scared: Masculinity and the Representation of the Male Body* (Philadelphia: Temple University Press, 1993), 189.

41. Parveen Adams and Merck conclude that only the lesbian sadomasochist escapes the constraint of the phallic order: "For hers is a fetishism freed from all fixed reference, maternal as well as paternal." In this definition of fetishism it is recognized that no one has the phallus (Merck, *Perversions*, 242–43). This identity politics–based understanding of sexuality escapes, Adams argues, the pathology of the female sex where the girl is always under the sign of the phallus whether she accepts or disavows female castration. See Merck, *Perversions*, 237–43.

42. Watanabe Jun'ichi, *A Lost Paradise*, trans. Juliet Winters Carpenter (Tokyo: Kodansha International, 2000), 183. I have changed the name order and added macrons to the translation.

43. For a discussion of Satō Makoto's plays, see Mori Hideo, *Gendai engeki*

marukajiri (Shōbunsha, 1983), 76–105, and David G. Goodman's extensive dissertation, "Satō Makoto and the Post-*Shingeki* Movement in Japanese Contemporary Theatre" (Cornell University, 1982). A short dialogue with Satō Makoto and Akutagawa Hiroshi in which they discuss *Dogs* briefly appeared as "Kyoten de no aratana shibai-zukuri o" in *Teatoro*, no. 372 (February 1974), 46–58.

44. Freud addresses this dynamic in his essay "A Child Is Being Beaten." Discussing the stages of beating fantasies by children, he states that the child first imagines a rival being beaten and then switches to imagining himself as being beaten, thereby satisfying Oedipal urges. Here I am concerned not with individual subjects but the insistent relationship of masochistic desire to the imperial system posited within this play.

45. Kaja Silverman, *Male Subjectivity at the Margins* (London: Routledge, 1992), 187.

46. The play itself traveled around the "empire" like all performances of the Black Tent theater troupe, which performed in a traveling tent. The actress who played Abe Sada, Arai Jun, won the Kinokuniya Theater award for best actress the year she performed the role.

47. The theater scholar Ōzasa Yoshio expands on Sada's role in the play to argue that she is a symbolic subject unlimited by familial or social constraints; see *Gendai Nihon gikyoku taikai,* vol. 10 (San-ichi Shobō, 1997), 446–47.

48. Walter Benjamin, "Thesis on the Philosophy of History," *Illuminations.* Quoted in Satō Makoto, *Kigeki Shōwa no sekai: Abe Sada no inu* (Shōbunsha, 1976), 9.

49. See the afterword to Fukuda Yoshiyuki's *Majo densetsu* (San'ichi shobō, 1969).

50. David Goodman, *The Return of the Gods: Japanese Drama and Culture in the 1960s* (Ithaca, N.Y.: Cornell University East Asia Program, 2002), 3.

51. Kazama Ken, *Shōgekijō no fūkei: Tsuka, Noda, Kōkami no gekisekai* (Chūō Koron, 1992).

52. Silverman, *Male Subjectivity at the Margins,* 195.

53. Satō seems to follow Benjamin in suggesting both that an image must be understood as historical and imagistic and is involved in the historical acts of the production of meaning, and that history is not primarily of succession or causality.

54. Satō, *Kigeki Shōwa no sekai,* 12. Commercialism and totalitarianism are in cahoots. The photographer hands out business cards to potential buyers of his commemorative photographs. His selling of commemorative photographs illustrates the dependency of nationalistic and totalitarian discourses on commercialism and capitalism.

55. Goodman, *The Return of the Gods,* 112.

56. Ayako Kano discusses the Romantic School and transhistorical feminine in her fascinating essay "Japanese Theater and Imperialism: Romance and Resistance," *U.S.–Japan Women's Journal* 12 (September 1996).

Epilogue

1. *Popular Fiction: Technology, Ideology, Production, Reading,* ed. Tony Bennett (London: Routledge, 1990), 247.

2. Ibid., 249.

3. Belsey, *The Subject of Tragedy,* x.

4. Belsey makes this point regarding plays and domestic conduct books of England, which "betray an uneasy alliance between liberalism and patriarchy" (ibid., 193).

5. See the "Takahashi Oden" chapter by Ōba Minako in *Aizō no tsumi ni naku: Kindai Nihon no josei shi,* ed. Enchi Fumiko (Shūeisha, 1981), 92–93.

6. Belsey, *The Subject of Tragedy,* 185

7. Cornyetz describes a dangerous woman figure that developed in canonical modern Japanese literature: "Mountain witches, female shamans, snake-women, and other spiritually empowered women have been represented throughout the Japanese canon. . . . Powerful women can be found isolated in the mountains devouring or bewitching the hapless men and children who wander into their magical domains, communicating with the deities, or spiritually possessing other women. These women stand as a testament to a tenacious, yet peripheral, presence in Japanese literature of powerful women who confront the dictates of male dominance and familial need. However, modern renditions of the dangerous woman stand aloof from the archaic and medieval portrayals that preceded her. Although she is presented in the guise of, or is overtly referential to, a plurality of antecedent female literary archetypes long linked to eroticism and though she is empowered by her link to the uncanny realms of the spirits, the dead and the supernatural, there is an unmistakable series of transformations. . . . My term *dangerous woman* is thus meant to include the variable modern representations of powerful women that are culled from, and commingle with, certain archetypes of the premodern canon." Nina Cornyetz, *Dangerous Women, Deadly Words: Phallic Fantasy and Modernity in Three Japanese Writers* (Stanford, Calif.: Stanford University Press, 1999), 14–15.

8. Jonathan Mark Hall, "Unwitting Subjects: Psychoanalysis and Modern Japan" (Ph.D. diss., University of California, Santa Cruz, 2004), 36.

9. Slaymaker, *The Body in Postwar Japanese Fiction,* 5.

10. Joan Copjec, *Read My Desire: Lacan against the Historicists* (Cambridge, Mass.: MIT Press, 1994), 11.

11. Tomioka Taeko, *Hanmyō* (Kawade Bunko, 1982), 81–82.

Index

Abe Sada (poison woman), xiv, xxiv,
104–8, 141, 175–76; arrest and
conviction of, 116; deviancy of,
125, 126, 134–35; vs. the emperor,
163–70; as heroine, 140; as love
story, 161–63; masochism and,
150–61; medical examination of,
122–24; medical studies about,
110–12; nymphomania of, 111, 123;
physiognomy and crime, 122–24; in
postwar period, 136–70; as primitive, 127–28; psychoanalytic diagnosis of, 124–35; in pulp magazines,
136–46; as regressed, 127; and
satire of fetishizing writer, 146–50;
self-narrative confession of, 104;
sexual desire, 104, 109–11, 127–28,
135; sexual experience, 104,
109–10; sexual perversions, 130–31;
150–61; sexual transgression, 124;
as unrepressed, 126, 130–31; as
vixen, 148–49
Abe Sada's Dogs (Abe Sada no inu),
163–70
abjection: and exclusion, xxv; and
feminine, xxii; and transgression,
xviii–xix

Adams, Parveen, 203n39, 203n41
Akita Masami, 112
alienation, 158
All Bizarre Hunt (Ōru Ryōki) (pulp
magazine), 143, 144, 148
Allied Occupation Press Code, 137
Amaterasu Ōmikami, 168
Amorous Woman of Shōwa, The (Shōwa
kōshoku ichidai onna), 148–49
Anderson, Benedict, 40, 45
Apter, Emily, 132, 134
Armstrong, Nancy, xvi, 34
Asakura Kyōji, xviii, 47
Ashton, James, 18, 20
Auden, W. H., 65
Austin, J. L., 78
authoritarianism: and perversion,
169–70
autonomy: of self-narratives, 104; as
unfeminine, 11
autopsy, 13–14, 15, 16, 22, 182n24,
183n31

Beardsley, Aubrey, 131–32
Beecher, Catharine E., 13
behavioral aberration: and medical
observation, 132, 134

Belsey, Catherine, 64, 172, 173
Benjamin, Walter, 165, 197n22,
    204n53
Beverly, John, 70
Beyond the Pleasure Principle (Freud),
    130
Binding of Oden's Letters, The (Tōji-
    awase Oden no kanabumi, 6,
    57–58
biocentrism, 2
biosocial life: and crime, 115
Birdman of Alcatraz, The (film), 65–66
Black Tent (Kuro Tento) (experimen-
    tal theater troupe), 164
Blanchot, Maurice, xxi
blood: as sign of danger, 116
body: language of, 147; social, 111
Book on Erotomaniacs (Shikijō-kyō
    hen), 116
books of nature. *See zōkakiron*
Botsman, Daniel, 56
Brechtian-style post–new theater,
    165–66
buraiha (decadent school) writing, 143
Butler, Judith, xxii, xxv, 79, 193n55,
    199–200n63

Cabanes, Augustin, 132
Canguilhem, Georges, 8–9
carnal literature *(nikutai bungaku)*,
    138–41
carnivalesque: and morality, 180n18
castle topplers, 15
castration, 106, 109, 130, 159–60,
    200n83
Chiba Shigeru, 17–18, 21–22
Chikasumi Jōkan, 94
Childs, Margaret, 74
Chinese medicine, 30
Civilization and Its Discontents
    (Freud), 129–30
class: boundaries, abolished, xvii,
    182n16; and drugs, xiv; and gen-
der, 63–64; and poison women, 1,
    10, 59, 62, xx; and transgression,
    xviii–xix, 10, 180n14–15
commercialism: and totalitarianism,
    204n54
confession. *See* self-narratives, of
    female ex-convicts
Confession (Zangebanashi), 69
Confessions of Love (Osada irozange),
    144
Conjugal Life (Fūfu Seikatsu) (maga-
    zine), 138, 145
conjugal magazines, 138–39, 145–46
Cornyetz, Nina, 174, 205n7
counterhegemony, xxiv, 107–8, 164
crime and criminals: and biosocial
    life, 115; description of, 31–32;
    and emancipation, 136; in enlight-
    enment fiction, 28–35; evolution-
    ary model of, 112–22, 130; execu-
    tions of female criminals, xv–xvi;
    and fin-de-siècle, xvi; and heredity,
    9–10; as heroines, 136; and mar-
    ginalization, xx; men, crimes
    committed by, xv, 118; and mod-
    ernization, 2; and nation-building,
    xv; in newspaper stories, xxiii; and
    physiology/physiognomy, 2, 22,
    116–24; political, 121; in postwar
    popular culture, 146–50; romanti-
    cized, 146; and sexuality, xvi, xxiv,
    1–2, 4, 13–15, 103–35, 244; and
    social change, xvi; and social sym-
    bolic order, xix, xviii; as stereotype,
    139; and submission, 11; and tech-
    nology, 28–35; and transgression,
    11; and women, 112–22. *See also*
    deviance/deviants, female; poison
    women *(dokufu)*
Crime Research (Hanzai no kenkyū)
    116
Crime Stories (Hanzai Yomimono)
    (pulp magazine), 139

Criminal Psychology, The (Hanzaisha no shinri), 116–17
Criminal Science (Hanzai Kagaku) (journal), 112–13
Criminology (journal), 115
Cruel Story of Youth (Seishun zankoku monogatari) (film), 155, 157–59
cultural narratives: stories of social deviants as, xvi, 2
cultural truths, xxv

Dai Nihon Bunmei Kyōkai (Great Japan Cultural Association), 115–16
Dark Night's Passing, A (Anya kōro), 97–100
Darwin, Charles, 69
Death by Hanging (Kōshikei) (film), 155
decadent school of writing *(buraiha)*, 143
Deleuze, Gilles, 159–60, 161
Demon *(yasha)* Oden. *See* Takahashi Oden (poison woman)
Derrida, Jacques, 54, 55
desire, female. *See* sexual desire and sexuality
deviance/deviants, female: and abnormal behavior, 17; and crime, xvi, 13–15, 117–20; cultural narratives of, xvi, 2; evolutionary theory as basis of, 118; as heroines in pulp magazines, 136–46; and hormonal imbalances, 117–18; idealization of, 144–45; medical discourse on, 111–13; and sexual desire, xvi, 9, 13, 110, 112; *See also* crime and criminals; poison women
devotion: and imperialism, 167–69
Diary of Shimazu's Soul, The (Shimazu Masa bodai nikki), 77
differend, 180n21
differentiation: and subjectivity, xxii;

and transgression, xxi. *See also* gender difference; sexual difference
discipline: and power, 169
disenfranchised, 70
distanciation: in post–new theater, 166
dokufu. *See* poison women
dokufumono. *See* poison women stories
domestic woman: motherhood and wifehood, 201n1; sexual desire of, 137; vs. transgression, xxv
dominance and domination: and imperialism, 167, 169; and masochism, 167, 169; and patriarchy, 163–64; and social relations, xxv
drama: and speech act, 192n32
drugs, xiii, xiv
Duggan, Lisa, xvi, 2, 24
Dyer's Hand, The, 65

Eagleton, Terry, 180n18
Eisenstein, Elizabeth, 53
Ellis, Havelock, 132
emancipation, 136
empiricism, 8. *See also* imperialism
enlightenment: and crime, 28–35; and early Meiji literature, 2–4, 25–28, 32, 33; in fiction, 28–35; in newspapers, 39, 40–48; and poison women stories, 9, 10–11, 25–28, 30, 35; technology and crime in, 28–35; and women, 46–47
erotic grotesque literary culture, 112, 113, 196–97n20
erotic novels: in pulp magazines, 143–44, 201–2n7
eroticism: need of, and crime, 120; and other, xix–xx
Essays on the Novel of Manners (Fūzoku shōsetsu ron), 194n75
evidence: rhetoric of, 30–31, 30–32
exclusion: and abjection, xxv
exotic: and transgression, xix

fascism: and masochism, 163–64
female criminals. *See* crime and
    criminals
female deviance/deviants. *See* devi-
    ance/deviants, female
feminine and femininity: and abjec-
    tion, xxii; and autonomy, 11;
    domestic models of, 137
Feminists Theorize the Political, 69–70
femme fatales, 99; as heroines, 170; of
    Ming fiction, 15; as ultimate trans-
    gressors, 170; voice, eradication of,
    149–50
fin-de-siècle: and female criminals, xvi
Flaubert, Gustave, xvii–xviii, 36, 37
Flax, Jane, 131
Foote, Edward, 18
Foucault, Michel, xviii, 24–25, 65,
    184n49, 193n55
Foucault/Blanchot (Foucault), 65
Franklin, Benjamin, 87
Freedom and Popular Rights Move-
    ment, xvii
Freud, Sigmund, 126–30, 132, 134,
    193n55, 199n58, 199n61, 200n83,
    201n85, 204n44
Fujii, James, 71, 86, 100–101
Fukuda Hideko (political prisoner):
    masculine self, 89–90; memoir as
    confessional self-narrative, 68, 69,
    70, 76–77, 84, 86–94; self-reform
    and social action, 89
Fukuzawa Yukichi, xv, 186n4,
    189–90n62
Funabashi Seiichi, 143
Fusei Ito (poison woman), 114
Futabatei Shimei, 94, 193n53
Fuyuki Takeshi, 143

gender: and class, 63–64; and genre
    outlaws, 1–5; and literacy, 188n13;
    and national ideals, xviii
gender difference: and confessional

self-narrative, 92, 94–97; of poison
    women stories, 172; of readers,
    45–46; and subjectivity, xxii; and
    transgression, 114. *See also* sexual
    difference
gender politics: and body politic, 24;
    postwar period, 158, 170
Gender Trouble, 199–200n63
gengo geijutsu (theater of linguistic
    art), 165
genre outlaws: and gender, 1–5
gesaku literature, xxii, xxiii, 3, 25–26,
    27–28, 34–35, 181n4, 185n56. *See
    also* Meiji literature, early
Gilman, Sander, 17, 132
gōkan literature, 3–4, 5, 7–8, 9, 17, 25,
    34, 35
Goodman, David, 164, 170
Gotō Kichizō (victim), 5
Great Treason incident, 103, 121
Grosz, Elizabeth, 198n35

Habuto Eiji, 116
haishi, 27, 185n53
Half My Life (Warawa no hanseigai),
    69, 76–77, 86–94
Hall, Jonathan, 134
Hanada Kiyoteru, 173
Hanai Oume (poison woman): appar-
    ent lunacy, hysteria, and drunken-
    ness, 82–83, 192n41; confessional
    self-narrative of, 66, 69, 70, 79–86,
    90, 93, 97, 98; sexual desire and
    crime, 111, 114, 121
Hanai Oume's Story of Repentance
    (Hanai Oume zange monogatari),
    69, 79–80, 85
Harada Okinu (poison woman), xiii,
    xiv, xv, 7, 30–32, 39, 66, 114,
    192n29; beheaded, 15, 31–32,
    181–82n13; in pulp magazines,
    139, 143
Hegel, G. W. F., xix

hegemony: and personal power, 165.
  See also counterhegemony
Hell of Oden, The (Oden jigoku), xxiv
hentai. See perversion
hentai seiyoku (sexual perversion), 148
heredity: and crime, 9–10
*Her Name Too Infamous: Poison Woman
  Takahashi; A Strange Tokyo Tale*
  (Sono na mo Takahashi: Dokufu
  no Shōden: Tokyo kibun), 5, 7,
  36–37, 38
high culture: and narcotica, xiv; and
  popular culture, xxv
High Treason incident, 103, 121
Hirata Yumi, 6, 32, 34, 80
Hirota Masaki, 11
Hirshfeld, Magnus, 132, 134
historical materialism, 165
historicism, 165
History of Sexuality (Foucault), 24–25,
  184n49
History of the Twelve Perversions, The
  (Hentai jū-ni shi), 113
Hobbes, Thomas, 183n32
Holmes, Sherlock, 171
Hori Seitarō, 12
hormonal imbalances: and deviant
  behavior, 117
Hoshi Getsuya, 68
humanity: evolution of, 129

Ihara Saikaku, 74, 143–45
Impassioned Woman of Love (Jōen
  ichidai onna), 143–45
imperialism: and devotion, 167–69;
  and dominance, 167, 169; and
  masochism, 150–51, 154, 159–60,
  163–70; modern, 112; and perversion, 159, 164–67, 169–70; and
  submission, 167, 169
Ino Kenji, 33
In the Realm of the Senses (Ai no
  koriida) (film), 150–61, 169–70

Iroha (small newspaper), 50
Ishida Baigan, 191n12
Ishida Kichizō (victim), 104, 128,
  150, 161
Ishii Kendō, xxiv, 17
Itō Kyōtō, 4, 27–28, 66
Itō Senzō, 4, 28
Iwata Itei, 59
Izumi Kyōka, xv

Jacob, P. I., 132
Japanese Romantic School (Nihon
  Romanha), 170, 204n56
jitsuroku fiction, 27–8, 143, 185n56
jūsōteki hyōgen (multilayered expression), 165

kabuki theater, xv, xx, 6
Kafka, Franz, 54, 55, 169
Kaibara Ekiken, 21
kairyō (reform), 2, 5, 26, 89, 94–97
Kamei Hideo, 56–57, 94, 96, 97
Kanagaki Robun, xxiii, 2, 4, 5,
  6–7, 16, 28, 32, 66, 114, 124,
  176, 192n29; and newspapers,
  6, 26, 37, 39, 42, 50, 57–58; on
  Takahashi Oden's criminal nature, 8–26
Kanayomi newspaper, 173; and books
  of nature, 18, 19; enlightenment
  rhetoric in, 39, 40–48; founding
  of, 6, 26; ironical, critical style, 25;
  in national press market, 43–44;
  popularity of, 42; transgression
  and the law in, 48–55; vernacular
  language in, 53–54; and women
  readers, 37–38. *See also specific
  newspapers*
Kaneko Fumiko, 103–4, 121, 130,
  173
Kaneko Junji, 116–17, 200n81
Kanno Suga, 103–4, 121, 173
Kano, Ayako, 204n56

Kara Jūrō, 166
Karatani Kōjin, 193n47
kasutori shinbun (pulp newspapers), 137
kasutori zasshi (pulp magazines), 148; as carnal literature, 138–41; conjugal magazines, 138–39, 145–46; cult of female deviants, 136–46; erotic novels in, 143–44, 201n7; female criminality in, 136–46; poison women in, 139–46; sales of, 201n5
Katayama Heisaburō, 19
Kawaguchi Matsutarō, 80
Kawamura Taiichi, 72
Kawatake Mokuami, xx, 6, 53, 57–58
Kawatake Shinshichi, 53
Kazama Ken, 166
Kimura Ichirō, 143, 144, 148
Kinoshita Naoe, 68, 94, 95
Kishida Ginkō, 43–44
Kishin Omatsu (Pirate Omatsu), 6
Kobayashi Hideo, 96
Kobayashi Kinpei (victim), 7
Kokueki Shinbun (National Newspaper), 84–85
kokuhaku (confession). *See* self-narratives, of female ex-convicts
kokuhaku shōsetsu (confessional novel), 68–69, 94, 95, 100
Kōno Kensuke, 137
Koschmann, Victor, 142
koshinbun (small newspapers), xxiii, 40–42
Kōzō, Shinoda, xxiv
Krafft-Ebing, Richard von, 115–16, 126, 132, 199n60
Kubota Hikosaku, xxiii, 4, 9–11, 52, 82, 114, 192n29
Kuga Chigaharu, 94–95
Kunieda Kanji, xxiv
Kuramochi Eikichi, 95
Kurita, Kyoko, 59

Ladies' Journal (Fujin Kōron), 124–25
Lancaster, Burt, 65–66
Latour, Bruno, 183n32
law, the: in newspaper stories, xxiii, 36–40, 48–64; and poison women, 2, 36–40, 55, 56–64; and transgression, 36–40, 48–55
Layman's Book of Nature, The (Tsūzoku zōkakiron), 18, 21–22
LeGuin, Ursula, 36
Lehman, Peter, 161
Lessons for a Cultivated Life (Yōjōkun), 21
Life of an Amorous Woman, The (Kōshoku ichidai onna), 74, 143–45
literacy, 42–43, 188n13
Literary Marketplace (Bungei Shijō) (journal), 113
Loftus, Ronald, 193n57, 194n66
Lombroso, Cesare, 117, 120
Lowe, Lisa, xvi
Lukacs, Georg, 70
Lyotard, Jean-François, 180n21

Madame Bovary, xvii–xviii, 36, 37
Maeda Ai, 2, 47, 61–62
Makihara Norio, 46
male subjectivity: and masochism, 164; and transgression, 177
Mantei Ōga, 189–90n62
Marcuse, Herbert, 159
marginalization: and drugs, xiv; and female criminals, xx; of poison women, 47; and society, xvii
Markus, Andrew, 3
Maruyama Masao, 141
Masa. *See* Shimazu Omasa (poison woman)
masochism, xxiv, 136–70; and dominance, 167, 169; and fascism, 163–64; and imperialism, 150–51, 154, 159–160, 163–70; and male subjectivity, 164; and militarism,

154, 163–69; parody of, 163–70; and patriarchy, 159, 162–64; and perversion, 164–67, 169; and phallic order, 161, 163; romanticized, 162, 169–70; and sadism, 128, 160, 161; and submission, 167, 169; and subordination, 170; and subversion, 160, 169–70; and totalitarianism, 136, 159, 160, 164, 169; and transgression, 136, 170
Matsui Junji, 184n41
Matsumura Shōfū, 139
Matsumura Shunsuke, 44
Matsuyama Iwao, xvii, 78, 93
McKeon, Michael, 53
McLaren, Anne, 15
Medical and Surgical Reporter (Philadelphia), 12
medical jurisprudence books, 184n41
medical narratives, 111–13, 196n19
medical observation, 132, 134
medical reports, 122–24
Meiji Culture Research Society, 17
Meiji literature, early, xxii–xiii, 2–5, 10–11, 172, 174, 183n34; and enlightenment science, 204, 25–28, 32, 33; and novelistic style, 27; and popular literature, 26–27; vernacular in studies of, 194–95n83. *See also gōkan* and *gesaku* literature
Mellen, Joan, 158
menopause, 116, 117–18
menstruation, 116–17, 123–24
Merck, Mandy, 160, 203n39, 203n41
militarism: and masochism, 154, 163–69
The Mirror of Female Physiology (Fujo seiri ichidai kagami), 12–13
misogyny: and sexuality, 15; and social revolt, 157–59
Mitamura Engyo, 4
Mitchell, Alice (murderess), 24
Miyako (newspaper), 124

Miyazaki Koshoshi, 94
Miyoshi, Masao, 150
Mizuno Yōshū, 94
Mobius, P. T., 118
Modern Criminology series (Kindai hanzai kagaku), 116, 135
Modern Japanese Autobiography (Kindai Nihon no jiden), 91
modernity, imperial, 112
modernization: female criminal discourses of, 2; pressures of, and crimes committed by men, 118; and women, 189–90n62
Monthly Reader (Gekkan Yomiuri) (magazine), 140, 141
moral justice, 32
morality: and carnivalesque, 180n18; and reading, 36
Moretti, Franco, 171
Mori Ōgai, 94, 100, 115
Mori Sannosuke, 80
multidimensional linguistic space, 165
Murakami Ume: confessional self-narrative on stage, 71–72
Muramatsu Tsuneo (ex-convict), 122, 135
murder: and sexual desire, 105, 108–12, 135; scientific knowledge and investigation of, 30
Mutō Tadao, 23

Nagai Kafū, xx–xxi, 180n18
Nagasaki Bunji, 128, 130, 132
Nagata Mikihiko, 140, 143–44, 146
Nakamura Kokyō, 115, 116
Nakamura Masanao, 186n4
Nakamura Mitsuo, 96, 194n75
Nakamura, Takafusa, 197n21
Napheys, George H., 12
narcotica. *See* drugs
narrative authority: in self-narratives, 4–5, 100–102
Narushima Ryūhoku, 41

nation-building: and female criminals, interest in, xv; and narrative of woman, 172–73; by newspapers, 43–44; and poison women, xvii–xviii, 174; and poisons/drugs, xiv–xv; pressures of, and crimes committed by men, xv, 118; and women, 172–73

national ideals: and gender, xviii

nature, books of. *See zōkakiron*

New Edition of Dokufu Stories Past and Present (Shinpen kokon dokufu den), 66

New Edition of the Meiji Poison Woman Stories (Shinpen Meiji dokufu den), 66

Newly Edited Poison Woman Tales of the Ages (Shinpen kokon dokufu den), 28, 31

New Tale of Seafaring Street Minstrel Omatsu, The (Torioi Omatsu kaijō shinwa), 4, 7, 9–10, 58, 82

newspapers: crime in, xxiii; editors in authority role, 46; enlightenment rhetoric in, 39–48; the law in, xxiii, 36–40, 48–64; and nation-building, 43–44; and print revolution, 53; reading and readership, 36–64; sales of, 41–42; serial articles and novels, 48, 52; travel narratives in, 58–60; women readers, 36–64

newspapers, small. *See koshinbun*

Nietzsche, Friedrich, xiv

Nightly Read Newspaper (Yoru Yomu Shinbun), 139

Night Storm *(yoarashi)* Okinu. *See* Harada Okinu (poison woman)

Night Storm Okinu (Yoarashi Okinu), 66

Night Storm Okinu's Flowery Dream of Revenge (Yoarashi Okinu hana no ada-yume), 7

Nihon Romanha (Japanese Romantic School), 170, 204n56

Nikkei Shinbun (Economic Newspaper), 161–62

nikutai bungaku (carnal literature): in pulp magazines, 138–41

Nikutai no mon (Gate of the Flesh), 142

Normal and the Pathological, The, 8–9

Nozoe Atsuyoshi, 116, 117–20, 125, 135, 198n39

nymphomania, 111, 123

occupation Japan, 136–46, 149, xxiv. *See also* postwar period

Oda Makoto, 18

Oda Sakunosuke, 140, 143, 146–50

Oden. *See* Takahashi Oden (poison woman)

Oedipus complex, 130, 132, 135, 159–61, 163–64, 204n44

Ogawa Ichitaro (victim), 5, 78

Ogawa Tameji, 46–47

Ohatsu (poison woman), 114

Ōi Kentarō, 87

Oka Kōji, 80

Okamoto Ichirobe, 77

Okamoto Kisen (Kanzō), 5, 7, 14, 15, 28, 36, 38, 66, 192n29

Okamoto Shinjirō, 107

Okamura Tsukasa, 94

Okuno Takeo, 186n70

Omasa (Shimazu). *See* Shimazu Omasa (poison woman)

Omasa (Uchida). *See* Uchida Omasa (poison woman)

Omatsu (poison woman), xiv, 4, 7, 39, 40, 52, 58, 60–62, 82, 111, 114, 119, 188n29, 189n47; heredity as source of criminal behavior, 9–11

Omi Hiroshi, 112–13

One Hundred Stories of Women from the Bakumatsu and Meiji Eras

(Bakumatsu Meiji onna hyakuwa), 93

On Man and Woman (Danjo jiei), 23

On Sexuality, 199n61

Onuma Kuma (poison woman), 114–15

Origin of Things Meiji, The (Meiji jibutsu kigen), 17

orthography, 3

Osaka incident, 87

Ōshima Nagisa, 150–61, 164, 167, 170, 176

Oshin (poison woman), xv, 66, 73, 76, 139

Otake (poison woman), 114

other: eroticization of, xix–xx; and self, xix; and transgression, xix–xx

Ōtsuki Kenji, 124, 127–28, 199n56

Otsune (female bandit), 50–52, 188n29

Ōzasa Yoshio, 166

Panizza, Oskar, 132

Paradise Lost (Shitsurakuen), 161–63

Parisian society, xvi

pathography, 132, 134

pathological behavior, 8–9

patriarchy, 173–74; anger and resentment toward, 85; and dominance, 163–64; and masochism, 159, 162–64; and perversion, 159; and subversion, 160; and transgression, 163; and violence against women, 158

personal power: and hegemony, 165

Perspective of Rumor, The (Uwasa no enkinhō), xvii

Perverse Psychology and Crime (Hentai shinri to hanzai), 116

perversion: and authoritarianism, 169–70; *hentai,* 115; and imperialism, 159, 164–67, 169–70; and masochism, 164–67, 169; and pa-

triarchy, 159; of poison women, 15; in poison women stories, 113; as romantic, 59; sexual, 148; vs. subversion, 150–61; and transgression, 126; and transhistorical, 170

Pflugfelder, Gregory, 21

phallocentrism, 161, 163

Phantom Otake. *See* Otake (poison woman)

Phenomenology, xix

photography, 28–35

Physical Life of Woman, The, 12–13, 182n21

physiology and physiognomy: and crime, 2, 22, 116–24; discourse of, 4; and transgression, 2

poison women *(dokufu):* as anomaly, 111–12; as antihero, xv; as barbaric, 11, 35; as cultural icon, xiii; as dangerous, 112, 116, 131, 136, 173–74, 205n7; modern girl, comparison, 1; punishment of, 113–14; as social symbolic, xix, xviii, xx, xxi; term, usage, xiii; and youthful optimism, xx. *See also* crime and criminals; deviance/deviants, female

poison women stories *(dokufumono),* xv; 1870s–1880s, xxii–xxiii; beginnings of genre, 40; as cultural diagnoses, 111–12; detectives in, 171–72; as escapist, xiv; realism of, 53–54

poisons. *See* drugs

Pollak, Otto, 117

Poovey, Mary, xvi

popular culture: and high culture, xxv; of postwar period, 137–38; reform of, 26; transgression in, xxv, 142–43

postwar period, xxiv, 149, 174–75; crime, 146–50; gender politics, 158, 170; and popular culture,

137–38; liberalism of, 137; pulp
magazines of, 136–46. *See also*
occupation Japan
power: and discipline, 169; and hegemony, 165
pregnancy, 116–17, 121
prostitution, 120, 143, 147–48, 161
psychoanalysis, 112, 124–35
*Psychoanalytic Diagnosis of Abe Sada,
The* (Abe Sada no seishin bunsekiteki shindan), 124–35, 200n81
psychological self/subject: and transgression, xix
Psychology of Perversion (Hentai Shinri)
(journal), 115
*Psychology of Perverted Sexual Desire,
The* (Hentai seiyoku shinri), 115–16
Psychopathia Sexualis (Krafft-Ebing),
115–16, 132, 199n60
psychopathology, 115
puberty, 116–17
pulp magazines. *See kasutori zasshi*
pulp newspapers. *See kasutori shinbun*

Quilt, The (Futon) (confessional novel),
68–69, 94, 95, 100

Raddeker, Helene, 104
rationality, male vs. female, 122
reading: and gender difference, 45–46;
and immoral behavior, 36; literacy rates, 42–43; of newspapers,
36–64; and transgression, 36–40;
by women, 36–64
recollection. *See* self-narratives, of
female ex-convicts
Record of Abe Sada's Behavior, A (Abe
Sada gyōjō-ki), 143
*Record of Miss Shimazu Masa's Conver-
sion/Repentance* (Shimazu Masa-jo
kaishinroku), 69, 72–77
Red and Black (Aka to kuro) (mental
science magazine), 138

Red Tent (Aka Tento) (experimental
theater troupe), 166
reform *(kairyo),* 2, 5, 26, 89, 94–97
regression, 126, 128, 135
rehabilitation. *See* self-narratives, of
female ex-convicts
religious conversion. *See* self-
narratives, of female ex-convicts
remorse. *See* self-narratives, of female
ex-convicts
repentance. *See* self-narratives, of
female ex-convicts
Repentance of Evil Deeds (Akuji
kaishun), 72
representation: and social life, xvi
repression, 126, 129, 130–31, 134–35
resentment. *See* self-narratives, of
female ex-convicts
restriction: and subjection, 193n55
Rinbara Sumio, 62–63
romanticism: of carnal ideology,
138–39; of crime, 146; hero as
protagonist, 59; and infatuation,
148; of masochism, 162, 169–70;
perversion as, 59
Ronell, Avital, xiv, xviii, 36

Sacher-Masoch, Leopold von, 167
sadism: and masochism, 128, 160,
161; and submission, 162
sadomasochism, 148
Saeki Shōichi, 91–92
Saitō Yozue, 113
Sakaguchi Ango, 107, 140, 143, 147,
149
Salome complex, 131–32
Sansantei Arindo, 25
satire: of festishizing writer, 146–50
Satō Makoto, 163–70, 176, 204n53
Sawada Junjiro, 111, 116
Scott, Joan W., xxii
Secrets of Nature, The (Zoku zōka hiji),
19

seduction: in pulp magazines, 138
Seinan war, xv, xxiii
seiyoku. *See* sexual desire and sexuality
Seki Reiko, 92–93
· Sekine Hiroshi, 107, 151
self: and other, xix; masculine, 89–90;
    and social action, 89
self-narratives, of female ex-convicts,
    xxiii–xxiv, 173; authorial discourses,
    complicity with, 69–70; authority,
    narrative of, 4–5, 100–102; au-
    tonomy of, 68–69, 94, 100, 104;
    as bold and unapologetic, 68,
    103–4; confessional novels, 95;
    disenfranchised collectivity of, 70;
    empowerment of, 97; and gender
    difference, 92, 94–97; by male
    contemporaries, 92; political im-
    prisonment memoir as, 68, 86–94;
    as recollection and remorse, 65–102;
    rehabilitation in, 65–66, 67–68,
    84, 89–90, xxiii; and religious
    conversion, 94; as repentance or
    confession *(zange)*, xxiii, 66–102,
    149, 173, 193n47; resentment in,
    91–92; sexual memoir as, 103–4;
    and social action/reform 89, 94–97;
    as social documents, 84–85; tran-
    scribed confessions, oral to written,
    73–74
sensationalism, 25
sexual desire and sexuality: and crime,
    xvi, xx–xxi, xxiv, 1–2, 4, 13–15,
    24, 103–35, 244; and deviance,
    xvi, 9, 13–15, 110, 112; of domes-
    tic women, 137; Meiji sexology,
    83n34; and murder, 105, 108–12,
    135; normalcy of, 137; of poison
    women, xx–xxi; vs. self-control,
    121; and transgression, 8, xxv; and
    women's role in society, 171, 174.
    See also transgression
sexual difference: and the body, 111;

and female power, xvi; and gender
    articulation, xvi; and social rela-
    tionships/identities, xvii. *See also*
    gender difference
Sexuality and Its Discontents (Weeks),
    103
sexually transmitted diseases, 19
Shapiro, Ann-Louise, xvi
Shiga Naoya, 97–100, 193n47
Shikitei Sanba, 3
Shimazaki Tōson, 94, 96, 101
Shimazu Omasa (poison woman),
    58–59, 192n38; confessional self-
    narrative, 69, 70, 71–79, 84, 85,
    87, 89, 90, 92–93, 93, 97–100
Shingaku, 71, 77, 93, 191n12
shingeki (realist new theater), 165–66
Shinoda Kōzō, 6, 93
Shinryūsai Teisui, 66
shōgeki (little theater), 164–66
Sievers, Sharon, xvii, 87
Silver, Mark, 58
Silverman, Kaja, 166
Slaymaker, Douglas, 140, 175
Smiles, Samuel, 186n4
Smyth, Ethel, 101–2
social action, 89, 94–97
social life: and representation, xvi
social relations: and domination, xxv
social revolt: and misogyny, 157–59
Society of Murderers (Satsujin shakai),
    113
soldiers: as masochistic, 166–69
Stallybrass, xviii–xix, 180n14–15
stereotypes, 33–34, 139
Stories of Early Modern Poison Women
    (Kinsei dokufu den), 113
*Strange Story of Enlightenment: The Re-
    venge of the Photograph, A* (Kaimei
    kidan shashin no adauchi), 4,
    28–35, 31
Street minstrel Omatsu. *See* Omatsu
    (poison woman)

subjection: and restriction, 193n55
subjective narrative: vs. objective
   reality, 53
subjectivity: and gender difference,
   xxii; and transgression, 177. *See
   also* male subjectivity
sublimation, 19
submission: and abnormality, 9; and
   crime, 11; and imperialism, 167,
   169; and masochism, 167, 169; and
   sadism, 162
subordination: and masochism, 170
subversion: and masochism, 160,
   169–70; and patriarchy, 160; vs.
   perversion, 150–61; and social
   body, 111
Suzuki, Tomi, 68, 96

taiyōzoku (sun-tribe), 157
Takabatake Ransen, 26–27
Takada Chūryō, 124
Takada Giichirō, 116, 120–21
Takahashi Oden (poison woman),
   xiii, xiv, xv, 2, 4, 5–8, 36–37, 38,
   56–58, 78–83, 173, 174, 186n2;
   Abe Sada compared to, 108; autopsy, 13–14, 15, 16, 22, 182n24,
   183n31; beheaded, 6, 181–82n13;
   and class discrimination, 62;
   comparisons to, 66, 78–83, 108;
   congenital guilt of, 111; criminal
   nature, proof of, 8–25; evil nature
   of, 9; final days of life, 14; in prison, 93; masculine behavior, 11–12,
   12; murder as revenge killing, 6;
   in pulp magazines, 139; physical
   abnormalities and sexual desire,
   21, 22; physiology/physiognomy
   and crime, 2, 22, 24, 122, 124;
   as popular, long-standing object
   of interest, 5; reproductive organs
   preserved and studied, 14, 22, 24,
   76; sexual desire and crime, 13–14,

21, 22, 110–11, 113, 114, 120, 121,
   122, 132
Takahashi Tetsu, 124, 126, 131, 132,
   134, 138
Takeshima Takegorō (male ex-convict),
   72
Takeuchi Ryōchi, 97
Tale of Demon Takahashi Oden, The
   (Takahashi Oden yasha monoga-
   tari), 2, 4, 7–25, 30, 32–33, 37,
   56–58, 114
Tamura Taijirō, 141, 142
Tanaka Noboru, 109, 150–61, 167
Tanaka Yuko, 20
Tanizaki Junichirō, xv, 80
Tashiro Kidoku, 20
Tayama Katai, 68–69, 94, 95, 96, 100
technology and crime: in enlighten-
   ment fiction, 28–35
testimonies. *See* self-narratives, of
   female ex-convicts
testimonio, 70
theater, xv, xx, 6, 52, 79, 164–66
Three Essays on Sexuality, 199n58
"Times, The" (Sesō), 146–50
Tokito Kensaku, 97–100
Tokyo Akebono (newspaper), 13–14
Tokyo Asahi (newspaper), 71, 106
Tokyo E-Iri Shinbun (Tokyo Illustrated
   Newspaper), xvi
Tokyo Girls' School, xvii
Tokyo Imperial University Medical
   School, 122
Tokyo Nichi Nichi Shinbun (news-
   paper), 13, 42, 43–44, 108
Tokyo Psychoanalysis Research Insti-
   tute, 124–25, 128
Tokyo Shinshi (journal), 17
Tomioka Taeko, xxv, 104, 175–77
totalitarianism: and commercialism,
   204n54; and masochism, 136, 159,
   160, 164, 169
Totem and Taboo, 127–28

toxins. *See* drugs
Toyama Army Medical School, 22
transgression: and abjection, xviii–xix;
    and antiauthoritarian power, 170;
    and class, xviii–xix, 10, 180n14–15;
    and crime, 11; and differentiation,
    xxi; vs. domestic, xxv; economies
    of, xviii–xix; eroticization of,
    xix–xx; exoticized, xix; gender,
    114; indispensability of, xix; and
    the law, 36–40, 48–55; and male
    subjectivity, 177; and masochism,
    136, 170; and other, xix–xx; and
    patriarchy, 163; and perversion,
    126; and physiology, 2; in popular
    culture, xxv, 142–43; and read-
    ing, 36–40; and regression, 126,
    128, 135; and sensationalism, 25;
    sexual, xxv, 8, 24, 118, 124, 159;
    as social, xx, 112; and society, 159;
    and subjectivity, 177; supplemental
    to everyday life, xix. *See also* sexual
    desire and sexuality
Traveling Actor Oume (Tabi yakusha),
    192n41
travel narratives, 58–60
True Story (Jitsuwa) (magazine), 143
True Story of Abe Sada, The (Jitsuroku
    Abe Sada) (film), 109–10,
    150–61
Tsubouchi Shōyō, 27, 34
Tsuchiya Reiko, 42, 50, 53, 187n6
Tsurumi Shunsuke, 142
tsuzukimono (serial novels): first con-
    temporaneous identification of
    literary form, 62–63; sensational
    temptress in, xiii; and serial news-
    paper articles, 48, 52
Turim, Maureen 157–58

Uchida Omasa (poison woman): con-
    fessional self-narrative of, 66–69,
    80, 89, 97–98

Uchimura Kanzō, 193n47
Ueda, Atsuko, 27
Ueno Chizuko, 20–21, 183–84n38
Umehara Hokumei, xxiv, 113,
    197n22, 197n23
underclass. *See* class
Uno, Kathleen, 201n1
utilitarianism, 32–33

Venus in Furs, 167
Victorian England: transgressive
    women in literature, xvi
Viper Omasa. *See* Shimazu Omasa
    (poison woman); Uchida Omasa
    (poison woman)
Viper Omasa (Mamushi no Omasa),
    66, 80
voyeurism, 122, 138, 150

Watanabe Jun'ichi, 161–63, 176
Watatani Kiyoshi, 71, 93–94
Weber, Max, 20
Weeks, Jeffrey, 103
White, 180n14–15, xviii–xix
Wilde, Oscar, 131–32
Woman as Sexual Criminal, 119–20,
    198n39
Woman Tearstained in Passion (Aiyoku
    ni nakinureta onna), 143
women: and crime, 112–22; and
    enlightenment, 46–47; instincts,
    as uncontrollable, 118–21; and
    modernization, 189–90n62;
    and nation-building, 172–73;
    as passive/aggressive, 119; ratio-
    nality of, 122; as readers, 36–64;
    role in society, 171, 174; social
    position and power, source of
    debate, xvii; and Westernization,
    189–90n62
Women and Crime (Josei to hanzai),
    116, 117–20, 125
Woolf, Virginia, 101–2

World of Comedic Showa, The (Kigeki
   Shōwa no sekai), 164–65
Wulffen, Erich, 119, 198n39

Yamada Asaemon, 6
Yamaji Aizan, 94
Yamamoto Taketoshi, 44–45
Yamamoto Yoshiaki, 27
Yanagida Izumi, 185n56
Yokohama theater, 52, 79
Yokose Yau, xxiv, 93, 113–15
Yomiuri (newspaper), 41, 44, 53

Yoshida Kou, 72
Yoshino Jirō, 80

zange (repentance or confession). *See*
   self-narratives, of female ex-convicts
zangeroku (repentance narrative). *See*
   self-narratives, of female ex-convicts
Žižek, Slavoj, 99
zōkakiron (books of nature), 17–22,
   19–20, 23, 182n24, 183n34,
   183n37

Christine L. Marran is associate professor of Japanese literature and cultural studies at the University of Minnesota.